100 Anime

100 ANIME

BFI Screen Guides

Philip Brophy

 Publishing

First published in 2005 by the
British Film Institute
21 Stephen Street, London W1T 1LN

The British Film Institute's purpose is to champion moving image culture in all its
richness and diversity across the UK, for the benefit of as wide an audience as
possible, and to create and encourage debate.

Cover design: Paul Wright
Cover image: *Akira* (Katsuhiro Otomo, 1989, Akira Committee)
Series design: Ketchup/couch
Set by Fakenham Photosetting Limited, Fakenham, Norfolk
Printed in the UK by The Cromwell Press, Trowbridge, Wiltshire

British Library Cataloguing-in-Publication Data
A catalogue record for this book is available from the British Library

ISBN 1–84457–084–3 (pbk)
ISBN 1–84457–083–5 (hbk)

Contents

Acknowledgments

Andrew Lockett for originally commissioning another thoroughly a-literate book; Keith Mansfield and Rebecca Barden for supervising the edit of this organism; the Museum of Modern Art, Sydney (especially Leon Parroisien, Bernice Murphy, Erica Drew and Peter Thorn) for allowing me to curate *KABOOM – Explosive Animation from America and Japan* back in 1994, through which I contacted and was aided by numerous people in Japan who have continued to help me with research in *anime* and *manga* since (including Hiromi Aihara at Japan Film Mart, Takayuki Matsutani and Yoshihiro Shimizu at Tezuka Productions, Kiyo Joo at Company Gold, Manabu and Keiko Yuasa, Satoru and Nobu Higashiseto); more recently contacted people in Japan who have been gracious in fending my queries over the last few years (Tomoyuki Sakurai and Yasuko Furuichi at the Japan Foundation, Shigeki and Yoshimi Chiba); the Melbourne International Film Festival (Tait Brady, Sandra Sdraulig, James Hewison and Brett Woodward) for accepting various curatorial proposals on *anime* events over the years; the Japan Foundation, Sydney (especially Masafumi Konomi) for being supporters of many *anime* ventures in Australia; Asia Link for granting me an arts residency in Tokyo, 2004; Madman Entertainment (Paul Weigard and Tim Anderson) for supplying numerous DVDs; Judy Annear; Chiaki Ajioka; Bruce Milne; Maria Kozic; Lorraine Hellar-Nicholas; and a final extra-special thanks to Tetsuro Shimauchi (translations and credit checks) and Rosemary Dean who have been invaluable supporters of my Japanese research as well as very dear friends. Death to dubbing.

Introduction

Pop implosion

Asian and pan-Pacific post-war cultures are no longer confined to their territories on the global map. They progressively transgress, invade and impregnate Euro and Anglo societies. Consequently, their absorption of mass ephemera from beyond their shores is redefining the notion of 'popular culture', transforming our understanding of the concept in strange and compelling ways. While some prefer the East to exclusively remain a charade of traditional rituals and ancient ceremonies, others discover an unlikely contentment in the chaos released by collisions between East and West. If one is acclimatised to this environment – a kind of post-modern air-conditioning in a post-colonial airport – one need not be adversely affected by post-modernism's so-called 'collapse of meaning'.

This is not news. Nor does one have to undertake a course to know it. Time has well passed for the need to analyse pop culture, as if it were a frustrating closed system of signs proliferated through each wave of subcultural commodification. Pop culture is too pervasive, rampant, eclectic and polyglottal to be unravelled and remade into an academic macramé pot holder. Yet this is not a generation gap defined by the hip and the square; it's a *cultural* gulf defined by differences in view of how cultures are transforming and mutating through transnational activity. Pop – more than anything else – is the implosive point around which these gulfs form, and the nexus of their attraction.

Ground zero

Japanese post-war pop culture stands as a prescient ground zero for this phenomenon of mutation. Somewhere between the mid-40s' nuclear decimation of old world Hiroshima and the early-60s' electronic reconstruction of new world Tokyo lies a dimensional warp. The new and the old fold into each other, unrolling Japanese fabric as a hybrid polymer of exacting tradition and radical invention. Influences centuries old are cross-wired with inspiration reaching centuries ahead. Japan's modern industrial veneer – that fascinating 'empire of signs' – is a panorama of a retooled, redesigned and re-imagined application of foreign influence. Nothing is as it appears; all is apparition. Smell the old in Japan – it gleams like new; rub the new – it sounds old. Sense, experience, legibility and meaning are melded into a living 'sense-surround' which can make you feel simultaneously engulfed and detached in its urban and rural spread. It can be imagined as a transcultural hologram, sent to us in the West as a concentrate that liberates sign from signification. You neither read nor analyse this: you ingest it.

Anime (Japanese animation) and *manga* (Japanese comics) are among the most immediate and potent signs of Japan's post-war pop culture. After your first random fifteen minutes of any (non-dubbed) *anime* you're bound to be overwhelmed by its otherworldliness. You will encounter a different gravity, an unlikely atmosphere, an unexpected moisture. Tangible one moment, it melts into a strange texture the next. Once caught by its ocular excess and sonic gestalt, your sense of the imaginable future is radically changed. The growth in Western audiences for *anime* over the past decade testifies to the addiction these worlds induce. You too can be easily snared by the sexy danger of it all, as you stand before a world of paranormal engines, metallic succubae and cute weapons. Dive in – things become viscous, shiny, loud. This is the appeal, the fascination, the allure of *anime*.

Hand made in Japan

An especially endearing aspect of *anime* is how flat its images appear before us, almost in denial of their impulse to 'animate'. It's a graphic hand-drawn super-flatness that communicates with great depth – one that iconically, formally and materially views its surface as a universe for its encoding and layering. The absence of any photographic aura globally scars animation and *anime* equally, segregating them somewhat from cinema and leading them to be slightly stigmatised and perceived as 'not-cinema'. This in itself is not a problem, though becoming conscious of how deeply ingrained this differentiation is aids in comprehending the 'animatic grain' of *anime*.

Not as modern an invention as presumed, photography brought to life the Renaissance dream of light, depth and perspective. This 'hands-free mechanical-eye' feat of capture has since magically cast cinema as being beyond rendering, leaving animation gripped by a manually mediated appearance. Impinged by late nineteenth-century orthodoxy, photography, cinema and 'cinegraphic' computer-generated images (CGI) live the dream of looking out the window to the world, while comics and animation look like they are still contemplating themselves on the drawing board. While Western photography and cinematography have progressed through either embracing or contesting the camera's predisposition towards actuality and 'realism', *anime* maps alternative dimensions of 'unreality' on its plane of materiality, intensifying the graphic and nullifying the photographic. The power of the pen and the boldness of the brush guide *anime* as a motion medium born of *manga*, where the act of drawing by hand is viewed as a powerful mode of narration.

Beyond *manga*, Japanese culture is abundant in ways that the hand made and hand operated are acknowledged. Manual dexterity and physical manipulation are signs and processes of a primary interfacing between human creativity, technological application and material connection. Accordingly, the hand is technological and the machine is organic, positing them feverishly interchangeable. As ritualised in the way that department stores wrap their parcels delicately by hand, manual dexterity, physical touch and material tactility are cosmologically aligned with the everyday, no matter how technologically advanced its exchanges.

As such, an asynchronism in sensibility forges a rift between *anime* and the recent rise of CGI in American animation and live action: *anime*'s hand-made production simulates machine-made manifestations, while Hollywood's computer-generated production insinuates human-generated manifestations. Even if computers are employed in *anime* (as they increasingly are), they will appear hand-drawn, to express the Japanese sense of physicality. Conversely, Hollywood's CGI spectacles archaically transform the cinema into a Sistine Chapel, claiming closeness to the godly touch of unmediated perfection in lifelikeness.

Sensorial otherness

While *anime* has risen to unimagined heights over recent years, the celebration of the art form has been somewhat deflated by an unnecessary mode of contextualisation whereby everything Japanese is compared to an American counterpart. Miyazaki becomes the Japanese Walt Disney; Japanese sci-fi owes everything to *Star Wars* (1977); the stories are a bit too complicated; the genres are often mixed up; there are not enough high-end computer graphics; the music is in the wrong place; morality is deemed shady and lacking; and we are continually warned that *anime* is 'not for children'. This covert Americanisation of *anime* is angle-mirrored by a peculiarly British fixation on the wackiness of Japan, embarrassingly paraded by journalists on TV in particular. The last decade has witnessed a pathological desire to understand *anime* by reducing it to recognisable forms, examples and models – all of which serve to prevent a wider critical audience from apprehending the sublime Otherness and intellectual confoundedness which throb within *anime*'s alien heart.

This book threads a counter-ideology through its words to address this bias towards numbing transliteration. Responding to the giddy

Gestalt of *anime,* it aims to follow the cultural indentations rendered by the fungal spread of *anime* over the last forty years. The result is a sensorial critical text, designed to allow one to feel the spongy deeper levels of meaning in *anime* without reducing it to familiar terrain. Ultimately, *anime* is enduringly strange and microcosmically weird – and all the while being surprisingly grounded in dramatic and audiovisual craft. In engaging with some of the art form's most perplexing and overwhelming titles, we shall trace these titles' distinctive schisms to their broader cultural and historical forms, without anthropologically reducing the titles to mere customs and rituals that represent 'the Japanese'. This book's approach neither knows 'the Japanese' as the Nippophile claims, nor is afraid of the differentiating Otherness *anime* extols to *gaijin* ('the non-Japanese'). It deprioritises the ideals and delusions of translation, and instead exacts and proclaims the powerful cultural difference that produces plastic beings, intelligent metals and beautiful amoeba.

Engineering *anime*

Much historical and modern writing on Western animation takes pains to wear long pants and stand tall next to its big brother, the cinema. Here we fortunately need not aspire to gain such flawed respect: *anime* is a heady essence of Western animation from which new hybrids are formed. In this sense, *anime* simultaneously benchmarks animation, and moves beyond those achievements. It constitutes a specific cultural mode of production so much so that in Japan – despite denials and claims to the contrary – *anime* can be regarded a meta-set within which cinema is a subset. Film historians and theorists might scoff at this inverted idea, but it is offered here to be critically employed as a perspectival tool that can help illuminate the medium of animation, and hence *anime*. If anything, it may help account for the explosive quality of *anime* and its acceptance within Japan in ways historically unimagined in the West.

Animation is the contextualising mode of the 'apparently visual' world. Redirecting the photographic impulse, it shows and reminds us that the world we see around us can be viewed not as things, but as the markings and recordings of energy fields, transmissions and events. From the concentric rings tabulated to estimate a tree's age to the volcanic formations evaluated to gauge major geological transformations, the world can be diagnosed this way – especially when documented or simulated through time-lapse animation. Once one accepts that all matter is but momentarily held in place by unseen energies and forces whose change alters its composition, then the visuality of things is no more than a slight optical algae: slippery, alive and essentially non-objective. What we 'see' is a disconnected moment from a more expansive and enveloping continuum of events.

The mechanics of animation highlight how all cinema is founded on frequency relationships in time and space. How fast or slow, how deep or grounded, how sharp or blurred, how static or active – our perception of movement in films is the result of people moving framing devices and recording devices in rhythmic, counterpointed and contrapuntal control. These methods of pre- and post-production constitute an 'animatic apparatus' that points to cinema and animation's *dynamic* design. The production of cel animation requires all sounds and images to be calculated and engineered according to temporal and spatial ratios of variance. Before any sense, meaning or effect can arise from an animated sequence, time (speed, rate, duration) and space (foreground, background, periphery) have to be arranged, orchestrated and conducted. Simply, the world has to be engineered through metaphysics before it can be visualised in motion.

While this is deftly conveyed through the acute timing and musical command of the wartime and post-war work by the Disney and Warner Bros. studios, the medium's potential for further mobilising and radicalising the animatic apparatus initially becomes evident in the boom of *anime* in the early 80s. It is in *anime* (Japanese cel animation – lately with ancillary computer processing and manipulation) that the dynamic interaction between gesture, event, sound and image reaches its apogee, combining extreme mannerism with post-atomic contemplative states.

Consequently, organic energies (air, water, steam, fire, smoke) modulate and/or fuse ethereal energies (psychic, cosmic, extraterrestrial, spiritual, ectoplasmic). While we can easily see people, vehicles and buildings around us in the real world, characters in a wide range of *anime* genres just as easily sense psychic beams whose visual markings exist in an immaterial domain. *Anime* excels in depicting these other worlds.

Figuring *anime*

If *anime* is a body, no existing medical practice is suited to examining it. This corpus of *anime* is a 'post-human' thing: neither ideal creation nor accidental mutation, but a transcendent being who has become something else. This notion is central to our coverage of *anime* for two reasons. First, 'transcendence' is the state by which Japanese spirituality is posited on a mortal plane devoid of Judeo-Christian morality. As many of the titles discussed will demonstrate, the 'being' of a person (which can be one's soul, mind, blood-line, weapon, limb or organ) is always caught in modes of transition. Acts of transformation, reconstitution, replication and attaining consciousness are all indications of transcendence. Second, 'becoming' is a key determining principle in animating, where each frame is drawn so as to advance and be replaced by that which it becomes. A fundamental realisation of this as a dynamic principle (rather than a recourse to realistic representation) underpins the awe-inspiring effects powered by *anime*'s uniquely polyrhythmic momentum.

The fusion of these two ideologies allows one to 'unconsider' cinema and its anthropological documentarian fix which returns us too predictably to the real and the natural. In place we will consider *anime* as a self-contained, self-refracting and self-sustaining field of audiovisual possibilities for figuring the unreal and the unnatural. As many titles discussed will demonstrate, 'transcending' and 'becoming' are malleable and interchangeable at every textual level of an *anime*. Most importantly, where the history of Occidental animation is writ large with the vocabulary of art and craft – promoting the same contra-photographic desires that instigated Impressionism over two centuries ago – *anime* remains resolutely 'unpainterly' in its Popist flatness and mediarised iconicisation. *Anime* has garnered only miniscule pockets of validation within contemporary critical evaluations of the cinema and animation. This book seeks to define *anime*'s attributes as both peculiar to their Japanese cultural production, and separable from the channels both cinema and animation have pre-assigned for explaining *anime*.

And so to mapping the post-human genomic body of *anime*. No slight analytic metaphor, this book accepts *anime* as a being from another world, offered to us for a prognosis that will extend the above notions of 'transcendence' and 'becoming' and serve as a guide for warping between the 100 titles of the book. Here, you will be asked to recognise *anime* as being enlivened, developed and monitored by multiple systems which channel life within the medium's corporeality. The operations performed upon these systems constitute the conditions under which *anime* will be discussed:

- the *energised form* created by rewiring the synaptic system;
- the *calligraphic momentum* activated by extending the musculatory system;
- the *sonic aura* arising from retuning the auditory system;
- the *decorative surface* rendered by realigning the optical system;
- the *mannequinned form* shaped from re-armaturing the skeletal system.

Like hyper-nervous networks, these systems both react to and affect each other to generate the audiovisual dynamism of *anime*. They are matrixed across genres, between audiences, within scenarios and throughout serialisations. The analytic framework proposed here may well be the result of ingesting too much *anime* over the years, but such intoxication is sympathetic to the sensational, spectacular and sexual palpitations that remain unregistered by either reading *anime* solely as Western dramatic form intensified, or dissecting *anime* using liberal, ideological and psychoanalytic models.

The energised form

Perhaps more than any other medium, filmic animation – the hysterical unleashing of dynamic movement resulting from the wilful animation of the inanimate – is precisely suited to visualising the invisible lines and fields of energy which exist in our physical reality and beyond. *Anime* is founded on a discursive metaphysical visuality, combining animist beliefs (the notion that all things contain a spirit of existence) with the medium's fantastic flexibility. While these ideas are symbolically delineated in *manga* from Japan's immediate post-war period, the visual tempo, orchestration and polyphony of post-60s' *anime* expresses a high-keyed formal interplay between energy and its depiction.

Specifically, energy is manifested as the registering, graphing and recording of the invisible. Scenes abound where lightning bolts crackle across the screen, breaking up space, objects and people. Very often, this energy comes from a character or from an object acquired by a character. Their psychological states are similarly outlined by superimposed swirling lines and imported optical backgrounds – visual devices transposed from a long legacy in *manga*. But while *manga* often uses these devices to describe interiority, *anime* exploits the dynamism of movement to affect the real world directly and physically, and to graphically thrust upon us this collision between energy and its depiction. These manifestations of invisible energy are demonstrated by the tangible transformation of the atmospheric conditions of a spatial environment – where a force leaves the body, mind, psyche or soul, and energises space.

Always, *anime* shows that these transformations are an interaction between bodies and the space they inhabit. From transgressed domains to invoked planes to incurred dimensions, the nexus of being and location construct the stage for *anime*'s dramatisation of erupting energies. Most *anime* narratives are predicated on this, writing into their stories a series of shifts and relocations of forces and powers that move through bodies and between spaces, accounting for the noticeable 'dimensionalism' in so much *anime*. Yet this is not merely evidence of the art form's reliance on fantasy as a vehicle for its outlandish spectacles. The spatio-corporeal nexus is marked by a Zen interconnectedness of things, wherein space itself is an energy. Humans (as bodies, characters, entities, things) are not actors on stage, but merely synaptic occurrences in the matrix of space.

Extending this Zen notion of form and space, *anime*'s depiction of any personified or objectified container is the result of 'rewiring its synaptic system' so that the body of a character is either capable of changing spatial environments, or of being hyper-sensitive to invisible changes occurring in those environments. More often than not, both character and narrative mystify the occurrence, leaving them and us wondering where precisely the energy lies: within the person or throughout their surroundings. Hair will float outwards; bodies will gradually levitate; roads will crack and expand; tentacles will sprout forth. These are some of the typical ways in which *anime* will visualise the synaptic activity across the body – replete with patterned arcs emanating from the body's halo of energised fluorescence.

The calligraphic momentum

Anime employs a concept of linear energy, where a causal vein of energy is contracted from one point to the next in either dispersive wave form or directed beam form. While Occidental thought will readily exemplify this by analogue systems like electricity (where man tames nature through 'inventive containment', then allows energy to territorially pass along a controlled line), Oriental thought provides a more immediate and corporeal model: *chi*, the energy that exists in anyone and anything. It can be hidden, exposed, tapped, exercised, abused. From the many martial arts through to disciplines like t'ai chi, one channels energy as a linear flow coursing through the body. This type of transference of invisible *chi* occurs in a range of energy manifestations in physical reality: from the stature of one's standing body, to the slice of the samurai sword, to the brushstroke in calligraphy. All are marked embodiments of channelled energy. Each example – the shape of the body, the slice of the sword, the calligraphic character – is a visual mark which is held in place by the latent dynamics of an invisible energy controlled by the body.

The calligraphic momentum of *anime* is a particularly self-reflexive condition. If we take calligraphy to be not only the traditional art of expressive brushwork but also the ways in which *chi* leaves its mark on anyone and anything, *anime* is the graphing and encoding of how things exist in the most fundamental sense. While the history of Western art – both the art itself and the ways in which it 'sees' non-Western art – is a para-evolutionary charting of progressive visualisation according to optical paradigms of 'how things look', *anime* is a dynamic graphing of the same but with attention paid to 'how things are'. Across six centuries of Japanese visual art, the brush has been used less as a tool and more as a 'musculatory extension' of the body/arm/hand. It is the instrument for channelling energy so that any act of depiction is more properly the recording of energy that simulated an actioning of its form. This advanced philosophical awareness through manual dexterity underpins the bulk of Japan's traditional practices – so much so that the representational and the ideogrammatic are reversed. The ideogram idealises the energy of a thing due to its calligraphic inscripture, leaving the representation to be merely the surface effect of that energy's documentation.

This supplanting of the representation with the ideogram is at the heart of how *anime*'s sense of motion differs from Western animation derived equally from da Vinci's vanishing perspective and Muybridge's photographical analyses. *Anime* literally animates brushstrokes, not things. Its formal characteristics are based less on watching things move and more on observing the frequency, range and ratio of their momentum. The resulting 'calligraphic momentum' never closely matches how things move or appear in the real world, yet *anime* is remarkable in its evocation of movement itself. Spiralling colons of billowing smoke, lapping waves of agitated water, shimmering fields of windblown pampas grass, even passing through a fluoro-lit underground freeway tunnel – these are among the many poetic moments of motion in *anime*.

The sonic aura

Not surprisingly, the sonic – that most invisible yet most palpable energy – surfaces to govern the audiovisual textuality of *anime*. Far from having the soundtrack submerged by *anime*'s imagery, image is immersed in *anime*'s soundtracks. This inversion of audiovisual logic (where convention dictates that sound subscribe to image) forwards a neumonic logic, whereby sound is both material and referent (recalling the calligraphic binary of energised ideogram and visual representation). Neumonic effects are the law court's hammer bang and AM radio's electronic whoops that command our attention; theatre's off-stage rooster crow and cinema's off-screen crickets that locate us within the story's time frame. These are not simply 'sound effects' which are interpreted at a base semantic level, but sonic effects which buzz our aural consciousness and signal that a sign is being signified. Our reading of them is as self-reflexive as *anime*'s calligraphic base. And just as how the materialisation of energy is narratively foregrounded in *anime* through its energised form, so too does *anime*'s audiovisualisation textually evidence and neumonically signify the nature of sound in our physical reality.

Again, sound in Japan is inversely defined by Western standards: silence becomes a crucially interconnected principle of sound, just as bodies cannot be separated from spaces. Silence in *anime* – as per its place in a long history of traditional Japanese music – evokes two conjoined concepts. First, silence represents the space within which one becomes aware of oneself through being isolated and divorced from one's surroundings. Second, silence symbolises the desire for that space when one cannot achieve it within a congested environment. *Anime* is certainly noted for its aural explosiveness and its unrelenting detonations, but it is equally capable of creating paradigms of spiritual quiet.

Yet still, binaries of noise/silence function differently in *anime* from their brace in Western cinema: in *anime*, noise can be cleansing and silence can be deafening. The *anime* soundtrack abounds with amplified erasures, screaming pauses and razor-thin detonations. It belies an aural cartography that references many archetypal neumonic devices from Japanese cinema, from the warm clickity-clack of a distant train in the cinema of Ozu and Mizoguchi to the chasm gorged by Kurosawa's Shakespearean *chambara* (swordplay movies) and their alternation between gasps of silence, spurts of blood, slices of resonance, and deep passages of nothingness. Come the 60s' *denka* (electronics) explosion and its onslaught of electronics, the sonar field of Japanese life had profoundly transformed the Japanese soundtrack into something more akin to Stockhausen than Korngold, and in the process 'retuned the auditory system' of the movie listener. It is hard not to hear this 'Nippon noise' equally in the transistorised 60s'/70s' cinema and the radiophonic bombast of 80s'/90s' *anime*.

Apart from the aural atomisation that landscapes sound as an atmospheric condition of *anime*'s plane, its placement of music is notably opposed to the European symphonic tradition which characterises dominant forms of Western cinema. *Anime* scores declare their function and purpose through multiple voicing, pluralistic stylisation and thematic duplicity. Music in *anime* – as in Japanese cinema generally – rarely functions as mood accompaniment, barely performs with historical authenticity, and hardly syncs to evident emotional expression. As if Wagner's programmatic synaethesia never happened, the *anime* score is an unmoving mask that suppresses emotional imprinting – similar to how music complexly functions in Japanese socio-theatrical traditions, from *kabuki* to *karaoke*. It might sound like disco, *enka*, glitch or Chopin, but despite such categories, the presence of music in *anime* will exude emotional disjunction, psychological heterogeneity, fatalistic enrapture, pastoral evisceration and karmic retribution.

The decorative surface

The arts in Japan have long promulgated a non-hierarchical articulation of 'surface' and 'depth' in contrast to the familiar notion that surface is but the insignificant exterior while depth embodies more substantial meaning. For when surface and depth are not readily separable, meaning is distributed across the two equally. The epidermal detailing, textural brocading and decorative totality of the history of Japanese visual art bear only scant relation to the optical reflectivity that inspires European visual discourse. Japanese art does not so much 'reflect' a visual reality as it barometrically monitors seasonal changes and anatomically deconstructs socio-cultural exchanges: from river currents and bamboo groves depicted like weather charts, to villages and castles dissected like bodies. In as much as Japanese language is ideogrammatic at base, Japanese art is diagrammatic in form. The surface is less a representation and more a drawn map to be traced, a drafted chart to be read, an assembled model to be explored.

No mere ornamental dressing, patterns are totems, icons and glyphs that evidence life forces and energies manifested through elemental contours. Pre-kaleidoscopic in its patterning, Japanese art – including *anime* – emboldens visual pleasure at surface level while presenting the dense data-encoding that resides within its superstratum. Appreciation is thus predicated on an aesthetic awareness of maps, charts and models, and how their informative patterns surpass traditional decorative function. From scrolling paper prints to hanging ink drawings to folding screen paintings, the decorative surface is always foregrounded, never allowing you to forget the flatness you are witnessing. Instead of rejecting this, *anime* embraces it wholly, importing those screen, scroll and print devices to hyper-decorate the animated image. Depth in *anime* is best characterised as an arrangement of flat decorative screens which appear to be progressively behind each other while contrarily declaring that the implied depth is but the limited expanse of the staged image.

From vermillion-lacquered wooden bowls to heshin-roped body parts, and from concrete-embanked river ways to light-festooned semi-trailer trucks, so much in Japan is covered – overlaid, dyed, imprinted, adorned – because everything is philosophically within – contained, grounded, sited, enshrined. Some view this as an artificial and destructive suffocation of natural elements and forms with corrosive, agitational or artificial materials. Others can discern an animistic principle of how the spiritual/mystical existence of any 'thing' is innately sited within, marking its exterior to be not a disposable shell but an integrated ornamentation that abstractly represents an inner state. Exciting a love of surface, *anime*'s allure enraptures those who thrill equally to plastic and pinewood, ducco and stucco. *Anime* is thus only superficially an allusion to the real or natural world. Ultimately, its decorative surface requires a 'realignment of one's optical system' in order to focus on its depth.

The mannequinned form

Somewhere within the slo-mo tornado of coloured patterns of the *kimono* floats a beautiful human body. Similarly, the feudal military attire of the war lord is a castle of armature which imprisons a heaving human body. In both instances, the outline of the body is negated and treated as an amorphous life force which is 'shelled' within an incorporated construct. This view of the body is crucial to the depiction of clothed and naked human form in Japanese art and theatre, and the mobilisation of that form within *anime*.

It is in bodily representation that *anime* heavily subscribes to a thesis of 'post-humanism' – the re-imaging, re-inventing and reconfiguring of all we assume humanity and humanism to signify. The body in *anime* is aggregatively sculpted under the conditions resulting from the previously noted operations performed on the form's systems, creating a contra-photographic, mega-ornamental, hyper-extended figure. Clean of any collaging of classical and archaic parts, the *anime* body is a new species, holistic in form and genetically manipulated according to *anime*'s encompassing of the history of human form as perceived within Japan.

Clearly the body in *anime* is of its own type: lips, hips, head, legs, eyes, fingers, hair – each are connected via a logic of proportion that is alien to Western post-da Vincian perspectives of 'accuracy'. Yet the drawing of *anime* bodies results from anatomical analysis and internal investigation, ironically not dissimilar to da Vinci's own cadaverous considerations. The difference is that *anime* chooses to gesticulate the body into an algorithmic figure that reflects these analytical findings, positing bodies as 'energy-covered' skeletons of form. Again, *anime* chooses to render things not 'as they look', but 'as they are' on both surface and within. The existence of bodies – how they are energised, mobilised, channelled, materialised, tested, empowered, thwarted, engaged and penetrated – is revealed and detailed in *anime*'s monstrous males, anorexic angels, gorgeous guys and flaming females, all of whom can be stoic statues of solidity or fluid morphs turned inside-out. They are interchangeable vessels, instruments and purveyors of these energies.

Anime not only perceives the human body through '*anime* vision' but also redefines bodily capabilities in the characters of its stories. Mixed in with 'humans' are aliens, robots, cyborgs, androids, mechanoids, replicants, simulations, newtypes, mutants, chimera, apparitions, spirits, entities, ghosts, gods, demons – all of whom may appear indistinguishable from 'humans'. While sometimes disorienting to follow, *anime*'s tracking of the many shifts between human, inhuman, non-human and post-human is governed by the longstanding Japanese attraction to puppets, automatons, dolls, figurines and idols. This latter collective is instilled with complex cultural notions of self-identity, psychological visage, group uniformity and public persona that allows all and any depictions of humans to be read primarily as mannequins. Upon this stage, humans simply do not exist.

This is possibly the most liberating aspect of *anime*: the subjugation of human-centric mandates of dramatisation which urges an inner probing of existence that enlivens its characters. Characters in *anime* are not based on 'people we know', but on possibilities of what people could be. Glitches in a robot's memory are thus more exciting than the preconditioned predictability of human behaviour. *Anime*'s reliance on mannequinned form and its animation of multifarious guises, masks and faces presents the human as skeletal architecture, plasticised flesh and neural matrixes. Sublime in its post-humanism, *anime* tells the story of a human who dreamt of being a robot – and whose dream one day came true.

Trouble-shooting

100 Anime is a selection of widely ranged titles which evidence the above notions of how *anime* is engineered and figured. It is neither a 'top 100' nor an introduction to the 'world of anime'. Such approaches are best left to tourist guide books: their usefulness is in their signposting, not in their postulation. This book seeks to retain the inexplicability of *anime* as framed by non-Western formations of Japanese history and culture – and argues for being disoriented yet seduced by *anime*'s graphic audiovisual form. I have experienced these titles many times, and their beauty lies in their elusive complexity despite what some might perceive as crass, kitsch or offensive artistry. Not concerned with pantheons and paradigms, I'm more interested in how the profusion of *anime* titles indicates an incredible well-spring of cultural energy pouring from post-war Japan. Just as the French and Dutch were amazed by the disposable Edo-prints used to wrap goods exported from Japan, I am spell-bound by the formal qualities and conceptual tropes of *anime*, and invite one to sense this book's titles similarly.

Adolescence of Utena (*Shojo kakumei Utena Adoresensu Mokushiroku*)
Japan, 1999 – 75 mins
Kunihiko Ikuhara

The lament over Barbie goes unheard in Japan. Her impossible figure, her intimidating stature, her sexualised passivity – all are ignored by Japan's longstanding investment in dolls, puppets and figurines. And when Western eyes have been cast over the increasingly elongated and mannequinned *bishojo* women of startling beauty in modern *shojo* (girls') *manga* and *anime*, the Barbie spectre clouds their vision again, blinding them to a salient difference: dolls in Japan are not bodies to become but idols to be worshipped.

The cult of idolatry runs deep in Japanese doll culture, but its most recent and maximal manifestation can be found in *Adolescence of Utena*. A feature film born from a TV series based on a *manga*, it presents an erogenous private-school world within which Utena – dressed in faux-military boy's attire combined with a micro-mini peplum – swirls around romantic and erotic entanglements in modular soap-opera format. Her ongoing 'affairs' with the subservient Anthy and the riveting Kiryu form spirals of love/hate frissons that encircle the school. Classes and studies are there merely to frame trysts, gossip and scandal. Sports and recreation are there only to cover a secret fraternity of sword battles in which Utena partakes regularly. The school itself is not merely a hermetic social sphere but a Russian doll of interior and disguised realms of sexual conflict and gender multiplicity: its architectural design is a mind-boggling visualisation of the school's dimensional mania. And throughout is Utena: striking poses, scaling heights, rushing forward, wielding swords, flowing hair, pressing lips. Idealised and idolised, her presence within *Utena* is that of a hyper-doll high on melodrama.

Utena's impossible beauty is manifold. As a neo-*bishojo* action figurine distilled and decanted from a long line of *shojo manga*, she is the animated impossibility of human form – a post-Barbie hystericalisation of bodily possibilities. *Manga* posterises these idols, but *anime* brings them to life. Consequently, a post-sexual state is attained by Utena's reinvention of human form. She is a hybrid morph of hermaphroditical duality, amplifying the sexuality of each gender rather than cancelling them out. Utena's conflation of gross femininity with genteel heroicism renders discrete and oppositional gender identity and history as inappropriate and ineffectual. As she soars through the air in a rain of roses, flushed with love and valour and holding her illuminated blade on high, her new angelic pose as a post-human meld of ingénue and gymnopede is breath-taking.

As a cinematic extension of the TV series, *Utena* is a maturation and ripening of the latter's nascent *amour*. The film replaces Cupid with Eros, intensifying all acts of transformation central to the original story. In short, everything is engorged: the erotics are more palpable and less decorative; the action is more physical and less suggestive; and the languid humidity of the TV series is turned up to a hothouse of desire and passion. Come the outrageous finale of the film when Utena breaks out of the school zone into a bizarrely imagined 'beyond', she shape-shifts into a transmogrified futuristic car, realigned as a sexual engine between Anthy's thighs. It's as if Barbie never happened. And in Japan, she didn't.

Feature

Genre: Gender Melodrama

Dir: Kunihiko Ikuhara; **Prod**: Toshimichi Otsuki; **Scr**: Yoji Enokido; **Anim**: Hichiro Kobayashi; **Chara**: Shinya Hasegawa; **Score**: Shinkichi Mitsumine, J. A. Seazer; **Manga**: *Shojo kakumei Utena* (*Adolescence of Utena*); **Wr/Art**: Chiho Saito (Be Papas).

(*Next page*) *Utena*: a hothouse of desire and passion

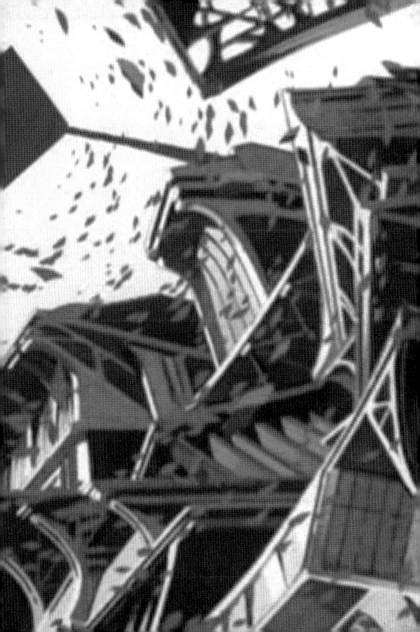

AD Police (*AD Porisu*)
Japan, 1990
Akira Nishimori, Takamasa Ikegami, Hidehito Ueda

Law enforcement evolves not of its own accord, but because of growths and changes in crime. The law is always reactive and reactionary; the criminal element is the dynamic organism to the law's control. *Anime*'s propensity to re-imagine any social order has led it to vividly imagine how the law might develop in the future to deal with permutations of crime. *AD Police* follows the exploits of a special police force – the Advanced Police – who have been created to combat Boomers: renegade robots of unstoppable destruction. The quaintly named 'Normal Police' take care of human crime.

    AD Police's concentrated polis refigures the collapsing cities of American 70s' crime films of the blaxploitation, mafia and psycho subgenres. This is not through characterisation, but in its depiction of the city as a cesspool of crime formed by the creeping decay of social order. Alienating skyscrapers, blinding fluorescents, defective subways, filthy tunnels, grafittied buildings – these signs of societal demise mark the 70s' televisual city and *AD Police*'s Mega Tokyo in 2027, suggesting that progress will be very slow in coming. But *AD Police* imports the societal malaise of America's wonderfully decrepit 70s' cinema not for social commentary, but for the vividly dissocialised psychopaths born from its narratives. It employs these types as signs of the slipping between humans and cyborgs, and how the contracted gap between the two beings is indicative of the contracting space of the congested city. The psychological ramifications of this 'psycho-physical transitioning' are graphically depicted, clashing social metallica and sexual metabolism in disturbing ways. Comprised of three episodes, each clarifies this in its study of how gender intensifies sexual behaviour, fusing the psychopath, the sociopath and the serial sex killer under extreme compression.

    'The Man Who Bites His Tongue' is *AD Police*'s presentation of the cyborg-becoming of the male body. Ex-boxer Billy has been reassembled so much that the only human component of his being is his tongue. Now a major fighter for the AD Police, existential crisis grips him following his rage at killing Boomers in frenzies of self-loathing. To return to human consciousness, he bites his tongue. Only by feeling this pain can he feel human. Becoming addicted to drugs administered by his creator, Dr Manabe, he becomes unstable and is eventually shot down by his ex-lover and fellow officer Jeena. He implores her to shoot him in the tongue.

With most intensity, 'The Ripper' is the cyborg-becoming of the female body. The ideal *OL* (office lady), Caroline Evers has her complete womb removed in order to stabilise her slope in productivity during her menstrual cycles. With cyborg replacement of her sexual organs, she can still achieve orgasm, but has developed an extreme 'menstrual envy' that transforms her into a serial killer who eviscerates human prostitutes patrolling the Paradise Loop subway. AD officer Ailis tracks the Ripper and is convinced the killer is a female human due to the anger of the crimes. In her pursuit of Caroline, Ailis identifies her own slipping towards 'human otherness', fearful that her approaching eye-replacement will cause her to eventually lose the ability to cry – a crucial expression of the human condition.

OVA (3)

Genre: Future Crime

Dir: Akira Nishimori, Takamasa Ikegami, Hidehito Ueda; **Prod:** Satoshi Koizumi, Tsutomu Sugita, Takanori Yaegaki; **Scr:** Aikawa Noboru; **Anim:** Tony Takezaki, Toru Nakasugi; **Chara:** Fujio Oda, Hiroyuki Kitazume; **Score:** Kaoru Mizutani; **Sound:** Fusanabo Fujiyama; **Manga:** *AD Porisu* (*AD Police*); **Wr:** Suzuki Toshimichi; **Art:** Tony Takezaki.

Ai City (*Ai Shiti*)
Japan, 1986 – 100 mins
Koichi Mashimo

Japanese language is a semantic amoeba. It employs a discrete ideogrammatic alphabet – *katakana* – for foreign words ('television' is reformed phonetically as *terebi*) but once a *katakana* word has been incorporated into usage, wonderful multi-layered flowerings of meaning are allowed. *Ai City* is a sci-fi *anime* also known as 'Love City' due to *ai* meaning 'love', but in sci-fi 'ai' is also an acronym for 'artificial intelligence'. This duality of meaning signified in *Ai City*'s title braces the central issue explored by the series: the conflation of genetic attraction (DNA) with chemical emotion (love).

The 'city space' of *Ai City* is dimensionally multiplied along these lines. Following a psychic battle between two Headmeters (beings endowed with super-ESPer power whose foreheads digitally display their energy levels), K blasts J into a counter dimension. The fabric of existence is literally torn, revealing the city to be but an illusory scrim to the neural wiring and DNA coding firing under the city's skin. This warping moment occurs as K – a defector from the nefarious Fraud organisation – escapes harbouring the young child Ai and the private detective Raiden. Once J has been jettisoned dimensionally beyond the city limits, alarms are sounded at Fraud where humanoids work to repair the Phase Dimensional Barrier under the fascistic control of the fearful Mr Lee, a hulking humanoid with terrifying psychic power.

That's just the first of many battles in *Ai City*. Multiple twists and turns abound thereafter, enveloped by flashbacks in K's mind where he relives moments during his internment within Fraud. But *Ai City* is more an emotionally charged stage than a military playground. There isn't a single battle which doesn't present an emotional consequence for those engaged in mighty psychic fights. The evil Tuned Men – stealthful hitmen brothers Rian and E – are shown to break down in tears at one point; the ruthless assassin J has her memory reconfigured once she is released from the grip of Fraud; and even the soulless Mr Lee reveals an unexpected side to his maniacal personality. *Ai City* posits all human existence regardless of its mutated composition as a flickering flame controlled by flux beyond its combustion. It presents a human story where love contracts define human interaction beyond the evolutionary proposition of life being essenced through DNA.

To enforce this, *Ai City*'s futuristic levels of existence are ultimately uncovered as the after-effect of present-day scientists altering DNA and creating a form of 'bio-pollution', which in turn develops a Genetic Alloy that eventually redesigns existence according to new genetic laws. The final showdown that occurs between the Genetic Alloy and what effectively is 'life itself' is of hyper-apocalyptic proportion. Surprisingly, while all human life is but transitions of existence, it is the Genetic Alloy alone that is pure through its innate corruption. Even as it is finally being destroyed through its own evolutionary self-cannibalisation, it cries out, asking why human life that abused the laws of genetics is allowed to live, while it in its supreme mutation is condemned to die.

Feature

Genre: Cyborg Action

Dir: Koichi Mashimo; **Prod:** Hiroshi Kato; **Scr:** Hideki Sonoda; **Anim:** Torao Arai; **Chara:** Chuichi Iguchi; **Score:** Shiro Sagisu; **Sound:** Noriyoshi Matsuura; **Manga:** *Ai Shiti* (*Love City*); **Wr:** Shuho Itabashi; **Art:** Shuho Itabashi.

Akira
Japan, 1989 – 124 mins
Katsuhiro Otomo

Typical of the wider chronicles of Japanese consciousness, *Akira* is set after the Third Nuclear War and in the supposedly futuristic city of Neo-Tokyo. The illusion of futurism is a cynical bluff: *Akira* is a world modelled entirely on Tokyo in 1964 as the city was being transformed for its rebirth for the Tokyo Olympics. The critique etched into *Akira*'s dystopian canvas is that the future never came: the future will thus be nothing but the existential wait for its non-appearance. Kaneda, Tetsuo, Kei and their delinquent gang are a new breed of sceptic philosophers biding their time in a city that never came.

Superficially, Tetsuo symbolises the hope to be found in the act of waiting. He has become blind to the fact that he and Akira are themselves the future which everyone awaits: they are the post-nuclear psycho-genetic beings born of the past's technological mistakes, though destined to live beyond those technologies. Yet *Akira* portrays Japan as a complete race of such beings – scarred by a nuclear past yet fully capable of transcending that past.

The opening title sequence to *Akira* exemplifies this. A flash appears on the horizon's edge, a huge ball of black energy grows and expands its circumference in sheets of white fallout, gravitating silently towards our location and engulfing the screen in searing white. Rather than staging apocalyptic scenarios for spectacle, *Akira* positions us to experience a nuclear blast – and live through it. Its white silence is a deathly visitation in the act of narration: we witness, we die, we become the future. The white screen gives way to an aerial cartography; but this time the city is reborn, with the frail remnants of central Tokyo held by thin bridges connected to the mainlands. The shimmering red and orange, the sinuous bridges, the pulpy morph of Tokyo's remains all evoke the image of a heart. And at its dead centre: the monstrous gaping crater left after the bomb drop which created Neo-Tokyo.

Akira: we witness, we die, we become the future

Accompanying this black void is the truly earth-shattering sound of *taiko* drums uniformly pulsing in single metronomic explosions. Herein lies a major pneumonic signifier that shapes the fantastic, post-nuclear textuality of *anime*. The crater we see is the still and dead recording of an energy event (the bomb drop) which has left a physical impression of its energy field. Just as the surface of a drum skin is traumatised and elasticised by the force brought to bear on its surface, so too do a nation's landscape and its inhabitants undergo an analogous psycho-geological scarring. This is how *Akira*'s present reverberates its past. And this is the crux of its take on sci-fi.

Japanese sci-fi is a catalogue of how the present will be cultured into the future, and *Akira* is the first and most prescient form of this approach. Less speculative fiction and more extrapolated perspective, *Akira*'s industrial design, urban planning and architectural manifestations resonate with a distinctively Japanese sense of grounded imagining: the images it projects are case studies of the present's capacity to live beyond itself. The future, therefore, is not what will be, but how things will end up.

Feature
Genre: Psychic Sci-Fi
Dir/Chara: Katsuhiro Otomo; **Prod:** Shunzo Kato, Ryohei Suzuki; **Scr:** Izo Hashimoto, Katsuhiro Otomo; **Anim:** Yoshio Takeuchi, Hiroaki Sato; **Score:** Shoji Yamashiro; **Sound:** Susumu Aketagawa; **Manga:** *Akira*; **Wr/Art:** Katsuhiro Otomo.

All Purpose Cultural Cat Girl Nuku Nuku (*Banno Bunka Neko musume*)
Japan, 1992
Yoshitaka Fujimoto

Anime is surprisingly similar to Japanese cuisine. Flavour and taste in Japanese cooking is grounded in the sequencing of discrete and disconnected taste sensations, contextualised by the neutralising elements of plain rice or noodles and *dashi* (seaweed) stock. The fusion of flavour happens more within the mouth than in the composite recipe alone. Through this arrangement of unmodified sensations, an expanded range of connectable flavours can harmonically co-exist, which – if meshed together through a singular processing – would degenerate into sickly hybrids. Even the simplest *sushi* is a micro-narrative of flavour as it swirls around your mouth prior to ingestion.

The 'recipe' for many seemingly hybrid *anime* will be made along similar parameters. *All Purpose Cultural Cat Girl Nuku Nuku* has the following ingredients: a boy (Ryunosuke) who mourns the accidental death of a stray cat; his scientist father (Kyusaka) hired by a giant company (Mishima Heavy Industries) to develop military robotics; his estranged wife (Akiko) hell-bent on securing final custody of the boy from the father; her hired assistants (Ari and Kyoko) who operate frightening weaponry and machinery in their many attempts to kidnap Ryunosuke for Akiko; and Nuku Nuku – a humanoid fused with the spirit of the dead cat and a prototype android skeleton. Simply arrange all ingredients and ingest.

The 'clashing' that might be assumed in combining these elements never occurs. Gags, memories, violence, desire, schizophrenia, sex, hilarity, abuse, absurdity – all are released in each episode of *All Purpose Cultural Cat Girl Nuku Nuku*, yet they never cause 'narrative indigestion'. This is because the switching and swapping between dramatic, comic and emotional moments in the ongoing story form an outlaid matrix across which the audience is teleported. The over-used and highly simplistic metaphor of being taken on a 'journey' in the televisual experience is majorly inappropriate here: narrative space to be travelled in *All Purpose Cultural Cat Girl Nuku Nuku* is never so linear. Like the emotional concatenations and mood swings which govern everyday life, there is never any clear way of preparing the narrative pathway to the next dramatic incident.

The amazing feat achieved by *All Purpose Cultural Cat Girl Nuku Nuku* lies in how the psychological 'verticality' of each of the series' elemental ingredients is never weakened, flattened or diluted. The commitment of Kyusaka both to protecting his son and preventing his research from being ethically abused by corporate concerns is unwavering; the bond between Ryunosuke and his sexy guardian Nuku Nuku is one of sublime attraction; and the anger and hurt that drives and possess Akiko to destroy everything in her path (often literally) in order to be close to her son are of a frightening intensity. Sardonic and self-deprecating exchanges are thrown between everyone at lightning speed, but these flashes never affect or redirect the primary emotional energies which motivate the series' key characters. Overall, *All Purpose Cultural Cat Girl Nuku Nuku* is only superficially an 'anarchic' series. Courtesy of the riotous familial bombast that binds its units together, it exudes a bittersweet taste that lingers long after the absurdity dies away.

OVA (12)

Genre: Cyborg Comedy
Dir: Yoshitaka Fujimoto; **Prod:** Kyoko Kobayashi, Shiichi Ikeda, Hiroshi Kato; **Scr:** Hiroshi Yamaguchi, Chinatsu Hokujo; **Anim:** Kenichiro Katsura, Yuji Moriyama; **Chara:** Seiji Kishimoto; **Mecha:** Hiroshi Ogawa; **Score:** Kenichi Fujita, Hiroshi Matsuda, Hioki Otomo; **Sound:** Jun Watanabe; **Manga:** *Banno Bunka Nekomusume* (*All Purpose Cultural Cat Girl*); **Wr/Art:** Yuzo Takada.

Angel Cop (Enjieru koppu)
Japan, 1989
Ichiro Itano

On the surface, *Angel Cop* contemporises the traditional 'lone wolf' of Japanese lore. This figure appears in historical figurative fiction derived from the seventeenth-century spread of *ronin*: 'lordless' wandering *samurai* seeking ways to apply their skills in a post-feudal epoch. The *ronin* is put into mythological overdrive by the saturated cycles of *chambara* (swordplay) and *yakuza* (gangster) films from the late 50s to the early 70s. These solitary figures are Japan personified: a rock, an island, an impassive isolationist force so in tune with its 'oneness' it lives on a separate post-social plane of existence. Not surprisingly, their tragic spectacles of existential expulsion also gain unlikely footholds in *anime*.

Akane Mikawa in *Angel Cop* is draped in the *ronin* costume, redesigned to present her as an urban detective fighting 'super-crime' perpetrated by a variety of cyborg and *ESPer* criminals. Not a super-human herself, she must dig deep within her psyche to synchronise with her foes' heightened energies, configuring *Angel Cop* as a story of human resourcefulness battling post-human might. True to the *ronin*, she is a loner: personally, she shares no close relationship with anyone; socially, she's a woman in a man's world.

While *Angel Cop* clearly sets itself up this way, it gradually disrobes its *ronin* costumery and pulls back to reveal a wider picture of gender conflicts. Akane's 'woman-with-balls' is actually not a socially displaced oddity: her conflicted gender status is simpatico with the mutated gender status of the criminals she tackles – many of whom end up her allies after much government duplicity. The childlike apparition of Flare is that of an antique eighteenth-century European doll: a pre-*gosurori* ('Gothic Lolita') replete with golden curls and taffeta bows. She is the psychic ESPer shadow to the looming Asura: a hysterical vision of heavy metal femininity with a mountain of ringleted hair and a sweeping black cape. Like a pair of doomed cosmic lovers, they materialise within and without scenes in space-warping walls of flames. The ultimate villain Lucifer is a steroid nightmare of gender confusion. Overcome by musculature to the extent that gender identification is impossible, this mega-breasted eye-lined platinum-blonde behemoth is the most grotesque gender mutation, and a nemesis that pushes Angel onto a plateau of possibilities she never thought existed.

The face of *kabuki* hovers like a meta-mask for these proceedings. While societal exchange in Japan can be viewed as exceedingly 'pre-modern' in its many sexist channels, bridges and underpasses, gender in its dramatic depictions constitutes a post-modern veil draped across the invisible fourth wall of theatre. Masks abound at multiple levels upon such stages, usually with gender being the diffusing principle for refracting the drama – *kabuki*'s feminised make-up of male actors being most notable. *Angel Cop* is a tantalising touch of that gender veil as it is stretched across the drama of urban crime and cybernetic aberration. Akane's lone she-wolf floats across the surface of it all like a textual *deus ex machina*, revealing all that is masked by gender.

OVA (6)

Genre: Psychic Crime
Dir: Ichiro Itano; **Prod:** Yasushi Nomura; **Scr:** Noboru Aikawa, Ichiro Itano; **Anim:** Yasuomi Umezu, Satoru Nakamura, Yasuhiro Seo; **Chara:** Nobuteru Yuki; **Mecha:** Masaharu Tomoda, Nobuyasu Moriki; **Score:** Hiroshi Ogasawara; **Sound:** Nobukazu Yamada; **Manga:** *Enjieru koppu (Angel Cop)*; **Wr:** Noboru Aikawa; **Art:** Taku Kitazaki.

Armitage III (Amiteji za saado)
Japan, 1994
Hiroyuki Ochi, Takuya Sato

Chimera of form is an essence of *anime*. Its ability to render complex human drama through the calligraphic sweep of its emotional engagement presents *anime* as possessing cinematic depth despite its graphic flatness. Its dramatic templates seem to function as a quoted theatre of morals, yet a pervasive amorality unties plot and character lines to trace floating notions of self and society. Simultaneously, *anime* is the discomforting resolution of this same chimeraesque state: *anime* always seems to be something despite being what it is. The cyborg in *anime* is but one of many figures which 'personify' this as both generic type and dramatic container. Armitage of *Armitage III* is a multi-layered chimera: childlike yet resolute; naive yet focused; innocent yet deadly. Like so much of Japanese

Armitage III: a neo-human image of the body dislocated from itself

popular culture, her label reads: 'not to be taken on the surface'.

Armitage is a standard amalgam of the cute killers and sexy assassins that populate cyber-*anime*, but her *kawaii* (cute) countenance is foregrounded as mere design effect. Her surface is no index to either her own troubled sense of self, her hidden energies, or the fatalistic paths she must follow throughout the story. Her outward guise as a cybernetic 'Necro-Lolita' relates to the stealth and subterfuge which create underground political divisions in the supplanted utopia of Mars. As she teams with the manly semi-bionic hunk of Ross to track terrorists using re-programmed cyborgs as killing machines, she slowly perceives the dystopia sheathed within the cyborg design of the beautiful world she inhabits and protects. Of course, the predictable yet nonetheless fascinating ethical quandary faces Armitage: what exactly makes her different from the hacked cyborgs she must terminate? Is she too not the result of programming? Could she not be a potential hack of herself, and if so, what becomes of that former self?

The chimera of *anime* is raised here by the *kawaii* mask of Armitage deep in thought over these issues. Western sci-fi will speculate broad socio-political issues in allegorical form, but a defining characteristic of sci-fi *anime* is its embrace of the philosophical and its propensity to define selfhood and identity away from the larger charting of society. That it does so through cyborgs and not humans only amplifies the human drama resulting from such characterisations, and *Armitage III* excels at combining these ideas with hard action and violence. This is particularly evident in the way Armitage's indestructible body is ravaged by serious handgun artillery. Bearing large titanium-tearing welts in her soft-yet-hard skin, we glimpse the metallic underlining of her being, melted into sores bored by white-hot leaden bullets. At this point, her apparent cuteness either confuses, repels or disorients: her body is just mechanical covering to her, giving us a neo-human image of the body dislocated from itself, just as Armitage is dislocated from her 'self'. Despite its high-octane momentum, *Armitage III* is an inquiry into how consciousness is codified through programmed directives. Revoicing Astro

Boy's eternal pondering from whence he came, Armitage is an orphan of humanity.

OVA (4)

Genre: Cyborg Action

Dir: Hiroyuki Ochi, Takuya Sato; **Prod:** Kazuaki Morijiri, Hiroaki Inoue, Yasuo Hasegawa; **Scr:** Chiaki Konaka, Akinori Endo; **Anim:** Kunihiro Abe, Koichi Hashimoto, Shinya Takahashi, Naoyuki Onda; **Chara:** Hiroyuki Ochi; **Mecha:** Atsushi Takeuchi; **Score:** Hiroyuki Namba; **Sound:** Masafumi Mima.

Astro Boy (*Tetsuwan Atomu*)

Japan, 1963 (B&W), 1980 (Colour)

Osamu Tezuka, Gisaburo Sugii, Daisaku Sakamoto, Eiichi Yamamoto, Osamu Dezaki, Yoshiyuki Tomino, Minoru Okazaki, Fusahito Nagaki

The most accessible route to the fantastic futuristic visions unleashed by *anime* is through the angelic face of the pre-pubescent robot, Astro Boy. The *Astro Boy anime* TV series has created not only a major post-war icon for Japan, but also a strangely attractive post-baby-boomer figure in Occidental countries where dubbed versions of the first TV series played.

The original *Astro Boy* was produced in black and white and remains a strong favourite with baby-boomer Americans. Its nostalgia value is high, and its naiveté is its charm. The colour remake of *Astro Boy* is an update of the original series and features a karaoke-disco version of the theme (true to the Japanese theme but with English words). To a different generation, this series now has a great early-80' retro appeal, while the colouring is wonderfully garish. Many changes to the original series are evident in this slicker version, but the themes are largely intact. The main shift is in the focus on Astro Boy's robotics. This time his seven powers are described not in humanitarian terms but in machine-power terms (trailing the late 70s' boom in robot *anime*). And just as Godzilla became a good guy in the Toho cycle of films through the 70s, Astro Boy in this second series would develop strong friendships with many of his mortal robot enemies, thus retaining a key theme from the *manga*: robots, monsters, spirits and animals are OK – Man is the problem.

The origins of Astro Boy in both the first two *Astro Boy* series and the *Tetsuwan Atomu manga* are consistent. Professor Temma aspires to create a new wonder robot with the aid of extensive R&D by the Science Ministry. He names the robot after his recently deceased son, Tobio. But Professor Temma becomes disillusioned with the almost-perfect nature of the ageless boy-robot and in a rage sells him to a circus. There he is rescued by Professor Ochanomizu, who educates Tobio and renames him Tetsuwan Atom. With new social skills, advanced robotics and a memory bank of human-affected experiences, Tetsuwan Atom commits himself to serving humans – but forever ponders his relationship with them. This is Pinocchio retold through Asimov, but with a molecular explosion of themes and dichotomies to do with the essence of soul, the imagination of children, the gender of plastic and the morality of cuteness.

Interestingly, both the Japanese and American production companies employed a woman to voice Astro Boy for both these series. (The 2003 series features an American male kid whose aggressive golly-gosh wisecracks are entirely opposed to Astro Boy's character.) The first two series' unusual softness for such a powerful robotic being is crucial to the character of Astro Boy as an innocent untainted by human foibles and their abuse of power. Despite the TV-reduced plots of both series the context, culture and form of the animated *Astro Boy* resonate with a peculiarly Japanese configuration of trans-gender post-war neo-human traits not usually explored by traditional social-conscience photo-cinema. Those vibrations are felt somewhere in all *anime* produced since.

TV

Genre: Robot Melodrama
Dir: Osamu Tezuka, Gisaburo Sugii, Daisaku Sakamoto, Eiichi Yamamoto, Osamu Dezaki, Yoshiyuki Tomino, Minoru Okazaki, Fusahito Nagaki; **Prod:** Osamu Tezuka; **Scr:** Osamu Tezuka, Noriyuki Honma, Masaki Tsuji, Kenichi Takashi; **Anim:** Daisaku Sakamoto; **Chara:** Osamu Tezuka; **Score:** Tatsuo Takai (theme song); **Sound:** Matsuo Ono; **Manga:** *Tetsuwan Atomu* (*Mighty Atom*); **Wr/Art:** Osamu Tezuka.

Baoh – The Visitor (*Baoh – Raihosha*)
Japan, 1989
Hiroyuki Yokoyama

When Ikuro awakens from a fluid incubation chamber at the beginning of *Baoh – The Visitor*, he is a nobody full of nothing. As he emerges/merges into a psycho-genetic killing machine known as Baoh, he becomes an anti-body and a hyper-thing. This reinvention of 'somebody' into 'something' recurs with alarming regularity in *anime*. *Baoh* is blunt in its take on such creation-through-nullification. The story has neither space nor time for pondering whether Ikuro himself ponders his past, present or future. He has simply become an unstable fluctuating organism. Human, humanism and humanity are flattened to a ground zero of existence, a void-space that withholds the supreme nothingness which guides his psyche.

Invented for the all-powerful all-funded Doress organisation by geneticist Dr Kusuminome, Ikuro is the first completed test subject of the Baoh process: an implantation of a horrendously powerful parasite that lives within the brain. Its effect upon Ikuro's brain grants him radical transformations of his bodily form. In place of standard principles of genetic mutation, which remain unalterable and only activated through generational procreation, the Baoh parasite works like a micro-geneticist within the brain's signal-processing centre, sending out commands to parts of the body to 'become' something terribly Other. As with all such experiments in the *anime* lexicon, the mind's interface with the brain and its controlling mechanisms throws chaos into the designer's projected picture. Once Ikuro has arisen, the rage he generates is a cycle that cannot be stopped.

Ikuro's only impulse is to protect himself and the young ESPer Sumire – herself an incarcerated child stolen for experimentation by Doress. Effectively lobotomised of any parental heritage, Ikuro becomes a surrogate parent to Sumire, as they are both mysterious orphans voided by the world which they roam. On the run, continually confronted with threatening situations, forced into moments of unchecked anxiety, Baoh stands in line with those tragic shape-shifters lost to their own transformative energy. More werewolf than cyborg, Ikuro is pushed to points whereby his metamorphosis cannot be reversed until he has depleted his newly activated resources and capabilities. In doing so, he passes through Dr Kusuminome's various pre-programmed Armament Phases, where Ikuro's arms develop blades, hands shoot forth spikes and chest cavity hurls thunderous balls of quaking force.

Being the product of one's environment is a quaint modernist social thesis that drifts by momentarily in an *anime* like *Baoh*. When one literally has been engineered, one's status is all-product, so quibbling over deviation from definable humanism is petty. *Baoh* reverses the environmental conditioning paradigm by Ikuro becoming the environmentally transforming product Baoh. The extreme violence he unleashes – melting faces with his bare hands, squeezing arms into black pulp, slicing torsos into volcanic geysers of viscera – equates his enemies' inner violence, which they bear through their being part of the insidious Doress organisation that created Boah. No simple matter of familial or corporate revenge, Ikuro as Baoh enacts a considered form of balance that matches his internal nothingness with the external nothingness his eviscerated enemies become.

OVA (1)

Genre: Psychic Action

Dir: Hiroyuki Yokoyama; **Prod:** Reiko Fukakusa; **Scr:** Kenji Terada; **Anim:** Michi Sanaba, Masayoshi Tano; **Chara:** Michi Sanaba; **Score:** Hiroyuki Namba; **Sound:** Noriyoshi Matsura; **Manga:** *Baoh – Raihosha* (*Baoh – The Visitor*); **Wr/Art:** Hiroki Araki.

Barefoot Gen (*Hadashi no Gen*)
Japan, 1983 – 85 mins
Masaki Mori

Visions of the end of the world come in many guises. A memorable image in *Barefoot Gen* is a horse running down a main street. The horse is on fire. This is Hiroshima; it's 1945 and the atomic bomb has just been dropped. That flaming horse speaks volumes of mythic proportion. It is a beast from Hades possessed and enflamed with the desperate desire to destroy, unleashed in the mania of war. It is one of the four horses of the Apocalypse – the second possibly appeared at Nagasaki, the other two prevented from appearing following Japan's surrender. Within *Barefoot Gen*, it is a singular surreal moment; an impassive document of how the world is being transformed at that precise moment.

Barefoot Gen relives the past without hindsight. As in the original *manga* written and drawn by survivor Keiji Nakazara, the memory of the lead-up to the A-bomb drop and the chaos that ensued is frozen in the present tense. While much *anime* has breath-taking leaps backwards and forwards in time – across eons, between epochs, within parallel continuities – *Barefoot Gen* is grid-locked in a tight linear development. Its momentum might appear slow and pedestrian, but it is an incremental progression from an event that has stopped time, erased space and utterly transformed atmosphere. The plain quality and tone in both *Barefoot Gen*'s *manga* and *anime* is integral to this grappling reportage of the unreal environment created in the bomb's immediate aftermath.

Autobiographies are attuned to details, allowing perspective to be shaped from their accumulation. *Barefoot Gen* recalls all the tactile experiences young Gen (representing author Nakazara) encounters and undergoes in the months that follow the fateful drop. They're not mere incidents: he helps deliver his mother's baby – and buries it shortly after. He attempts to save others only to have their flesh fall apart in his hands. Mostly though, Gen's 'journey' is devoid of heroics and is forged by the

Barefoot Gen: chaos frozen in the present tense

slightest physical occurrences: securing a handful of rice; finding a barely running water-pipe; scavenging wood, blankets, matches. *Barefoot Gen* evolves into a terse testimonial, eschewing poetry, metaphor and symbolism for a simple and unadorned depiction true to the title of the *manga* in its formative stages – *Ore ga mita* (*I Saw It*).

    Barefoot Gen functions as an important contextualising prop for *anime*'s futurist speculation. Terms like 'dystopian', 'post-apocalyptic' and 'mutation' cannot be applied to *Barefoot Gen*. It is not 'dystopian' because its flayed social malaise is not the result of any utopian impulse (save for Japanese imperialism of which the *anime* and *manga* are openly critical). It is not 'post-apocalyptic' because it takes place as the bomb was dropped and as people were desperately trying to figure out their predicament. And it does not deal with 'mutation' as metaphor because the story observes precisely how the physical body suffers and contorts through radiation. Futuristic *anime* may be comparatively 'ungrounded' and 'unrealistic', but they echo the phrasing of *Barefoot Gen*'s reportage and invert it into modes of allegorical flow and archetypological patterning.

Feature

Genre: Historical Drama

Dir: Masaki Mori; **Prod/Scr:** Keiji Nakazawa; **Anim/Chara:** Kazuo Tomisawa; **Score:** Kentaro Haneda; **Sound:** Susumu Aketagawa; **Manga:** *Hadashi no Gen* (*Barefoot Gen*); **Wr/Art:** Keiji Nakazawa.

Battle Angel Alita (Gunmu)
Japan, 1993
Hiroshi Fukutome, Rin Taro

A 'Pinocchio effect' – the desire to create a living being from an anthropomorphic doll – is sutured within the Japanese culture of puppets just like Pinocchio's own invisible strings. *Astro Boy* is the seminal modern text, rewiring Pinocchio with Asimov and Zen and envisaging a post-human child as the logical extent achievable through robotics. *Anime* could be regarded as a medium of puppetry with its myriad alignments of machines with humans, mechanics with consciousness. This would explain why so much cinema history and film language falls off *anime*'s corpus like an ill-fitted costume.

Battle Angel Alita is a whirlpool of puppet mythology that sucks in European and Japanese currents, forming a transcultural blend of animatrics. Gally (Alita in the English versions) is neither born, conjured nor invented: she is assembled bit by bit from parts scavenged in a huge cyborg junkyard by Dr Ido. Her conglomerate status is a reflection of the myth-recycling which brings her story to life. Set in the obligatory dystopian future, created from an ecological wasteland that grants human life scarcely a foothold to eke out an existence, Gally is both a mystically resilient life force and an undying testament to the Pinocchio effect.

Constructing robotic form and designing intelligent function in Japan has naught to do with the European heritage that chains Icarus to Prometheus to Frankenstein to *2001: A Space Odyssey* (1968) in a single God-fearing cold sweat. Making robots is how post-humans breed in a non-Judeo-Christian incubating system. The serious industrial pursuit of robotics, the aesthetic crafting of anthropomorphic semblance in any machine, the animistic belief in life force in all things, plus the acceptance of spiritual, mystical and hidden energies within dolls, figurines and idols – these form the sedimentary layer that holds *Battle Angel Alita* as a socio-cultural tradition as much as a cine-generic invention.

The world *Battle Angel Alita* depicts and how Gally fits into it are then issues of more importance than the precepts of her animatronic being. Gally attains cyborg consciousness in the world from which she has been assembled: a cruel terrain populated by renegade machinery, dysfunctional robotics and aggressive devouring forces. Scrap Iron City is bereft of civilisation as we know it and deadly conclusive laws of the junk jungle govern all life forms. Yet this society is no more than humanity devoid of its positivist stance and progressive flag-waving. It is arguably the essence of humanity – especially when one sees that the upper classes of human and cyborg alike are now secluded in a gigantic suspended metropolis kilometres above the ground. A metallic disc structure the size of a continent, Sky City Zalem tapers into a central colonic chute that literally excretes all form of waste from the ruling classes, dumping it onto the spread of Scrap Iron City below. If you are what you eat, you are also what you defecate, and from this technological excreta Gally arises. Initially unbeknown to her and Ido, she harbours psychic-martial abilities which are a compression of the disused energies the ruling classes have left fallow below them. Gally thus becomes a deadly Pinocchio who dreams not of being human, but of becoming post-human.

OVA (2)

Genre: Cyborg Action

Dir: Hiroshi Fukutome, Rin Taro; Prod: Kazuhiko Ikeguchi, Joichi Sugito; Scr: Akinori Endo; Anim: Futoshi Fujikawa; Chara: Nobuteru Yuki; Score: Soichiro Harada, Kaoru Wada; Sound: Yasunori Honda; Manga: *Gunmu*; Wr/Art: Yukito Kishiro.

Beck (Beck – Mongolian Chop Squad)
Japan, 2004
Osamu Kobayashi

It's a shame that dramatic forms rooted in the teen world are so often presumed to be transitory, disposable and reactive. *Beck* is all these things – not in terms of its status as entertainment product (being a TV series developed from a long-running *manga*) but in the way it shapes the emotional moods of its characters and their situations.

Despite the setting of *Beck* being a surprisingly accurate reflection of the hipper-than-thou, starry-eyed yet freshly cynical world of inner city Japanese alt.rock bands fantasising about American-style fame while pouring their lives into making their band happen, one need not be into this subcultural realm to appreciate the series. More than many might perceive, *Beck* is an intense and simmering study of how a group of young kids work out their interpersonal and antisocial connections to assemble the band as a vehicle for their aspirations, shortcomings, delusions and frustrations. In some respects, it's the standard individual being shaped through team spirit, which is common in *anime* script templates, but the weight, texture and transparency *Beck* conveys through its rock milieu and characterisation is always engaging, convincing and affecting.

Central core to the claylike lump of the unformed band is fourteen-year-old-Yukio. Across the series, he is the springboard, instigator and conduit for the unseen and unknowable circumstances which map out the groundwork upon which the band is slowly built. His chance meetings with the slightly older and brooding Ryusuke and his fiery sister Maho, Yukio's childhood friend Izumi, and failed Olympic swimmer Mr Saitou (a British Beat fan in his forties who teaches Yukio to play guitar) – these momentary intersections slowly lurch towards the inevitable making of the band called Beck (named after Ryusuke's dog).

Yet *Beck* does not achieve this through script alone. Scenes of Yukio learning guitar, having his guitars smashed through accidental and malicious actions, and melding his guitar with the band sound are conveyed with sonic precision and palpable energy. When Yukio bonds with Ryusuke, Maho and Yukio, instruments, voices, backing, ambience and tonality are all foregrounded in profoundly symbolic ways that prove that *Beck* is a sonically literate drama, and no mere Broadway-style vaudevillian mime of rock debauchery and pyrotechnics.

The foregrounded poetics of the music's materiality point to the sedimentary drama mined by the series, from which the symbolic elements of the story's subcultural setting are aligned. The band is centred as the socialising unit for the drama; its formation is the means to draw out the narrative; the guitar is wielded as the transformative instrument that actions the drama; even a guitar pick is held as a mystical token. Whereas rock mythology is usually staged pompously as having religious significance (its idols and gods, its believers and fanatics), *Beck* drains rock music of all its invested mythology and in place returns it to a small-scale social world. A rare *anime* in its attunement to the power of song, the projection of voice and the headspace that amplifies the world in which one lives.

TV

Genre: Teen Drama
Dir: Osamu Kobayashi; **Prod:** Shukuri Takeshi, Yoshimi Nakajima; **Scr:** Osamu Kobayashi;
Anim: Madhouse; **Chara:** Motonobu Hori, Osamu Kobayashi; **Score:** Taku Hirai;
Sound: Yukio Nagasaki; **Manga:** *Beck*; **Wr/Art:** Harold Sakuishi.

Black Jack (Burakku jyakku)
Japan, 1996 – 93 mins
Osamu Dezaki

Modern American comic books are synonymous with 'super-heroes' to such an extent that most American heroics in popular culture are synonymous with comic-book approaches to narrative. By comparison, *manga* is decidedly post-human, preferring to create either 'super-machines' in robots, cyborgs, androids and mobile suits, or densely complicated 'meta-heroes' who embody contradictions and conflations rather than distilling them into a hypo-mythic concentrate. One infamous instance is Black Jack, the renegade unlicensed surgeon of the long-running *manga*.

The film *Black Jack* builds upon the established characterisation of Black Jack as a calmed emotional torrent of disaffected grievances, simultaneously ruthless in his financial dealings with clients and violently ethical about the use of his surgeon super-skills. If doctors are generally aligned with gods through their life-granting actions, Black Jack is a soul

Black Jack: a calmed emotional torrent of disaffected grievances

in purgatory due to being more skilled than the gods. This dooms him as an outsider both metaphysically and socially; his super-skills place those who seek him in awe of his power, while medical boards of the world bristle at the mention of his name. Yet far from the composed physician of moral lore, Black Jack is a volatile figure. In *Black Jack* he is clinically cool as he performs an impossible removal of a tumour in the pituitary gland, yet bursts into an emotional rage when learning of the abuse that caused his patients their unnecessary suffering.

The plot of *Black Jack* pits his discerning and disconcerting medical super-heroics against Jo Carol Brane who has developed a drug capable of transforming normal people into 'super-humans'. Possessing talents as prodigious of those of Black Jack, she stands as a feminine mirror to his dark and brooding stature. However, her advances in developing the drug for her father's company Brane Pharmaceuticals push her into covering up the drug's side-effects years down the track, leading her to form an unholy alliance with Black Jack that ties their skills and ethics into a complicated psychological and ethical ball.

Jo Carol's 'super-humans' in fact create a phenomenon labelled 'super-humanism' after a spate of impossible records are created during the 1996 Olympics. Two years later, these same heroes of statistical achievement lie withering in a secret Brane Pharmaceuticals facility as their insides are literally eating them alive. These ex-super humans now require Black Jack's super-skills, creating a wry inversion of the 'super hero' convention of a mere mortal suddenly possessing super-human strength. In *Black Jack*, such strength is ultimately debilitating, and requires a super-intellect to battle its effects and save once-normal humans from their artificial endowments.

Within the broader portraiture of Black Jack, such situations are commonplace in the terrain across which he roams. Disconnected from social mores and their welcoming comforts, his outsider status matches the ways in which the sick body will often reside outside of both social and medical control. Only when all other avenues have been exhausted do people contact Black Jack, as does Jo Carol Brane in the film. Black

Jack's unlicensed status is the proper proclamation of his meld of hero, anti-hero and 'meta-hero'.

Feature

Genre: Psychological Drama

Dir: Osamu Dezaki; **Prod:** Kazuyoshi Okuhara, Takayuki Matsutani; **Scr:** Eto Mori, Kihachi Okamoto; **Anim:** Akio Sugino; **Chara:** Akio Sugino; **Score:** Eiji Kawamura; **Sound:** Etsushi Yamada; **Manga:** *Burakku jyakku* (*Black Jack*); **Wr/Art:** Osamu Tezuka.

Black Magic M-66 (Burakku majikku M-66)
Japan, 1987
Hiroyuki Kitakubo, Masamune Shiro

Only in *anime* could a secret department, buried deep within the military, engineer an unstoppable cyborg killing machine – and model it like a puppet. *Black Magic M-66* is the official moniker of this machine, and its design replicates the armature and interlocked mechanisms that afford movement in the puppet designs of *ningyo joruri*, a traditional form of puppet theatre. Mario is in fact a 'naked' puppet, unclothed and bare, replete with wispy white hair that evokes the white mane worn by shamanistic characters in Japanese folklore. While much American cyborg sci-fi attempts to frighten us with what ultimately are squeaky-smooth and algorhythmically manipulated CGI puppets, *Black Magic M-66* deliberately presents the physical puppet as a design through which terror emanates, linking the story closer to a nightmarish fatherless Pinocchio than any of the grand robot lineage of sci-fi.

As in the original *manga*, Mario escapes and becomes a dislocated wandering being. Following his premature activation after an army freight plane crashes, his sole purpose – to kill according to programmed directives – guides him toward Felice, the granddaughter of his creator Dr Masshu (who had entered her name into Mario's memory as an interim test). The military is forced into mounting a massive attack plan, tracking Mario and bombarding him ceaselessly, but to no effect. Mario is the child born of their destructive desires, and now freed of the army's paternal control, he becomes a ruthless robotic *ronin* stubbornly sticking to his pre-programming with deadly logic. *Black Magic M-66*'s titular titanium killer is a dehumanised simulation of human form, equipped with super-human strength, inhuman focus and post-human drive. His face evokes frozen innocence and heated impassivity as it stares not ahead but through everything: walls, buildings, armaments and people. Like an unstoppable heat-seeking missile, he homes in on the inner identity concealed within Felice, invisible to her and everyone except Mario and his steel gaze.

The magnetic attraction between Mario and the innocent Felice starts to resemble the *Frankenstein* movie archetype where the monster is attracted to the innocence of the young girl playing by the river, and similarly driven to possess the bride with reverse-necrophiliac desire. But wholly opposed to the demeanour of Frankenstein's 'created monster', Mario remains abjectly soulless. Frankenstein's creature in the novel and most films is surprisingly full of human emotion – far more than his creator. Mario is pure doll: incapable of a nano-wrinkle in his metallic skin. His animated form and mute stature strangely link him to the classic Frankensteinian mouthing and stumbling, yet *Black Magic M-66* rejects all morals which reduce and condemn the Frankenstein creation's manoeuvres.

Ultimately, Mario is a stateless, borderless, homeless being. The *anime*'s dramatic climax rises in reverse of the destructive collapse of the skyscraper where Mario has finally cornered Felice. In a superb series of spatial contractions, he chases Felice and the news reporter Sybel up floors, stairwells and elevators onto the rooftop – ultimate terrain of those who have nowhere else to go; final resting place for Mario's unstoppable purpose.

OVA (1)

Genre: Cyborg Action

Dir: Hiroyuki Kitakubo, Masamune Shiro; **Scr:** Masamune Shiro; **Anim:** Takayuki Sawaura;

Chara: Hiroyuki Kitakubo; **Mecha:** Toru Yoshida; **Score:** Yoshihiro Katayama;

Manga: *Burakku majikku M-66* (*Black Magic M-66*); **Wr/Art:** Masamune Shiro.

Blood – The Last Vampire
Japan, 2000
Hiroyuki Kitakubo

A partially 'lost' period of Japanese cinema is its early 60s' 'anti-American' films which – a decade on from the end of the American Occupation – were free to tackle themes and issues disallowed across the preceding decade. Both radical cinema and exploitation cinema of this period revelled in a savage Pop Art that furiously bathed in Americana only to cleanse itself in flames. Many of these films examined the heated dynamics that typified the modern culture clashes that shaped Japan into its current state. *Anime* has rarely connected to this period of cinema, one notable exception being *Blood – The Last Vampire*.

Blood is set in the mid-60s' midst of these 'anti-US' films' production, and laterally connects to the spirit and *Zeitgeist* of those films. The hybrid-animation technique of *Blood* is fast paced and multi-layered and seems initially more modern than its pre-Vietnam war setting, yet this stylistic clash is symbolic of the cultural clash at the time. A re-invented vampire tale, *Blood*'s central character is the precocious teen Saya: a haunting doll of a vampire hunter upon whose countenance one can read infinite emptiness and chillingly calmed soullessness. Not a vampiric being devouring blood for sustenance, she is 'fresh blood': a new type of being that has been born in the post-war hysteria wherein Japan is overcome by the shockwaves of what the nation had set into motion during World War II. An innocent of sorts, Saya represents the proceeding generations swept up in the tides of post-war as flotsam purely through their blood-line and racial connection to a country's war machinery that churns the ocean.

The Gothic effect in *Blood* is strangely muted. In place of the dank penumbra of fetid stylisation that signifies the Gothic, *Blood* is toned a dirty yellow (a problematising pan-Asiatic 'yellowing'), diffused through cyclone fencing, electrical wiring and faulty fluorescent lighting. The American bases and their curved corrugated hangars typify the landscape as bats in the belfry are replaced by B-52s above. The planes' ominous drone mingles with an endless ferrying of trucks, jeeps and railcars, orchestrating a noisescape which replicates the noise in Saya's head as she grapples with her violent impulses. These same impulses are being harnessed by an elite Japanese 'secret police' battling an insurgent vampire force who exist due to pre-war dealings with the government. Saya is a pawn in their grand plan, but she may also be the queen of the game.

Made so many decades after the American Occupation, *Blood* gives rise to reading contemporary Japan under similar forces. Saya resonates with today's problematised teens and the psychological difficulties they face as 'post-Bubble boomers', born in a dehistoricised era that complexly watermarks Japan–US and Japan–Asia relations from the preceding century upon the present day. Today's teens are like Saya,

Blood: a new type of being born of post-war hysteria

innocent but implicated. And like Saya, their maturation may not be through spiritual enlightenment (the primary metaphor in teen *anime*), but through a broader contextualised picture of how they fit in with a past of invisible socio-political forces which guide their movements.

OVA (1)

Genre: Goth Drama

Dir: Hiroyuki Kitakubo; **Prod:** Yukio Nagasaki, Ryuji Mitsumoto; **Scr:** Kenji Kamiyama; **Anim:** Kazuchika Kise; **Chara:** Tatsuya Terada; **Score:** Yoshihiro Ike; **Sound:** Keiichi Momose.

Blue Seed (Buru shiido)
Japan, 1994
Jun Kamiya, Kiyoshi Murayama, Shinya Sadamitsu

Anime thrills to the invisible. Energies, dimensions, beings, temporalities, sexualities – all are configured as vibrational forces unregistered by the eye. While the animated medium in the West is spurred onward to greater verisimilitude and lifelikeness, *anime* strives towards greater apparition and mysticism. Laterally linked to ecological exploration in much *anime*, *Blue Seed* is brimful of visualisations of invisible energies, yet it is also grounded in the earth. Literally.

Blue Seed extends its scenarios of mystical powers hidden in plants, flowers and seeds through an awareness of trees. Apparently still and inanimate, their visible form is the result of energised connections to two invisible zones – the underground soil where a tree's roots drink H_2O, and the overground air where its leaves breathe CO_2. The tree's overground matrixed sprouting mirrors its underground rhizome network. Accepting this state of the tree's life force and its territory, it's a

Blue Seed: part psycho-agrarian medium, part eco-social mediator

small twist to accord spiritual possibilities to trees. *Blue Seed*'s fantasy flora vibrationally summons Momiji who ends up helping the TAC Agency – a special division combating the increase of 'possessed' monster trees and insectoids known as the Arigami which erupt into orgies of destructive force, decimating all urbanised land within their reach.

This is a marvellous allegory of nature taking its revenge on culture. Hemmed into correct behaviour as parks, gardens and reserves, the cultivation of nature within any urban spread – but especially space-starved Japan – is allowed access to earth and air by restricted occupancy ordinances. *Blue Seed* imagines nature's rejection of such legislature, creating a new urban threat for its deruralised inhabitants. Coming in the mid-90s when ecological concerns were being progressively expressed, *Blue Seed*'s TAC Agency symbolises a Japan that is now having to deal with the after-effects of decades of corporate abuse of the environment. *Blue Seed* does not voice these concerns so outwardly, but themes of ecological balance are rooted in the series' drama.

Momiji is the 'blue seed' of *Blue Seed*. Due to the blood of the mystical Kushinada clan fuelling her veins, she carries the potential to avert disaster, navigate compromising situations and point to solutions. Part psycho-agrarian medium, part eco-social mediator, she is the voice of reason and the ears of sympathy that the TAC Agency requires if it is to save the city without destroying nature. Momiji's ability is seeded deep within her – her mysterious blue pendant with its 'halved' yin/yang symbol suggests she is aligned with a non-holistic system: nature living under modernity. Seeds symbolise heritage and lineage, just as roots symbolise the connectedness of things, and Momiji is the psychic connection bringing everything onto a plane of balance. Her counterpart – a genetic counterpoint to her stability – is the disturbed Kusanagi: a horticultured human mutation who once served the Aragami, his rage erupts through his limbs like cacti blades lashing out. The yang to Momiji's yin, he becomes an important part of her existence that allows them as mutant and psychic to atone for human intervention and quell the herbivorous invasion before the Earth truly returns to the Earth.

TV

Genre: Mystical Action

Dir: Jun Kamiya, Kiyoshi Murayama, Shinya Sadamitsu; **Prod:** Naohiro Hayashi, Masaki Sawanobori, Yukinao Shimoji; **Scr:** Toshihisa Arakawa, Masaharu Amiya; **Anim:** Nobuyoshi Habara; **Chara:** Yuzo Takada; **Score:** Kenji Kawai; **Sound:** Kazuhiro Wakabayashi; **Manga:** *Aokushimitama buru shiido* (*Strange Blue Seed*); **Wr/Art:** Yuzo Takada.

Bubblegum Crisis (Baburugamu kuraishisu)
Japan, 1987
Katsuhito Akiyama, Hiroki Hayashi, Masami Obari, Fumihiko Takayama, Hiroaki Goda

Cute babes; tight suits; big guns. The hyper-sexed construct of a woman with an incredible figure who is also a crack marksperson is a complex assemblage of male, female, gay, straight, heroic and S&M fantasies, equally distributed across the 'mytho-morph' of this popular icon in American entertainment. Much ridicule and disdain have been accorded this icon of absurdly female objectification, but that has never diluted its power or appeal.

Within *anime*, this American 'mytho-morph' has been retooled and customised, undergoing a new body-shop buff to complement Japanese driving conditions. The definitive *Bubblegum Crisis* series is based on an all-woman team and their mind-boggling eye-ogling hi-tech body-suit armoury (replete with mecha-stiletto power-boots). Celia, Priss, Linna and Nene form the Knight Sabers – a vigilante group of mercenaries in Mega Tokyo, 2032. They suit-up and disrobe their mecha-suits throughout, each of them distinguished by their colour. This colour-coded super-suited action-gang is a homage to the 70s' era of live action *tokusatsu* TV series: serialised action sagas that mixed martial arts, heroic pantomime and super-transformative beings whose suits and costumes signified their transformed state, mystical power and paranormal capabilities. The Knight Sabers of *Bubblegum Crisis* are high-throttled mecha-sexualisations of the same.

Yet this is not enough to characterise the super-sexy-suit phenomenon of *anime*. The suits of *Bubblegum Crisis* are essentially a denuding of the gendered body, reconfiguring its sexuality as an outer skin and psychic shell counter to the notion that sexuality resides within. By materialising sex, gender and power as a curvaceous yet crustaceous culturing of armour – an act not far removed from Japan's *daimyo*, *samurai* and *geisha*s' material enveloping of the body – *Bubblegum Crisis*

Bubblegum Crisis: reconfiguring sexuality as an outerskin

turns the body inside-out and the psyche outside-in.

Outrageously puerile and emblematic of 80s' *otaku* iconography, *Bubblegum Crisis* rises above its iconography and achieves something American babes-with-guns entertainment cannot: an unlikely respect for female characterisation despite and beyond its costumery and adornment. Erotically enshrining the Knight Sabers' bodies and suits throughout the series, *Bubblegum Crisis*'s spotlighting of Priss is the antidote to a consumptive malaise of sexualised femininity. The opposite to her moniker, Priss fronts a hard rock band and is a sullen solitary figure brimful of unresolved issues. She stands for 'rock' music in opposition to the *idoru* pop promotion of 'bubblegum' music, thereby giving deeper meaning to the series' title. *Bubblegum Crisis* may not be far removed from the American tacky-wacky of 70s' TV series like *Josie & the Pussycats* (1970) and *Charlie's Angels* (1976), but the psychological differences between the characters of *Bubblegum Crisis* make it comparatively more involving. Plus the series is concise in dramatising its female domain as one wherein women have no fear of technology; are capable in extreme and threatening situations; collectively work to deal with situations; and actively dismiss the mock-heroism of their male counterparts. At the end of the day those sexy suits are remarkably secondary to the women who wear them. A curious oddity in Western entertainment; an established code in *anime*.

OVA (8)

Genre: Power-Suit Drama

Dir: Katsuhito Akiyama, Hiroki Hayashi, Masami Obari, Fumihiko Takayama, Hiroaki Goda; **Prod:** Hiroshi Tazaki, Kinya Watanabe; **Scr:** Katsuhito Akiyama, Arii Emu, Toshimichi Suzuki, Hidetoshi Yoshida; **Anim:** Kinji Yoshimoto, Satoshi Urushihara, Masahiro Tanaka, Morifumi Naka, Masaki Kajishima; **Chara:** Kenichi Sonada; **Mecha:** Obari Masami, Shinji Aramaki, Hideki Kakinuma, Kenichi Sonada; **Score:** Kouji Makaino; **Sound:** Noriyoshi Matsuura.

Burn Up!
Japan, 1991
Yasunori Ide

Late twentieth-century televisual drama in the West would be nowhere without doctors, lawyers, cops and detectives. The fact that 'quality drama' is associated with productions centred on these types is deflating in its implication that they are the moral guardians of contemporary society. Such clichéd dramatic vessels are refreshingly absent in *anime*.

Burn Up! is a complete mockery of that legitimised televisual grip. It bears all the labelling and typecasting one can read on their Western live-action counterparts, but here they are irreverently dismissed as just another bunch of bureaucrats in dead-end jobs. Cross-hatched with super-hero patterning, *Burn Up!* shows cops to be not much more than a team of uniformed drones hampered by protocol and ineffectual in practice. Invisibly housed within this regime is a secret crime-fighting team of Maki, Remi and Yuka. Absurdly buxom babes in uniforms that could only exist in *anime*, the trio are a maverick unit with the 'balls' to handle situations beyond the limited powers of the police (a wry barb at the much-derided Japanese police force suffering government control).

Maki's boyfriend Kenji and his partner Banba are detectives on the same force, but they end up being far less effectual than Maki, Remi and Yuka once these buoyant bamazons swing into action. Maki in particular is more hot-headed than a division of macho men, always itching to discharge fire-power and get the job done hard and fast. The women (of course) don outrageous crime-fighting outfits which resemble that of a leather-clad dominatrix. In the hyper-design mode of *anime*, there is no attempt to qualify their costumery, giving us a sense of how ridiculous American 40s' crime-fighting attire must have appeared to those outside the West. The vertical lettering 'POLICE' down their thigh-high boots is a bizarre but titillating fusion of departmental signage and erotic tease.

The main assignment the team takes is to bust the Samuel McCoy white slavery ring. Working undercover, Yuka's life is in jeopardy now the gang has discovered she is a cop. Interestingly, 'white slave trade' was a staple element of American 30s' serials. However, it had also been a staple 'human crop' throughout most of Japan's abusive epochs, wherein daughters were sold by peasant families into prostitution in a practice that openly continued up to World War II. Despite the feverish comedic tone of *Burn Up!*, a slight pall hangs over 'female trade' being employed not for its exotic appeal but for its commonplace notoriety. Yet this is one of the many elements in *Burn Up!* that is deliberately flaunted in a tart and cursory manner. Swirling and splashing in pop culture mud, *Burn Up!* refutes the mandates of social commentary and progressivist solution. While it may suffer attacks from those who wish to ideologically demolish disreputable fare due to its 'ignorance of context', the rampant sauciness and sexiness of *Burn Up!* can be deemed a welcome respite to the self-important quality dramas used as ideological pornography by those who wish to sculpt artificial dioramas of self-validating concern.

OVA (4)

Genre: Future Crime

Dir: Yasunori Ide; Prod: Akio Matsuda, Susumu Miura; Scr: Jun Kanzaki; Anim/Chara: Kenjin Miyazaki; Mecha: Gasho Tano; Score: Kenji Kawai; Sound: Yoshikazu Iwanami.

Combustible Campus Guardress (*Bakuen kyampasu gadoresu*)
Japan, 1994
Toshihiko Nishikubo

With one of the most post-modern titles in the subgenre of 'wild school' *anime*, *Combustible Campus Guardress's* use of Japlish is a key to unlocking its energetic approach to narrative. It's as much a reflection of then-called 'New Wave' Japanese cinema's antisocial comedies like *Crazy Family* (1984), as a refraction of the contemporaneous US antisocial teen movies like *Rock'N'Roll High School* (1979). *Combustible Campus Guardress* is a multi-generic style-clash of the comic, cosmic, pathetic and tragic goings in your average Japanese high school. Sort of. The series simultaneously parodies and critiques not only what it depicts as the antics of the high school, but also the way the *anime* is constructed and formulated according to clichés and conventions which ordinate its 'wild school' subgenre. The employment of Japlish in its title is just one of many smoke-bomb screens of pranksterism which modulate the series' anarchic comedic thrust.

In clear demonstration of how high school is another world, the Tobira High School houses the Sakimori, a group of teens dedicated through heritage to fighting the Remnant: warriors of the Dark World seeking to break through the school's barrier to take over the world. The school is designed as a giant land-lock in the shape of a voyeuristic key-hole that rises upward and creates a series of tributary waterways to island its terrain and seal its inhabitants in a mortal conflict. But it's also a riotous piss-take on how Japanese isolationism might be taught in the classroom. Taking those metaphors literally, it lays claim to high school hell being a potent example of self-enforced isolationism. This reckless quasi-punk attitude is emblematic of 80s' Japanese pop culture, rejecting the leftist strategy of critique and obliquely making a link to the radical absurdist theatrics of films like *Emperor Tomato Ketchup* (1971) and its savage satire of social propriety in Japan.

As with the much maligned 80s' cycle of US teen movies, *Combustible Campus Guardress* cunningly disguises the respect and pathos it extends to its rowdy, confused and pressured kids via a series of internally coded modalities. This subcultural argot is the vernacular and vulgar 'voice of youth', and is an apt form of delivery which has coded teen *anime* for over two decades. Siblings Hazumi and Takumi and their classmates are interred in a psychic prison in acerbic replay of how school is a hermetically sealed social sphere that has little to do with the outside world. This accords with the well-documented 'terror of being taught' in the Japanese school system. Under its oppressive regime, individuality is supposedly drummed out of any potential freak in school – though those same freaks can end up as acclaimed artists in *manga* and *anime*. *Combustible Campus Guardress* is full of nothing but 'freaks', misfits and outcasts. That they swim in a gaudy goldfish bowl of contradictions is something ignored by acerbic Western analyses of Japanese schooling and its will-bending 'knowledge through indoctrination': these kids know it's hell, and live through it with the achievement of having survived hell.

OVA (4)

Genre: Teen Comedy

Dir: Toshihiko Nishikubo; **Prod:** Hiroyuki Yamagata; **Scr:** Satoru Akahori, Kazushi Hagiwara; **Anim:** Kazuya Kose; **Chara:** Noriyasu Seta; **Score:** Fumitaka Anzai; **Manga:** *Bakuen kyampasu gadoresu* (*Combustible Campus Guardress*); **Wr:** Kazushi Hagiwara; **Art:** Noriyasu Seta.

Cream Lemon (Kuriimu remon)
Japan, 1986
Kazuya Miyazaki, Bikkuri Hako, Ayako Mibashi, Yuji Motoyama,
Toshihiro Hirano

The slip from the erotic to the pornographic replicates the slide from metaphor to metonym: when the rose becomes a vulva, poetry evaporates and viscera materialises. But what of animated imagery of the body at its basest? Is it pornographic poetry or poetic pornography? *Cream Lemon* may have the answer, though uncomfortably supplied.

Openly erotic in its title, *Cream Lemon* is a series from the first wave of *anime* soft-core porn that erupted during the early 80s' OVA boom. Like conventional porn, the story is a prop for the incidentalising of sexual activity, allowing it to be packaged in modular serialised form. Each volume of *Cream Lemon* contains a clutch of short episodes (termed 'climaxes'), each being disconnected from the other save for their contribution to the ongoing series. This is not only symptomatic of porn – to maintain supply in order to trigger demand – but also a synchronous exploitation of the OVA phenomenon and its delirious serialisation outside cinema exhibition and TV broadcast, designed for private home consumption and collectability.

The notoriety and popularity of the *Cream Lemon* series gave rise to reconsidering if the veracity of the photographic image is the means for stimulating response in partaking of the pornographic, or whether an animated image's graphic nature could seduce the viewer. The series is surprisingly free of fetishistic and parafiliac content. Men, women, teen boys and teen girls are all rendered realistically; most episodes show them unpossessing of super-powers or psychic abilities; no situations in which they are engaged produce karmic recurrences or mystical resonances; and no bodily transformations or transmogrifications are unleashed by any sexual activity. In a sense, *Cream Lemon* is anti-*anime*: its novelty is its eschewing of the fantastic the form extols, and in place offering a banality rendered with the precision of technical diagrams.

This depiction of a flattened world of predetermined interaction between its plasticised sex-dolls and clinical sex-aids constitutes a joining of the calligraphic and the pornographic to foreground the sexually graphic: an erotic peculiar to the Japanese climate of imagification.

But this is not to say *Cream Lemon* is simply a celebration of the banal. While the series' episodes are almost perfunctory in their stratagems of arousal and satiation, two dominant mutations of image codes shift the series into the surreal. The first recurring device is the use of pixilated effects to cover labial lips, pubic hair and erect members – standard in live action, but highly ironic in *anime* where no camera exists as such. The second recurring device is the sudden territorial rupture of the graphic by the symbolic, when the unshowable needs to be represented non-graphically. In one memorable episode a woman entices an Alsatian dog to perform cunnilingus on her; as she becomes enflamed in waves of oohs and aahs, we see close-ups of the Alsatian licking … a rose. Metaphor and metonym copulating and exchanging each other's fluid effects in a way that could only happen in *anime*.

OVA (36)

Genre: Erotic Drama

Dir: Kazuya Miyazaki, Bikkuri Hako, Ayako Mibashi, Yuji Motoyama, Toshihiro Hirano; **Prod:** Fairy Dust (company); **Anim:** Hiroshi Tajima, Mamoru Yasuhiko, Bikkuri Hako.

Crying Freeman (Kuraingu Furiiman)
Japan, 1989
Daisuke Nishio, Nobutaka Nishizawa, Johei Matsuura, Shigeyasu
Yamauchi, Takaki Yamashita

Many lines stream outward with a contra-Japanese compulsion from
Crying Freeman. One cluster heads towards China. Set in the
netherworld of the Chinese crime syndicate 108 Dragons, the story
follows the creation of Crying Freeman, an infallible killing machine.
Originally Ko, a dedicated ceramics craftsman, he is reprogrammed to be
the clan's top hitman through intricate acupuncture control. Perversely,
he is also programmed to automatically cry at the moment he kills his
targets, reminding him of his inner humanity. Just as the triad clan make
over the Japanese kiln artist into a Chinese assassin, so does *Crying
Freeman* immerse its story in Chinese ideals of power, society, family and
contracts,

Another contra-Japanese flow of *Crying Freeman* leads to the origins
of its illustrative mode. In place of the foregrounded calligraphic
brushwork which marks *anime*'s look, *Crying Freeman* employs a pen-
based aspect to its visualisation. The style is noticeably Western through
its alignment with realistic life-drawing perspective in place of the iconic
styling and idealised forms typical of *manga* and *anime*. *Crying Freeman*'s
visual surface is closely modelled on its originating *manga* and its realistic
depiction of bodies in action. Furthermore, the body of Freeman is
aflame with a huge tattooed dragon – signage of his ownership to the
clan, but also a bodily inscription of his Chinese status in defiance of the
yakuza Japanese tattoo imagery.

Despite these major impulses towards non-Japanese lineage and
typing, *Crying Freeman* subtextually expresses its Japanese origins and
aspirations in complex ways. Freeman falls in love with the beautiful
Japanese Emu who was originally a target on his list due to her
witnessing one of Ko's hits. The power of their love, however, allows
them to become a couple within the 108 Dragons, with Emu being

tattooed and formally re-named Fu Ching Ran. Emu and Ko become major forces in the development of the 108 Dragons and together battle a series of non-Asian crime syndicates intent on possessing Ko's super-skills: Italian mafia, Japanese *yakuza*, Black American radicals, as well as the Chinese international diaspora. Ko's body was originally perceived by the heads of the 108 Dragons as being the perfect physical form to be used as a vessel for their neural possession, but within he is a bottomless reservoir of deeply distilled Japanese waters.

Within the iconic and symbolic procedures of *manga* and *anime*, *Crying Freeman* is not dissimilar to the subgenre of mobile-suit space dramas. Ko is ultimately 'not himself' yet is conscious of this state, and resolves his voided status to reach a higher plane of existence and action. *Crying Freeman* delights in warping time and space through the split-second timing that guides the precision with which Ko shoots, stabs and knifes his victims. Often they are depicted as still images – frozen in terror and incomprehension – while Ko remains animated and moves through them like a dimensional death wave. Ko's 'character' is less a socialised and identifiable type, and more a fertilised breed of dehumanised machinery, propelled by death drives and sex drives that chillingly portray the cold interior of the archetypal Japanese assassin.

OVA (6)

Genre: Samurai Drama

Dir: Daisuke Nishio, Nobutaka Nishizawa, Johei Matsuura, Shigeyasu Yamauchi, Takaki Yamashita; Prod: Akira Sasaki, Naoko Takahashi, Tomiro Kuriyama; Scr: Higashi Shimizu, Tatsunosuke Ohno, Ryunosuke Ono; Anim: Koichi Arai, Satoshi Urushihara; Chara: Ryochi Ikegami; Score: Hiroaki Yoshino; Manga: *Kuraingu Furiiman* (*Crying Freeman*); Wr: Kazuo Koike; Art: Ryochi Ikegami.

Dangaio (Hajataisei dangaio)
Japan, 1987
Toshihiro Hirano

An action-packed ride of intergalactic thrills, *Dangaio* reverberates with a deeper, darker tone. Tracing the core veins of sci-fi, fantasy and other dreaming/speculative genres, *Dangaio* replays a reconstructed 'theatre of life' in the name of 'human drama'. But through *anime*'s unique capacity to potently bring to life complete realms, its narrative assemblages and vertiginous *mise en scène* are more revisionist than speculative. In its synaesthetic recreation of 'being' in a new world rather than asking 'the reader' to imagine such things, futuristic *anime* like *Dangaio* is constructed as if it has been made in the future, and is looking back at historical and social conditions on earth.

Dangaio is only illusorily a sci-fi tale: it is covertly a war movie. But instead of retracing war from the cartographical power drafted by generals and strategists, it focuses on the mind of the soldier. This is a strong characteristic of all post-Occupation war movies from Japan. The individual's character is psychologically excavated, as if to retrieve the mental glitch that transformed Japanese individuals into the military mass engaged in World War II. Of course many countries have pondered and analysed this – but few countries continue to do so fifty years later in animated entertainment aimed at an audience not even born during the war.

Dangaio's plot is more a contrivance to conduct such a psychological examination. The seemingly evil Professor Tahsan claims to have 'invented' a quartet of super-androids, but in reality they are four teenagers from different planetary systems. Tahsan has kidnapped them for their super-psychic abilities, and has erased their memories so as to sell them to the space pirate overlord Captain Galimos of the monstrous Bunker fleet. But this teen group – Miya, Rol, Lamba and Pi Thunder – gradually regain their memories and discover that each comes from a war-torn world. A double level of war trauma and memory loss is then

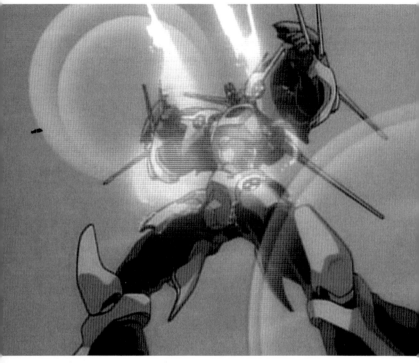

Dangaio: doubled levels of war trauma and memory loss

suffered by this group. First – after escaping from being sold to Galimos – they struggle to continue fighting while remembering their true inner identity, the dawning of which is a psychological interference to their tasks at hand. Second, once they remember who they are, they then suffer a new shell-shock which forces them as a group to return to each of their individual planets for closure and resolution to their problematised inner states.

Viewed this way, Tahsan – who after enraging Galimos joins the quartet on the run – is a therapist conducting an involved and multi-levelled treatment of their memory loss. Through their ventures, each comes to realise that despite having once had families and homes, they are now utterly alone. This is a post-Freudian plus for them: their joint psychic abilities – gained as much from DNA schisms as their realisation of being 'post-social' – allow them to merge and 'crossfire' their four individual fighter planes into the giant Dangaio meta-machine. Their teen/team spirit of *banzai* ferocity is signified by their call signs as they connect: 'Assemble!', 'Psychic Wave!', 'Plasma Typhoon!' and 'Spiral Knuckle!'. In the face of the ongoing global will to never forget the past, *Dangaio* radically proposes to remember to forget.

OVA (3)

Genre: Psychic Power Suit

Dir/Chara: Toshihiro Hirano; **Chara:** Junichi Watanabe; **Prod:** Makoto Asanuma, Toru Miura; **Scr:** Noboru Aikawa, Toshihiro Hirano, Koichi Ohata; **Anim:** Hideaki Anno; **Mecha:** Masami Obari, Koichi Ohata, Shoji Kawamori; **Score:** Michiaki Watanabe; **Sound:** Yasunori Honda; **Manga:** *Hajataisei dangaio* (*Evil Slaying Giant Star Dangio*); **Wr/Art:** Toshihiro Hirano.

Demon City Shinjuku (Makai toshi shinjuku)
Japan, 1988 – 80 mins
Yoshiaki Kawajiri

Apocalypse-101 is perfunctorily tagged at the opening of *Demon City Shinjuku*. Ten years earlier in the dead centre of Shinjuku, a battle between good and evil was waged that left the area a fallow inhuman terrain, soaked in brewing malevolence, waiting for an almighty ripening of dark forces in the present day. The landmark of this demonic realm is impossible to miss: the Shinjuku Keio Plaza towers are half-demolished, with one leaning angled upon the other. Police, military and government forces have attempted to take control of the deadly zone periodically, but have always failed. Though never depicted, the rest of Tokyo simply gets on with life as if nothing is wrong in Shinjuku.

The indefatigable delight of *anime* is the way the apocalypse is assumed to be commonplace. *Demon City Shinjuku* creates an alternative world complete with its interior ordinances, cosmic controls and necromantic strictures, and lands it hermetically in the midst of downtown Tokyo. Never is such a scenario regarded as ill-defined or implausible in *anime*; never does any character qualify, contextualise or clarify such situations. To some this might suggest an indifference to dramatic veracity, but philosophical notions of destiny, lineage and fate are deemed to eventually take care of matters. This clears the ground for the drama and action in *Demon City Shinjuku*'s modernisation of traditional *yokai* (ghost) legends and their vengeful tales.

Following Genichiro's loss to the maniacal Levih Rah during the pre-title set-up, our shuttle to the present ten years later finds Genichiro's son Kyoya to be the inheritor of advanced mystical control in the psychic art of *nempo*. But in less than a week, Levih Rah will rise from his dormant state renewed with power to wholly consume the mortal dimension and harbinge hell on earth. The prime minister is about to set Shinjuku into karmic realignment but is foiled by Levih Rah casting a spell that is slowly draining his life force. Kozumi's daughter Sayaka seeks out

Kyoya to aid her in fighting Levih Rah, and after reluctantly agreeing to help her, the two venture forth into the bowels of spiritual discontent that is Shinjuku.

The dimensional subdivision of Shinjuku from the original battle between Genichiro and Levih Rah is referred to as the Devil Quake. Levih Rah reconfigured the area as a vertical zone, tapping into the subterranean negativity suppressed by the overground's social planning. Having split the earth open, he slices the ground to create a vibrational mega-calligraphic line that cracks and delineates Shinjuku as a possessed zone. The final battle between Levih Rah and Kyoya is between the vertical and the horizontal, as Kyoya attempts to re-seal the demarcations carved by Levih Rah's summoning of dark energies. Interestingly, the transfixed state of Shinjuku is depicted through a blinding colourisation of blue and pink, as if the neon city of Shinjuku has been reconstituted by an ethereal night aura. Maybe the rest of Tokyo knew that as long as Shinjuku's neon haze was visible, it would eventually return to the mortal plane.

Feature

Genre: Mystical Horror

Dir/Chara: Yoshiaki Kawajiri; **Prod:** Kenji Kurata, Makoto Seya; **Scr:** Kaori Okamura; **Anim:** Naoyuki Onda; **Score:** Motoichi Umeda, Osamu Shoji; **Novel:** *Makai toshi shinjuku* (*Demonic Domain City Shinjuku*); **Wr:** Hideyuki Kikuchi.

Devil Hunter Yoko (Mamo no Hunta Yoko)
Japan, 1990–3
Tetsuro Aoki, Hisashi Abe, Haruo Itsuki, Junichi Sakata, Akiyuki Shinbo

As declaimed numerous times throughout *Devil Hunter Yoko* in a self-mocking tone, Yoko Mamano is the 108th Devil Hunter of the Mamano family. All the Devil Hunters have been women, and Yoko lives with her mother Sayoko and a feisty grandmother. The household is a matriarchal domain: a generational commune of women bereft of the domiciliation and servitude expected of households headed by men. While many fantastic fights with vicious demons abound throughout the series, the everyday world of the Mamano family is a microcosm of the symbolic all-female domain of *anime*, creating a maternal fantasy world governed entirely by female lineage and energy.

Yoko's world is one where men are only mentioned in terms of their sexual and romantic value. She must remain a virgin until her official transition to Devil Hunter once she turns sixteen – but after that both grandmother and mother encourage her to track down men for her own pleasure (with mother even supplying the condoms). Not a morning passes that doesn't start with Yoko on the verge of a wet dream caused by her many infatuations, and family discourse openly connects sexual virility in women to their ability to destroy demons. With all this talk of sex, *Devil Hunter Yoko* is undoubtedly in part an erotic fantasy, ranging from infantile sex gags to outrageous transformation scenes wherein Yoko has her clothes shredded mid-air as blinding light magically robes her in a hip-hugging bust-clutching Chinoise silk split skirt. But the series' scenarios exclude man/boy channels of desire, focusing instead on girlie-fixated dream worlds and proto-feminist male-crushing pyrotechnics.

Yoko's yin/yang symbol that covers her bulging breasts is emblematic of the gender battles she wages. She desires men who have been modelled as ideal fantasies of manhood within her fertile mind, just as she repels men who have been symbolically sculpted as monstrous nightmares of manhood within the spiritual world. A love–hate compulsion radiates from Yoko from which a yin/yang balance of sorts is struck. This is not precisely what happens in *Devil Hunter Yoko* plot-wise, but if she were placed on the psychoanalyst's couch, her wet dreams and fresh kills would appear to be seeking harmonic atonement.

While heritage dictates Yoko's abilities, duties and skills, and grandmother particularly talks about her past, no men are ever mentioned as part of the family tree. Their absence from the family's history is confoundedly total, inferring that the mystical strength of the Mamano clan comes from its erasure of men. When Yoko blossoms into full Devil Hunter, she reaches deep within her psyche to extract her Soul Sword: a definitive hyper-phallic instrument that becomes the customised inner self for each Devil Hunter. This act of self-empowerment is a virtual mime of self-procreation, suggesting that each woman embodies her own phallic ability. *Devil Hunter Yoko* itself (strictly a line of sequels rather than a self-contained OVA series) progressively self-procreates along similar lines, as each episode is made at least a year apart, leaving visible signs of stylistic maturation as it evolves.

OVA (6)

Genre: Mystical Horror

Dir: Tetsuro Aoki, Hisashi Abe, Haruo Itsuki, Junichi Sakata, Akiyuki Shinbo; **Prod:** Keiichi Onoki, Haruo Sai; **Scr:** Yoshihiro Tomita, Hisaya Takabayashi, Katshisa Yamada; **Chara:** Takeshi Miyao; **Score:** Hiroya Watanabe, Toshiyuki Omori; **Sound:** Yasuhiro Matsura; **Manga:** *Mamo no hunta yoko* (*Devil Hunter Yoko*); **Wr/Art:** Juzo Mutsuki.

Devilman (*Debiruman*)
Japan, 1987
Tsutumu Iida

Just as the Devilman is a traumatised reincarnation of the demon Amon in the person of young Akira, so too is *Devilman* a textual reincarnation of a lineage of religious dogma. Part post-war pan-generic entertainment, part Japanese embrace of religious multiplicity, part heady evolutionary psychic mutation, *Devilman* is a freeform mix of cultural voice and theological visage. In creating such a flagrant abomination of narrative form, it inverts the Western presumption of the demonic, and disavows the notional idea that 'devils' are the essence of all dramatisation of evil.

The character of Akira (often naked, always with captivating mascara-lined eyes) is central to an acidic transubstantiation of these conventions, digesting them and subsuming their contradictions into his mutated form. Condemned and afflicted with a demonic heritage, he must navigate both the netherworld underscoring visible human existence and the invisible cosmic dimension encasing human existence. His space-shifting location affects the duality of form he possesses, changing him from a healthy human into a hirsute horror. But no matter what state he appears in, Akira is at once devil and man: a hybrid unwelcome in either zone. The deeper tale of *Devilman* is one of cross-bred impurity. The binary divisions which attempt to lock Akira into a singular behavioural model are the limiting and oppressive forces with which he must contend, giving rise to a new interpretation of 'beyond good and evil'.

The most apparent generic seeding for *Devilman* is neither Nietzsche nor the Necronimicon, but the sprawling multi-plateaued vista of the gods in Hindu Sanskrit legends. The eternal wars among the gods and between their terrain and the pursuits of mankind contextualise the idea of a 'devil' central to *Devilman* (in the *anime* and especially in the much longer serialisation of the originating *manga*). In Hindu cosmic lore, gods, devils, beasts and man share cross-over dimensions of existence – sometimes causing territorial transgression, other times creating fateful or liberating zones of co-existence. Japan's fundamental breakdown of multiple planes of existence (spirits, man, animals) echoes aspects of the Sanskrit mythology, but minus its theological directives. Devilman is thus a rogue *Nihonjin* roaming the Sanskrit domain, amorally shifting from human pathos to spiritual atonement to soulless condemnation.

The second instalment of *Devilman* ('Siren the Demon Bird') erupts with gendered dualities and sexual multiplicity. Akira encounters, combats and even respects Siren, a karmic counterpoint to his own unstable virility. Breasts gleaming, crotch feathered, head crowned with majestic white wings, her womanhood is revealed as a mutation of wolverine, phoenix, vixen and swan – all while recalling the global folklore associated with such creatures. The long battle between Siren and Devilman becomes an extended orgasmic violence as they penetrate, evaginate and castrate each other with pornographic zeal. The Sanskrit aspects of the story become limned with kamasutra edicts, pushing the *Devilman* series into a heightened celebration of transcendence through animalistic sex as practised by god-demon souls. It really doesn't get better than this.

OVA (3)

Genre: Mystical Horror

Dir: Tsutumu Iida; **Prod:** Katsumi Hasegawa, Katsuhisa Kato, Koichi Murata, Ryohei Suzuki, Toshio Tanaka; **Scr:** Go Nagai, Tstumu Iida; **Chara:** Kazuo Komatsubara; **Score:** Kenji Kawai; **Sound:** Etsuji Yamada; **Manga:** *Debiruman* (*Devilman*); **Wr/Art:** Go Nagai.

DNA^2 (Dokonade nakushita aitsu no aistu)
Japan, 1994
Junichi Sakata

Despite its ethereal mystique, the symptoms of love are visible and physical. Depending on who provides the diagnosis, the root of love is claimed to be chemical, hormonal, even pheromonal. DNA^2 sites love at the molecular level – not to find a sublime explanation for love, but to comically clash earthy erogenous energies with the transcendental rush love generates.

Like a high-school biology lecture hijacked by a teen comedy, DNA^2 encircles the chaotic merry-go-round of thwarted desire and misled affection between Junta, an excitable but repressed boy; his close friend Ami; and her friend Tomoko. There's also a spunky alien, Karin, who has come from the future to neutralise the hyper-sex drive lying dormant in Junta. He is apparently destined to become the Mega-Playboy, and 100 years hence will have been responsible for fathering 100 sons who will also be Mega-Playboys, which in turn will precipitate a dangerous population explosion. The cause of it all is Junta's DNA, which Karin has been assigned to render impotent. Her plan: get Junta to happily settle down with Ami, despite the duo's relationship being purely platonic.

Like a Shakespearean comedy spinning in high-velocity revolutions, every imaginable switch and double-take is played out to hilarious ends. The Shakespeare connection is not gratuitous: in his era, the spleen was the seat of the emotions upon which love was throned. The history of literature and poetry abounds with metaphors that dance around the rising of the penis and the juicing of the labia. DNA^2 openly mocks that protracted choreography and visualises arousal as a transformative bodily process beyond one's control. Junta vomits whenever turned on by the sight of a girl's crotch, cleavage or butt. His cheeks swell up and his posture undeniably resembles a throbbing penile shaft with engorged head. His come shots are outrageous gushes and projectiles of vomit as he loses control. Not surprisingly, his unrealised true love is Ami, the only girl with whom his 'girl allergy' is entirely absent. Tomoko has a similar yet equally quirky allergy. Her proximity to boys brings on a nervous condition that leads her to fart uncontrollably.

Everyone in *DNA^2* is physically affected by love. While Karin scientifically argues from the stance of molecular cause and effect, it is also a ruse used by a real playboy-type early in the series. He claims that women are drawn to him because of his DNA-pull, and insists that they are powerless to this attraction. His galling persuasiveness causes women to swoon to an imagined DNA-effect. Junta, however, has been accidentally shot with an activating-DNA bullet by Karin (a moody fireball herself, she distractedly loaded the wrong bullet). This destabilises his DNA, turning him randomly into an actual Mega-Playboy. Like a bizarre fusion of *shojo manga* stars and dazzles and a Jekyll-and-Hyde psychological transition, Junta moves from smooth-talking, ultra-sensitive poet to moronic, nose-picking adolescent. Reflecting the hormonal instability of teens and their wildly vacillating throes of passion, *DNA^2* declares lovesickness to be the most affecting of all teen malaises.

TV

Genre: Teen Comedy
Dir: Junichi Sakata; **Prod:** Powhouse and Nippon TV; **Scr:** Tatsuhiko Urahata; **Anim:** Masaru Kitao, Eisak Inoue; **Chara:** Kumiko Takahashi; **Mecha:** Takeshi Koike; **Score:** Fuji Takano; **Sound:** Shigeharu Unno; **Manga:** *DNA^2 – Dokonade nakushita aitsu no aistu* (*DNA – His Thing He Lost Somewhere*); **Wr/Art:** Masakazu Katsura.

Dominion – Tank Police
(*Tokuso Senshatai Dominion*)
Japan, 1988
Koichi Mashimo, Takaki Ishiyama

Rays, shafts and beams of intense energy randomly fall across the metropolis in much post-nuclear apocalyptic *anime*, causing chaos and destruction, not unlike the infamous black rain of Hiroshima and Nagasaki. Such is the subtextual scarring which lines the underbelly of popular Japanese imagery, and *anime* remains remarkably attuned to the effect its past has on its contemporary 'psyche of the city'. *Dominion – Tank Police* exhibits this base impulse to re-imagine the destructive, wherein the city – its landscape and architecture – is treated as the surface across which an agent of destruction leaves its visible mark. Wry humour frames *Dominion*'s contemporary image of the city: the urban/domestic elements of police, citizens, robots and criminals are the agents of energy control and abuse. Rather than lines or waves of light and sound carving up the landscape, here it is people and machines that tear the social fabric and architectural blueprint.

Throughout *Dominion*, tactical police and the criminal element wage war, but the power and energy of each adversely affects the surrounding environment. The Tank Police is exactly that: a motley crew somewhere between *Police Academy* (1988) and *Hill Street Blues* (1981–7) who are called in when things get out of hand. They roll up in specially designed tanks which are so advanced they are incapable of moving on many roads as their powerful belts eat up the asphalt. This wry comment on disjuncture between design and planning in the bureaucratised metropolis is a key theme in the original *manga*, as is the story's focus on female rookie cop, Leona, who is fiercely proud of her own tank, nicknamed Napoleon.

Dominion is particularly concerned with the relationships between crime proliferation, law enforcement and military engagement, and how those relationships impact on both criminals and law enforcers. The story initially sets up a farcical relationship between the amoral adrenalin-pumped criminals Buaku, Unipuma and Annapuma, and the Tank Police. This is then diffused by a focal tie between one member of each – Buaku and Leona. Before too long, a whole side of Buaku is revealed: he is actually a genetically engineered droid searching for the origins of his birth, and it is Leona with her sensitivity to urban machinery (she seriously 'loves' Napoleon) who facilitates a deeper understanding of what drove the droid Buaku to crime in the unforgiving urban environment.

Dominion is typical of much serialised *anime* in the way it changes its tone from rambunctious parody to disquieting reverie. In Western theatre logic, this would be deemed distracting, unsure, defocused and ill-shaped. But to an Eastern dramatic sensibility, this is an 'a-moralised' removal of layers, where masks are held in place in order to deftly lower them – a gesture far reaching in many forms of Japanese theatre. *Dominion* is a procession of dramatic masks according to this logic, moving through diverse emotional states in order to enrich its social staging of an urban future.

OVA (4)

Genre: Future Crime

Dir: Koichi Mashimo, Takaki Ishiyama; **Prod:** Ritsuko Kakita, Kazuhiko Inomata, Tamaki Harada; **Scr:** Koichi Mashita, Dai Kohno; **Anim/Chara:** Hiroki Takagi; **Mecha:** Koji Ito; **Score:** D. Crew; **Sound:** Hiromi Kanbara, Daisuke Jinbo; **Manga:** *Dominion*; **Wr/Art:** Masamune Shiro.

Doomed Megalopolis (*Teito monogatari*)
Japan, 1991
Rin Taro

In futuristic *anime*, Tokyo is usually depicted as an urban orb of magnetic attraction that binds political, corporate, legal and criminal forces. As a 'megalopolis' of power, this notion is an extended symbol of the original fortresses of the Tokugawa regime: artificially constructed cities designed to contain, grow and spread the power of the shogunate and/or the state from a central concentrated source. But the fall of these fortresses that conduct the collapse of the Edo epoch returns Tokyo to its organic social geography: strewn villages which form the base to the urban palimpsest of prefectures that constitute modern-day Tokyo.

More historical horror than futuristic fantasy, *Doomed Megalopolis* 'rebuilds' Tokyo as a megalopolis by linking the millennial guardian spirit of Tokyo, Masakado, to the necromancer Kato who is hell-bent on reviving Masakado's soul in order to possess it and Tokyo. Across the series, Kato's actions sync to major incidents that peak at the closure of Tokyo's Meiji reformation in the first few decades of the 1900s. Technically coming a decade after the end of Meiji, the Great Kanto Earthquake of 1923 forms a spatio-temporal nexus for his attempts, siting both a destabilising of Masakado's rock-solid spirit and the building of the Tokyo subway system. Time and again, the ground on which people stand gives way: subterranean mountains rupture the earth and shoot skywards; yawning caverns materialise as deadly voids; terrestrial planes transform into spiritually reconfigured enclosures. The psychic and cosmic rezoning of land is central to *Doomed Megalopolis's* staging of its apocalyptic historiography.

Superficially, this can be read as *anime* exploiting Japanese history to pulp folkloric mythology, yet the series extends predictable historical events to trace how they are modulated by modern consequences. Signposted by the prefixed 'doomed' in its title, *Doomed Megalopolis* repositions a 'return to the past' as a looping of the past already forecast and foretold. A true dystopian vision rather than an affected one, it demonstrates how the Meiji rebuilding of an urban centre that ignores the historical cooption and coercion of power of the medieval past is not far removed from rebirthing the Tokugawa fortresses and their oppressive rule.

Perversely portrayed as an SS-style commandant, Kato is a caricature of the maniacal power that flickered deep within the demonic eyes of feudal war lords. His desire to control the city accordingly brings about apocalyptic destruction, drunk as he is on his own supreme energy that dooms his domain to implode again and again. His strategies range from direct demonic invocation of Masakado, to corporeal possession of Yukari and her daughter, to spiritual abuse of the Shinto priestess Keiko, to resurrection of an ancient dragon spirit, to all-out cosmic confrontation with the reincarnate Goddess of Mercy. Everyone and everything is but a 'thing' in his way, to be either destroyed or employed as a medium to channel negative energy towards the tomb of Masakado: ground zero of Tokyo's history. Yet within the schematic tropes of good-versus-evil, *Doomed Megalopolis* constructs Kato as the inability to erase the past, providing us with an angst-ridden text of those doomed to remember.

OVA (4)

Genre: Mystical Horror

Dir: Rin Taro; **Prod:** Akio Jissoji; **Scr:** Kaizo Hayashi; **Anim:** Kazuyoshi Katayama, Koichi Chigira, Kazushige Kume, Takashige Ichinose; **Chara:** Yuki Maisa; **Score:** Kazz Toyama; **Sound:** Masafumi Mitsuma; **Story:** *Teito monogatari* (*The Tale of the Capitol*); **Wr:** Hiroshi Aramata.

F3 – Frantic, Frustrated & Female (Nageki no kenko yuryoji)
Japan, 1994
Masakazu Akan

The spiralling politicised query of 'the gaze' is accelerated in *anime* porno with maddening centrifugal force. Pursuing who is being looked at and who is the looker, parsing the scopic to segregated genders, stratifying levels of ideological consciousness in voyeurism – such psychoanalytic methods applied to *anime* are likely to confound the prescriptive urge to separate the 'correct' from the 'incorrect' in erotica.

F3 – Frantic, Frustrated & Female is a 'comedy of tremors' centred on barely pubescent Hiroe who cannot achieve orgasm. The commonly assumed figure of the frigid should lend this premise to portray Hiroe as either a nymphomaniac or a male-repellent bitch. But in *F3* Hiroe embarks on a quest to orgasm purely for her own pleasure, connecting her character to the heroines of *anime* within whom narrative is centralised and from whom signification is dispersed.

This is so much so in *F3* that it starts to resemble an *anime* self-help sex manual for women – despite it being a base comedy seemingly oriented towards an audience of male voyeurs attracted to female bodily mechanics. After Hiroe's sister Mayaka spies on Hiroe using a dildo (the make of which Mayaka is familiar with herself), Mayaka undertakes to help Hiroe in the quest for orgasm. A bizarre but genuine bond exists between the two, emblematic of a feminine closeness nurtured by a 'big sister' helping the junior. Mayaka thus becomes a therapist of sorts, analysing Hiroe's problem and working through a range of experimental measures to ascertain the appropriate solution. Following the futility born of straight masturbation and sex-aids, Mayaka attempts sexual seduction of Hiroe as the two engage in a long bout of cunnilingus. This only serves to numb Mayaka's tongue while keeping Hiroe on the tiring brink of orgasm.

Realising that physical stimulation alone is useless, Mayaka figures Hiroe's mind is blocking the final stage of coming. She decides to hypnotise Hiroe, using an ancient Chinese tantric method of concentration. Again, nothing. Other methods follow, including visits to a psychic medium who witnesses the 'un-coming' souls circling Hiroe's aura, and a decrepit scientist whose multi-pronged mega-dildo machine Hiroe destroys through her insatiable appetite. The outrageous methods utilised in *F3* simultaneously mock the manifold pseudo-sciences deigned to repair Woman's problematic body, while positing Hiroe as a fountain of post-human sexual energy requiring stimulation beyond the norms available on the mortal plane. Hiroe herself is depressed by this state of Otherness, reduced as she is to having to fake orgasm for her boyfriend – a task she finds only magnifies her problem.

The solution accidentally found is that due to the earlier hypnotic experiment conducted by Mayaka, Hiroe can only come once her sister touches her. The gag is that Mayaka simply has to tap Hiroe on the shoulder, and Hiroe will be thrown into a Fuji-shaking orgasm. Almost indifferently bisexual, *F3* proposes that the hyper-phallic powers of man, his machines, his sciences and his religions might control Woman, but they cannot make her come.

OVA (3)

Genre: Erotic Comedy

Dir: Masakazu Akan; **Prod:** Yutaro Mochizuki, Kinya Watanabe; **Scr:** Aguda Wanyan; **Anim:** Kouji Hamaguchi; **Chara:** Ayako Uchimi; **Manga:** *Nageki no kenko yuryoji* (*Healthy School Student in Grief*); **Wr/Art:** Aguda Wanyan (Wan Yan A Gu Da).

The Fantastic Adventures of Unico (*Yuniko*)
Japan, 1981 – 90 mins
Toshio Hirata

Many sophisticated Westerners have bemoaned the prevalence – and undying increase – of *kawaii* culture in Japan: the terror of the 'cute' where everything is rendered bug-eyed, fat-limbed, big-headed and round-bellied. What is often missed in adult aversions to the cute is that *kawaii* is not simply a regressive childhood fixation (which could just as easily be cited globally in sport, business, war and politics – all of which demand its proponents to 'grow up'). More complexly, *kawaii* results from the oppressive regime of humanism – humanity's supposedly definitive trait – returning as a nightmarish spectre of affected affection. Anthropomorphism is the DNA of all forms of cute, and Japanese *kawaii* rewires the neotononical body into a grossly transmogrified container of cuddles, impregnating anything and everything with the possessive energy of 'cutification'. For a West that says 'let's hug', the East retorts 'hug this'.

If you want an audiovisual definition of what *kawaii* (cuteness) is all about, you can't go further than *The Fantastic Adventures of Unico*. It wields its beauty sincerely and perversely – and this mix of the two modes bears a distinctively Japanese mask. It drips with European kitsch of the same variety that clings like treacle to Disney's post-war work, centred as it is on the forest and its woodland creatures, suffering peasantry and devious royalty. But *Unico*'s style also distinctly leans towards *shojo manga* with its accent on dizzying visual sensations which depict both Romantic and Gothic emotional tropes. Typically Japanese, the characters of *Unico* are all of European heritage: the baby unicorn Unico (the diminutive 'co' signifies *kawaii* in Japan); the rascally kitten who becomes a girl, Chao; the fairy godmother-like Nishikaze no sei. Throw in the handsomely satanic Ghost Danshaku – menacing yet achingly seductive – and you have a prime force in propelling the melodramatic throb of the story.

Despite the ocean of cute upon which *Unico* floats, his characterisation presents him as a kind of empathetic flotsam. Unico is the innocent loner suffering unending abuse (malicious and thoughtless) at the hands of humans particularly, providing us with a social self-critique that quietly yet firmly rages in so much supposedly uncritical Japanese entertainment. The 'loner/lost child' in post-war *manga* and *anime* – of whom Unico is a cousin – is both an elegy for the defiled innocence of youth during Japan's imperialist mania and an apology to that same youth left stranded and scarred by the actions of their parents. Unico's plight specifically relates the tragic myth of the unicorn – left behind when Noah's ark set forth – to Japanese children left behind in the country's headlong rush into war. To presume *Unico* is saccharine, cloying and infantile just because it's a hyper-*kawaii* children's *anime* is not a simple case of cultural misreading: such a view is more likely a projection of the West's status of children's entertainment – restrictive, patronising, fearful, moralistic – onto a much more rounded Eastern version of the same.

Feature

Genre: Folklore Melodrama

Dir: Toshio Hirata; **Prod:** Shintaro Tsuji; **Scr/Chara:** Osamu Tezuka; **Anim:** Akio Sugino; **Score:** Yoshi Kitayama; **Sound:** Takashi Miyamoto; **Manga:** *Uniko*; **Wr/Art:** Osamu Tezuka.

Fist of the North Star (*Hokuto no ken – Seikimatsu Kyuuseishu Densetsu*)
Japan, 1986 – 110 mins
Toyoo Ashida

Based on a *manga* of the same name by the artist whose pen name is Buronson (in homage to Charles Bronson), both *manga* and *anime* of *Fist of the North Star* are predictably in love with violent Western movie culture. The *anime* resembles *Mad Max 2*'s (1981) Western-revision that has devolved into a desolate landscape of brutality, here placing the monolithic hero of Kenshiro to say little, remain aloof, and explode in a rain of punches when pushed too far.

But something else breathes behind this façade of pulped pyrotechnics and macho mania. Counterpoint to *Fist of the North Star's* screaming visual iconography of quotations is the stilling silence of its Eastern deployment of energy. Martial arts form the duel fuel on which this *anime* runs, shaping a common ideal of futuristic action *anime* through depicting a world entirely 'Westernised' on the surface but indelibly Eastern in its inscripture. Kenshiro might be dressed in black leather in a sexy mix of Japanese high-school thuggery and American biker beastliness, but his attire hides his symbolic duality as a disenfranchised *ronin* and a don't-mess-with-me Buddhist monk. Kenshiro's special martial arts skill comes from his titular technique, where his fists pummel an opponent's body in the constellation of the Big Dipper. This diagrammatic welt draws psychic cosmic energy from Kenshiro's own astrological heritage, allowing him to synchronise to a greater cosmological energy that he directs through his fists to disable (or decimate) his wrong-doers. Kenshiro is thus less a being and more an intersection of time and space, and in knowing this he is capable of strength well beyond his corporeality.

While Kenshiro respects his bestowed power, the marauding gangs he encounters bear no such respect to others or themselves. Here *Fist of the North Star* is most interesting: it perceives how the energy resulting from Eastern martial arts becomes diffused, reused and abused in a post-apocalyptic wasteland by 'foreigners' – those who roam and reterritorialise the once-defined and isolated notion of 'Japan alone'. Kenshiro battles hordes of mega-thugs under the fearful leadership of Jacky, who controls them like a feudal lord. But this unruly bunch resemble the most debauched *ronin* drunk on their own power, endlessly appeased by displays of their own intimidation of the weak. Jacky's ultimate body-guard is the ferocious Raou – a muscular monster of grotesque might. He is a thing of power – a post-human injection of martial arts energy, but devoid of any true sense of the purpose of that power. In marked contrast, the stoic Kenshiro never wields his power as a force, mostly carrying it deep within himself, and only calling it forth when abusive power like that displayed and flaunted by Jacky's troops threatens Kenshiro's determination to remain alone in a thankless world. While this might suggest a meta-xenophobia laces the spectacle of violence in *Fist of the North Star*, this *anime* ultimately ponders whether those with energies are truly destined to possess them.

Feature

Genre: Mystical Action

Dir: Toyoo Ashida; **Prod:** Shoji Kishimoto; **Scr:** Susumu Takahisa; **Anim:** Masami Suda; **Chara:** Masami Suda; **Score:** Katsuhisa Hattori; **Sound:** Hideyuk Tanaka; **Manga:** *Hokuto no ken – Seikimatsu Kyuuseishu Densetsu* (*Fist of the North Star – The Apocalyptic Legend of the Messiah*); **Art:** Tetsuo Hara; **Wr:** Buronson.

Five Star Stories (*Faibu Sutaa monogatari*)
Japan, 1989
Mamoru Nagano

There is something quintessentially Other about Japanese clothing. The shapes, forms and contours struck by costume and attire throughout Japan's medievalism virtually deny that a body resides underneath. From the platformed planks of *geta* shoes to the engulfing bondage-wrapping of the *kimono*, there is a distinct Otherness in how the Japanese body is perceived to connect to the ground, to the air, and to any clothing it touches. Modern and post-modern fashion design upholds this tradition dramatically, as does *anime* – maybe even more so.

It doesn't take much to see medieval *yoroi* armour in the mobile suit phenomenon of early 70s' *anime* space operas. But one has to look much harder at *Five Star Stories* to discern the human form in its bi-ped crypto-human machines, called Mortarheadds. These transfigured mobile suits of *Five Star Stories* are in fact 'immobile'. They can only be animated into action by the Fatimas, a lineage of psychic android maidens who can mind-sync with these huge machines as intermediaries with their internal pilots, called Headdliners. The Mortarheadds bear no semblance to aerodynamic design – the principal governing factor that has shaped the mobile suit lineage along the lines of planes and jets. The Mortarheadds are more like grossly extended formations of medieval court retinue, recalling the stately posture and garb of officialdom.

A military overlay is blended with the Mortarheadds' uniform, as they stand erect bearing monstrously enlarged lances, which they use to joust. These competitive spectacles are central to the drama and action of *Five Star Stories*, and in both *anime* and the originating *manga* the battling shapes of the Mortarheadds become a heightened abstraction of costumed form. In detailed swoops of 'fabric' (what are the Mortarheadds actually made of?) they recall butterflies and spiders, soldiers and cyborgs, angels and devils, morphing into one another as they clash with frightful force and graphic gusto. *Five Star Stories* is a 'futur-feudal' fusion of jousting and territorial conflict in a sci-fi narrative, and the mecha-design of the Mortarheadds embodies this wholly.

Gender and sex floats to the surface in *Five Star Stories*' pageantry of post-modern mannequins. Both the Mortarheadds mecha and their Headdliner pilots represent gross amplifications of male power which nonetheless requires the miniscule yet essential female voice to operate and mobilise their internal mechanisms. This is a perverse and engaging meld of the phallic with the erotic, as the Fatimas' inner voice shapes the outer bulk of the Mortarheadds, giving us a psychic-Jungian rewrite of the traditional 'chivalry' which splits gender onto ornamental planes and makes medieval mythology so sexually repressed (but makes it so endearing still in these undying conservative times). *Five Star Stories* mimics to a degree all the pomp and melodrama of the Arthur/Guinevere saga, but in *anime* such archetypes are put through the Japanese wardrobe department. There, male and female are reclothed in forms that simultaneously trace and obliterate the gendered body.

OVA (1)

Genre: Mystical Power Suit

Dir: Mamoru Nagano; **Scr:** Akinori Endo; **Chara/Anim:** Nobutera Yuki; **Score:** Tomoyuki Asagawa; **Manga:** *Faib Sutaa monogatari* (*Five Star Stories*); **Wr/Art:** Mamoru Nagano.

FLCL (Furi Kuri)
Japan, 2000
Kazuya Tsurumaki

Sociology is the cheapest of cinematic divining rods, but it must be noted that the spectre of teen suicide in contemporary Japan has peculiarly fuelled many fantastic film, *anime* and *manga* scenarios for at least a decade now. *FLCL* (homonym and acronym for 'furi kuri') accepts this terrain as a school in which one is interred, and therein builds a sci-fi project formally unclassifiable and deliberately self-problematised. The result is an ungainly mutation of debilitating teen angst with outrageous machinic interaction.

While much 90s' *anime* revisioned the 60s' boy-with-robot lineage, *FLCL*'s Naoto sprouts robots from his own head. This occurs after being bashed on the head by a Fender bass guitar wielded by wild alien Haruko, an unruly older girl riding a Vespa. And that's 'sprouts' literally – like an embarrassing erection. One of these sprouted robots becomes a mechanical externalisation of Naoto's inner power, and then periodically swallows the boy to transform into a mystical mecha-power.

This sounds linked to the visceral inveteracy of David Cronenberg, but *FLCL* is closer to the nightmare world of films like *The 5,000 Fingers of Doctor T* (1953), where children are trapped in realms so violently upscaled that they convey the subjective terror of being young: equally unable to control one's world and oneself. *FLCL* is emblematic of a third wave of *otaku* – connected less with childhood yearning or object fetishisation and more with social ostracism. Naoto's father is a grown *otaku* who still publishes *doujinshi* (parodic fan *manga*) which gather in unsold piles in the family home. *FLCL* sites Naoto as a sensitive barometer in the mediarised storm which spins around him.

Apart from its astounding artistry and densely compacted scripting, *FLCL* is notable for its radical use of music and sound. *FLCL* frenetically percolates with post-grunge power-pop J-style. Songs are mixed high, hard and happily, generating a freshness in mixing disallowed since John

Hughes' vilified pop-tracking. The largely instrumental song score is gloriously radiophonic in its saturation and density. The energy of the wall-to-wall tracks is solidly integrated into the drama and its many mood swings. And in seeming oppostion to this hyper-compression and fat rendering of pop noise, the tactile presence of amp hums, drum tunings and vocal sibillance is gorgeously foregrounded. True to the spirit of youth, the music sounds sparklingly raw and urgently alive.

FLCL: debilitating teen angst and outrageous machinic interaction

This breathing presence of electrified liveness carries over into *FLCL*'s sound design and its privileging of a potent silence: the digital recording of nothing. One continually hears mics left on to record the hum of unseen technology (fridge compressors, subway rumbles, stairwell rings, etc.), generating careful placement and modulation of the sonic grain of emptiness which filters urban and suburban Japan. Fluoro tubes at 3 a.m., aircon exhaust down a lane, and the poetic phoneme of a train shuttling in the distance: *FLCL* is a febrite recording of the Japanese psychological landscape today. Do not be fooled by its pop sheen and audiovisual bombast. They are signs of the noise that is Japan: a humming sonorum that holds its people in a psycho-sociological grip, to whom amplified silence is both a comfort and terror. Such is the headspace of Naoto and the narrative terrain of *FLCL*.

OVA (6)

Genre: Teen Robot Drama

Dir: Kazuya Tsurumaki; **Prod:** Maki Terashima, Hideki Uchino, Toshimichi Otsuki; **Scr:** Yoji Enokido; **Anim:** Hiroyuki Imaishi, Masahiko Otsuka, Tadashi Hiramatsu; **Chara:** Yoshiyuki Sadamoto; **Mecha:** Yoshitsune Izuna; **Score/Songs:** Nobuyoshi Mitsumune, Shinkichi Mitsumune, Running High, Happy·Bivuoac, The Pillows; **Sound:** Toru Nakano.

Galaxy Express 999 (*Ginga tetsudo 999*)
Japan, 1978 – 129 mins
Rin Taro

Galaxy Express 999 regales the saga of young Tetsuro and his quest for a mechanical body, accompanied by the haunting yet gorgeous Maitre. In a post-*Star Wars* era, that's the kind of summary that is used to describe the contents of cereal boxes these days, but *Galaxy Express 999* is decidedly different in two key respects. First, Tetsuro's quest is to attain a post-human state – a perfect mechanical being. This displaces him from the universalising humanism that pumps the *Star Wars* brand of heroics. Second, *Galaxy Express 999* remains true to the calming, existential tone of Kenji Miyazawa's 1922 source novel *Ginga tetsudo no yoru* (*Night on the Galactic Railroad*), which is less concerned with the conquest of outer space and more focused on the path to inner peace. Of course there is humour and action in the *anime*'s many unfolding chapters, but they are brought forth on waves of emotional intensity which ultimately float the story in a sea of tragedy.

Epicentral to *Galaxy Express 999*'s space opera is a pulsating heart of romance, fuelled by lost love, familial fracture and regretful remorse. The fateful legacy of Maitre, the unrequited love of Claire, the self-effacement of Ryuzu, the lost soul of Shadow – these are captivating and inspired portraits of loss. Contrasted against these incomplete beings who yearn and search for the impossible is Tetsuro who actually is comparatively more complete yet unaware of this. Motivated by familial traumatisation from watching the robot war lord Count Mecha kill Tetsuro's mother, he wishes to become a robot in order to have the super-strength to kill Count Mecha. Pathetic humanism and imperfect machines span the breadth of *Galaxy Express 999*, positing humans on a greater plane of existence with other living things, be they ectoplasmic entities, spiritual ciphers or mechanised humanoids.

A key feature of *Galaxy Express 999* is the seemingly bizarre mix of futuristic technology, World War II military design (derived from America,

Japan and Germany), Italian Westerns and imperial Russian costume design. Part *Doctor Zhivago* (1965), part *A Fistful Of Dollars* (1964), part *Metropolis* (1926), this is a potent example of how Japanese style promotes a daring and unique blend of elements which in the West are usually only acceptable in the guise of camp (which typifies Western space operas from *Flash Gordon* (1953) to *Star Trek* (1966) to *Star Wars*). Camp in the West often results from impure stylistic components being joined in a way that renders the individual components partial and unfinished, suggesting an amateurish execution and presentation akin to school pantomime or vaudevillian parody. But in the East, where the same components are primarily imported and understood to be incapable of full assimilation, the joining of disparate components is experienced less as active fusion and more as simultaneous digestion. Rendered as *anime*, *Galaxy Express 999*'s multi-faceted production, mechanical and costume design (all laid out in the original *manga*) relate to the Japanese tradition of foregrounding the decorative. Upon this stage the film resides as a well-grounded post-modern celebration of transnational culture and retro-future imagining.

Feature

Genre: Mystical Allegory

Dir: Rin Taro; **Prod:** Saburo Yokoi; **Scr:** Shiro Ishimori; **Anim:** Kazuo Komatsubara; **Chara:** Reiji Matsumoto; **Score:** Nozomu Aoki; **Sound:** Akihiko Matsuda; **Manga:** *Ginga tetsudo 999* (*Galaxy Express 999*); **Wr/Art:** Reiji Matsumoto.

Gall Force – Eternal Story (*Garu fosu – Eternal Story*)
Japan, 1986 – 86 mins
Katsuhito Akiyama

In Western audiovisual fiction in general, images of women receive scant exposure, promotion and celebration when compared to the innumerable ways in which images of men are consistently used as neutral vessels for depicting control, valour, foresight and success. Since its early 80s' explosion, *anime* has produced a remarkably low proportion of male hero images and scenarios. In fact, the bulk of all futuristic scenarios are centred on female protagonists or all-women groups and societies.

Celebrated as an icon of 80s' *otaku* culture due to its iconicisation of 'cute babes with laser guns', *Gall Force – Eternal Story* can be read in entirely opposite ways. What on the surface appears to be a condescending objectification of Woman is in fact a highly resonant encoding of how power can be visually and symbolically presented by foregrounding aspects of gender in the act of depiction. The open-ended illustrative possibilities of *anime* facilitate this with greater ease than live-action cinema, and *anime* explores the extremes to which these depictions of power and gender can be taken.

Gall Force depicts an 'all-woman domain' – yet one wherein women boldly drive gigantic vehicles, display sharp militaristic logic, and collectively operate more as a buddy-gang than a girlie-clique. While this would be an oddity in Western entertainment, in *anime* it is a dominant mode of depiction. In *Gall Force* it is a proposition of how gender is actualised in the social sphere.

It is likely that such readings of these scenarios are triggered primarily by imaging women in such roles. The *Alien* cycle, for example, is distinguishable mostly because Sigourney Weaver rather than Arnold Schwarzenegger is battling it out with female breeding aliens and their offspring. The plot template is standard macho sci-fi action, but the gendered traits of the fictional characters affect the reading of their actions and motivations. Similarly, *Gall Force* symbolically and ideologically suggests ways of reflecting on Western image codes by virtue of confronting us with images of women doing and thinking in ways which Western fiction tends to avoid, suppress, ridicule or reject.

Marking this clearly, the plot of *Gall Force* is centred on the power struggle between genders. Set (as late twentieth-century sci-fi invariably dictates) in a time well before our own, we encounter two interplanetary species who have warred for eons: the Paranoids, who look like human women dressed in tight but functional space suits, and the Zoenoids, slimy biomorphs with guttural male voices. A universal council decides that the only way for the war to end is through genetically mutating both species, to create a 'mutant' species which ends up being a human male. (The moment of impregnation of officer Patty by a Zoenoid 'slime-mass' is a mind-expanding rewriting of sexual-genetic copulation.) In a weird mix of the Jungian psychological concept of dual gender traits within each sex, and the Christian biblical tale of Adam and Eve, *Gall Force* casually proposes that men are mutations between feminine energy and monstrous power.

Feature

Genre: Gender Sci-Fi

Dir: Katsuhito Akiyama; **Prod:** Mitsuhisa Hida, Nagateru Kato, Toru Miura, Ikuo Nagasaki; **Scr:** Sukehiro Tomita; **Anim:** Nobuyuki Kitajima, Masahiro Tanaka; **Chara:** Kenichi Sonada; **Mecha:** Hideki Kakinuma; **Score:** Ichizo Seo; **Sound:** Noriyoshi Matsuura.

Gankutsuou – The Count of Monte Cristo (*Gankutsuou*)
Japan, 2005
Mahiro Maeda

Gankutsuou – The Count of Monte Cristo is hard to watch. Literally. If *anime* excels in drawing attention to its status as drawing – engulfing the viewer in a hallucinogenic overload of visible markings that eschew illusionism for expressionism – then *Gankutsuou* re-inscribes that base of *anime* and overwrites new layers of artifice and decoration with dizzying complexity.

Loosely – no, abstractly – based on *The Count of Monte Cristo*, *Gankutsuou* is set in an outlandish future on Earth and beyond that folds Dumas' elitist European milieu into a pompous utopian concoction of Florentine plazas, baroque churches and *fin-de-siècle* World Pavilions. It's the Japan that Japan most dreams about, laid out in *Gankutsuou* as if bombarded by a billion Bavarian Disneylands. Yet underneath its neo-olde-worlde décor is advanced hi-tech infrastructure of an impossible scale. The bulk of its architectural rendering is ironically generated through advanced 3-D computer graphics. Yet such technology is employed primarily as an unsettling backdrop for *Gankutsuou*'s characters. The Count, the two young male friends Albert and Franz, and the rich parade of nobles, decadents, paupers and thieves are all rendered in standard *anime* line-work – but their hair and clothing are rendered as purely flat fabrile surfaces. Imagine that sections of patterned wallpaper were used instead of filling in these areas with shaded coloured depth.

There is much signified by this bold design conceit. First, it symbolises the function of imported Gothic affectation in Japanese image culture. The fracturing between the characters' robes and their personal flesh marcates European fashion from Japanese physiology, clashing Edo figuration with Beardsley disfiguration. Second, if one observes closely the manifold fabrics engulfing all the characters, one will perceive how they literally wear themselves on their sleeves. Extending the signification of heraldic *kamon* crests, all manner of portentous symbols swirl in the fabrics which camouflage their wearers like ornate kimonos levitating against florid backgrounds. Third, the glaring decadence of the series and its heavily scented homo-erotic narrative thrills are only superficially European. Mostly, they are evocative of Edo's bisexual 'floating world' as depicted in the period's sensual scrolls and their decorative implosions.

Ringmaster to *Gankutsuou*, the Count is a living compendium of decadent symbolism and maudlin rhetoric. He breathes, gesticulates and poses as a multiple-personality imprinted by Machiavelli, Sade, Nietzsche, Wilde and Bataille. No mere Goth cartoon of Count Dracula, this Count's real name is Gankutsuou, meaning King of Dark Caves, and his voice is as dense as the reverberation generated by such cavernous quotation. The series is the lining of such psycho-geography: a diapasonic diorama of the Europeanesque as it can only exist within *anime*.

The near-abstraction of *Gankutsuou* is indicative of how deeply the Gothic has penetrated Japanese visuality over the preceding four centuries. Just as the mobile suit of sci-fi *anime* is the diamond-hard veneer compressed from centuries of feudal and military uniforms, so does *Gankutsuou*'s hyper-haberdashery gather its shape from an equivalent period of European toning, shaping and patterning tailored by Japan's unique sense of refashioning.

TV

Genre: Gothic Melodrama
Dir: Mahiro Maeda; **Prod:** Mahiro Maeda; **Scr:** Natsuko Takahashi; **Anim:** GONZO; **Chara:** Hidenori Matsuba; **Score:** Koji Kasamatsu; **Sound:** Yota Tsuruoka; **Novel:** *The Count of Monte Cristo*; **Wr:** Alexandre Dumas.

Gantz
Japan, 2004
Ichiro Itano

The most frightening part of *Gantz* is the opening subway station scene. Katou waits for his train. Having witnessed his behaviour at school we know he is desultory, solipsistic, withdrawn, repressed. The subway is 'real' but the soundtrack is hyper-real: we hear inside the heads of everyone, each in their own isolated world of banal, self-centred thoughts. Katou looks around him, his voiceover interpolated with the babble of others: in high Nietzschean mode, he scoffs at them all. Suddenly a street drunk falls on the track. The train approaches; no one does anything; the din of their voices continues.

Consistently, *Gantz* depicts life full of people in similar situations. One feels trapped by the narratives as if being tested: is this *anime* trying to hollow me out to register my emotional response to these complete dismissals of humanity? At the subway incident, Katou's friend Kurono jumps down to retrieve the drunk, and both he and Katou are killed – or so it seems. They find themselves in a nondescript apartment within which rests a large black orb, Gantz. Other people are also there. It's a fantasy island of sorts: everyone is possibly dead, but all are instructed by Gantz's teletext to partake in a survivalist game and capture designated aliens. It might be Earth. They may be dead, alive or 'faxes' of their selves. But the psychological torment of their situation is clear. Like lab rats, Katou and Kurono – plus another girl who has just attempted suicide, Kei – are subjected to the limits of their capacity to respond, to feel, to react.

The Gantz orb can be read as the inner sphere of existence in contemporary Japan: a black hole of emotional nothingness, turned inside-out as an orb to reveal the darker side of restrained protocol. In much *anime*, this void is floated on philosophical clouds, but *Gantz* slams it down to the social asphalt time and again. A mental self-cleansing is enacted each time, as Katou, Kurono and Kei reflect on themselves not through self-centred desperation, but through monitoring their proximity and distance to both those they desire and those they despise. Opposite to the smooth matt black surface of the orb, Katou, Kurono and Kei are rendered as prismatic splinters of humanity, schismatic in their identities and fractured in their make-up.

An indifferent sci-fi narrative permeates *Gantz*. The orb appears to be sent for some purpose, and those who are summoned to the orb afresh (as most die in their fight against the aliens) appear to be miming some sort of destiny, though the tone is disingenuous. Despite some erotically disorienting suits which operate like psycho-sexual skin-grafts, this is a super-hero story that can't even be bothered with defining humanity, marking it a disturbingly open scan of the cold heart of those beyond emotional touch. As Katou, Kurono and Kei 'return' to reality after having engaged in a 'game' for the Gantz orb, their social world is far from comforting. Like the 'real' world of the opening subway station, it's a living hell of frozen action and deafening silence.

TV

Genre: Psychic Sci-Fi

Dir: Ichiro Itano; **Prod:** Atsuya Takase, Hiroshi Nishimura, Yasufumi Uchida; **Scr:** Masashi Sogo; **Anim:** Hidemasa Arai; **Chara:** Naoyuki Onda; **Mecha:** Toshihiro Nakjima; **Score:** Natsuki Togawa; **Sound:** Hiroyuki Hayase; **Manga:** *Gantz*; **Wr/Art:** Hiroya Oku.

Genocyber (Genosaibaa)
Japan, 1993
Koichi Ohata

When young Elaine finally reveals her dormant power in *Genocyber*, she sprouts and spreads translucent angelic wings. This iconic Angel of Death has appeared in numerous *anime*, giving rise to a repeated trope of avenging beings who ultimately reveal themselves as an embodiment of past transgressions. In *Genocyber*, Elaine is a particularly gifted ESPer (preternaturally endowed with powerful psychic prowess) whose capabilities when she was an infant were clandestinely harnessed by the military to create a vicious weapon. Now a teenager, Elaine's pubescent state and developing consciousness of the world around her create a deep internal conflict which manifests in her frightening displays of uncontrolled energy.

But these *anime* Angels of Death differ from their European counterparts in two respects as exemplified by *Genocyber*. First, Elaine is not a third-party visitation of vengeful justice: she is central to the abuse and her sole suffering is suppressed to such an extent that it returns with magnified force. For Elaine, it's personal. Second, the biblical morality and its God-like effect can only superficially be sited in Elaine's explosiveness. Her actions are spurred by the need to redress imbalance and return her inner self and outer environment to an equilibrated home for her future growth. Her blindness to her past, her deafness to her self and her insensitivity to those around her are all to be tackled by her transcendence through monstrous form to become a harmonised self.

In *Genocyber* as in much hard sci-fi *anime*, balance is more important than sides – and balance is not struck simply by taking 'the right side' as if there is such an inalienable thing. In the liberal-minded critique which underscores most science-fiction within the Western tradition, its tediously voiced concerns stultify as much as define it. Ethical angst over degrees of scientific enquiry into genetics and species, artificial life and overcoming death, planetary design and extraterrestrial interaction – all tend to blur into one inflated Judeo-Christian spook-show. *Anime* pays lip service to many of these grand themes of sci-fi, but will always modulate them with waves of broader cosmological resonance and frequencies in psychological, cultural and mystical bandwidth.

Genocyber's notable resonance lies in Elaine's depiction as a wartime waif. While such a figure from cultures connected to the Allied Forces in World War II will evoke sympathy, the image of a Japanese waif bears a stalled duality – especially from the Japanese perspective. The Japanese waif that populates much dystopian *anime* is symbolic of how a society can neglect, disown and deny its own members, and thus ignites the shame of the parent. Like a ghost, the wartime waif of Elaine returns as a wartime wraith. Scarred by the forces and energies that created a previous wartime era (as most futurist *anime* is set after some sort of global devastation), these wraiths are the instruments through which balance is struck. Elaine in *Genocyber* was once an instrument for military research; she is now instrumental in military recompense.

OVA (5)

Genre: Psychic Sci-Fi

Dir/Mecha: Koichi Ohata; **Prod:** Masashi Abe, Shinji Aramaki, Shin Unozawa, Minoru Takanashi; **Scr:** Koichi Ohata, Noberu Aikawa, Emu Aril; **Anim:** Kimitoshi Yamane; **Chara:** Atsushi Yamagata; **Score:** Takehito Nakazawa, Hiroaki Kagoshima; **Sound:** Michnori Matsuoka; **Manga:** *Genosaibaa* (*Genocyber*); **Wr/Art:** Tony Takezaki.

Ghost in the Shell (*Kokaku kidotai*)
Japan, 1995 – 83 mins
Mamoru Oshii

You weigh near a tonne because you are made of titanium alloy. Your internal mechanics afford you incredible strength but massive weight. You move through a complex system of counter-balance that allows you to appear deft, light-footed, graceful, human. You are the female cyborg anti-terrorist major Motoko Kusanagi from *Ghost in the Shell*. To relax, you dive into the bay of New Port City and reconfigure your pressurised body capsule to be its Earth-bound weight. Sinking to the bottom of the ocean floor, you find the darkness warm, almost as if you can register temperature. Returning your pressure to 'normal' you shoot up to the surface and float. Through your goggles you notice droplets of water and slow-moving clouds in the skies above . . .

Ghost in the Shell: philosophical cyborgs battling demonised humans

This is how *Ghost in the Shell* imagines the 'mind' of the cyborg. Motoko is on the surface a lithe Amazon of a woman, replete with wig, lips, hips and breasts that forever remain impossibly perfect. But beneath her surface is a consciousness of emptiness, frozen still yet emotionally restless. For Motoko is 'the Japanese' – that strange beast endlessly scrutinised by the West, but here projected as a self-image within the *anime* of *Ghost in the Shell*. Motoko's cling to the ocean speaks volumes: an island of humanism, she returns to the womb of its oceanic infinity; she attains a fluidity and free-floating sensation that liberates her from form; and she is at one with the ocean's indivisible oneness. This is philosophical therapy of the highest order, and it runs as deeply and voluminously through the hyper-kinetic action drama of *Ghost in the Shell* as Motoko sinks in her bay-side reveries.

The urban metropolis of a 'contemporised' Tokyo (New Port City) provides the backdrop for Motoko's battle with urban terrorists – a breed of 'real' humans demonised and rendered inhuman by the Ministry of Foreign Affairs that wishes to suppress them. The premise of having cyborgs battle these 'inhumans' is ironical, but to Motoko it becomes philosophical as she takes her place in the great lineage of Japanese robots and cyborgs and starts to ponder her own existence. Again, this is Japan pondering its own existence – its role in the world and in shaping its own homeland.

A dystopian theological subtext pervades *Ghost in the Shell*. Motoko and her cohorts are tracking an ultimate 'foreigner' – a para-sentient software program whose 'artificially intelligent' status queries the existence of 'natural intelligence' and thus works to overcome human endeavour in New Port City. Motoko synchronises with this 'self-creationist' program in multiple ways: it not only mirrors her own post-sentience as a post-human, but she also eventually 'synchronises' with this software as an act of philosophical merger in a world where corporations and politics have become so merged that their processes and discourses are imperceptibly fused. A 'counter-fusion' to such local and global urban-modernisation, Motoko is reborn not only into a new cybernetic suit (tellingly of a child) but a higher level of cybernetic consciousness. As per its originating *manga*, *Ghost in the Shell* freely mixes the karmic with the psychic with the robotic, in a future that hasn't happened yet – because it is the present of Japan.

Feature
Genre: Cyborg Crime
Dir: Mamoru Oshii; **Prod:** Ken Iyadomi, Mitsuhisa Ishikawa, Shigeru Watanabe; **Scr:** Kazunori Ito; **Anim:** Toshihiko Nishikubo; **Chara:** Hiroyuki Okiura; **Mecha:** Shoji Kawamori, Atsushi Takeuchi; **Score:** Kenji Kawai; **Sound:** Kazuhiro Wakabayashi; **Manga:** *Kokaku kidotai* (*Attack-Shell Mobile Force*); **Wr/Art:** Masamune Shiro.

Giant Robo – The Night the Earth Stood Still (Gyaianto Robo, The Animation)
Japan, 1992
Yasuhiro Imagawa

Giant Robo – The Night the Earth Stood Still fuses many hallmarks of *anime*: the boy who operates a giant Golem (in this case, one designed with said Teutonic guise); a fantastical time-warped setting wherein retro meets futro with nitro; and a canny self-referentiality which skates across the sheen of Jap-Pop culture (*Giant Robo* is in fact a mutative remake of a *manga* and charming, clunky live-action series, *Tetsujin 28* from the late 50s). But what distinguishes *Giant Robo* is how its take on the 'Oriental Gothic' reveals much about how the old does not return to haunt the new as much as it conjoins it.

In a sublime fusion of the Gothic and the apocalyptic, *Giant Robo* opens with the huge church bells of Paris's Notre Dame Cathedral clanging with the bodies of dead scientists: the death knell of old science for the city of the future. Once the bells of Notre Dame have sounded, an expanding set of shock waves emanates from the central cathedral to eventually surround Paris. As a negative energy field drains the city of power, all lights are extinguished from the centre out to create a black hole. The knolling bells ring across the city and ominously signify the event of the energy drain; the blackout silently and visually follows the pattern of concentric circles which neumonically replicates a bell's own spherical wave formation. Typical of Japanese calligraphic consciousness, the visual is the recording of energy waves which rupture a material surface.

In actuality, the blackout is a macro-circle of energy drain that follows a micro-circle or internal circumference of Dr Shizuma's underground laboratory, which has risen to the surface to create a circular island of black energy, which then drains the surrounding area and later the globe. As in many horror and Gothic-inspired scenarios, the earth covers the past, the dead and the forgotten. While Occidental

Gothic sets its scenes near a graveyard of buried dead bodies who return to life to haunt the living, the 'Oriental Gothic' of *Giant Robo* functions according to a pan-Pacific logic: tectonic plates on the ocean floor are themselves markings of the Earth's life in a previous epoch, waiting to rise up and destroy the present through a cataclysmic earthquake. The earth 'is' the past. Dr Franken Von Fogle – presumed dead and buried in the past – returns (via his son) to haunt the prosperous city running on the Shizuma drives he co-invented by literally raising his underground laboratory to the surface to create a black hole of oppression.

Giant Robo's world is one of rivets, steam, iron and brick – all lovingly detailed and impressively styled in faux-deco. It imagines a para-Tokyo as an industrial giant whose landscape rose high and mighty like a *fin-de-siècle* metropolis. Although not as gleamingly futuristic as most *anime*, it nonetheless embraces the urban fantasy of much *anime* which paradoxically imagines disaster – buildings collapsing as gigantua promenade – as a relief to the limitations imposed on a city that is always on the verge of annihilation.

OVA (7)

Genre: Robot Melodrama

Dir: Yasuhiro Imagawa; **Prod:** Minoru Nakazawa, Takashi Ohashi, Minoru Takanashi; **Scr:** Mitsuteru Yokoyama, Yasuhiro Imagawa, Eiichi Yamamoto; **Anim/Chara:** Toshiyuki Kubooka, Akihiko Yamashita; **Mecha:** Makato Kobayashi; **Score:** Masamichi Amano; **Sound:** Yasunori Honda; **Manga:** *Gyaianto Robo*; **Wr/Art:** Mitsuteru Yokoyama.

Golgo 13 – The Professional (*Gorugo 13*)
Japan, 1983 – 94 mins
Osamu Dezaki

Some may find *Golgo 13*'s use of still panoramas, freeze-frames, multiplied images and camera-plane mechanisms a 'cheap' or 'inferior' approach to the craft of animation. But *Golgo 13* acknowledges that just because animation activates the movement of things, it doesn't have to keep everything moving all the time. As animation continues to be rail-roaded down tracks towards endless gratuitous motion (the CG 'fly-through' to nothingness), *anime* embraces a parallel history of stillness, where the lack of motion is purveyed for its stilling effect.

The stillness of *Golgo 13* is no mere stylistic conceit, even though it is heightened by a highly stylised *mise en scène* that hardly ever relates to any depiction of worldly physics. Renowned and undefeatable hitman Golgo 13 is essentially a frozen figure: his art of killing through the skill of sniping frames him dead-still as he brings death to those locked in his telephoto scope. Similarly, he remains a rock-hard emotionless wall when dealing with people. Everything is but pure business to Golgo 13. His sureness and confidence prevents him from ever rushing into something; everything is well prepared, allowing him to remain cool and collected throughout. This 'stillness' befits the extreme limited-animation of the film as it accents the precision and sharpness with which Golgo 13 approaches all his contracts.

Honouring the *manga* on which it is based, *Golgo 13* is more a graphic text than an animation text. It foregrounds *manga* conventions of narration, often using frames within frames, and replicating the pseudo-cinematic angling and multi-framing used by *manga*. Overall, the film appears as an animated *manga* rather than a fully fledged *anime*. Lens flares, slow-motion, diffused cinematography and tracking shots create a carnival of simulacra that steeps *Golgo 13* in a cool theatricality that brazenly flaunts its hyper-flatness in face of the medium's 'will to

Golgo 13: brazenly flaunting its hyper-flatness

move' – a stylistic strategy missed if one judges *anime* only by life like motion and illusory depth.

Once one accepts this freezing of narration in *Golgo 13*, one is better placed to perceive the film's unique momentum. Gorgeous gestures of movement are unfurled during Golgo 13's numerous erotic encounters. While he remains a macho dildo of sorts – expressionless yet capable of taking women to orgasmic heights – the scenes of these encounters become enveloped by swirls of light and movement which represent the feminine experience as an erogenous inertia of trembling thighs and gritted teeth. Typical of hitmen in 60s' *yakuza* films, Golgo 13 seems removed from his own love-making, leaving his sexual encounters to be staged and presented more from the tactile responsiveness of the women he beds for voyeuristic effect. Of course such hitmen are more in love with their guns, their work and the results they achieve. As established through its originating *manga*, Golgo 13 is a boldly brushed icon of the hitman, traced over Japanese *yakuza*, American mafia and British super-spy stereotypes. The stark, gaudy, chauvinistic visualisation of *Golgo 13* posterises him, highlighting sex, death and beauty in a pan-generic panorama of graphic action.

Feature

Genre: Crime Drama

Dir: Osamu Dezaki; **Prod:** Mataichiro Yamamoto, Nobuo Inada, Yutaka Fujioka;
Scr: Hideyoshi Nagasaka; **Anim/Chara:** Akio Sugino; **Score:** Toshiyuki Omori; **Sound:** Shizuo
Kurahashi; **Manga:** *Gorugo 13*; **Wr/Art:** Saito Takao.

Grave of the Fireflies (*Hotaru no haka*)
Japan, 1988 – 85 mins
Isao Takahata

Set during the horrendous fire-bombings of military and civilian Japan in the lead-up to the atomic bomb drops, *Grave of the Fireflies* follows two children orphaned in the Kobe attacks – Setsuko, aged five, and her older brother Seita, aged ten – as they try to survive on the streets. The story is told in flashback, opening with Seita's memorable voiceover: 'September 21st, 1945. That was the night I died.'

Despite its sombre tone, *Grave of the Fireflies* is a true celebration of life, using the animated image to poetically dwell upon life essences: the weight of fresh rice, the swirling of hot soup, the spray of clear water, the final flickering of fireflies. No other film comes close to according such respect to the basest of materials. Focusing on the minutiae upon which life precariously hangs, the film is imbued with a reverence for anything that is life-sustaining. To many, it's an unexpectedly potent emotional experience for an animated story. As we feel the deepening desperation that drives the starving Seita and Setsuko to survive, an unimagined force is evoked in this *anime*: loss. The ambience of absence and the landscape of erasure created by war cast its survivors as ghosts caught with one foot in the land of the living. Seita and Setsuko journey down this path, drained by every step they take.

An incisive and considered political rumination slowly materialises beyond the obviousness of the film's historical scenario and its emotional grip: a society is shown to be most cruel to its own members when overtaken by the hysteria of war. This is a noticeable theme running through the bulk of Japanese cinema critical of Japan's involvement in World War II: part apology, part redemption, part therapeutic grievance. *Grave of the Fireflies* at no point casts blame in any direction, but instead replays the circumstances in which people were placed as the result of their actions. Seita and Setsuko being 'children of war' are posed as innocents, yet the film folds them into the flows and seepages

Grave of the Fireflies: a reverence for anything life-sustaining

of life forces which ensue in the aftermath of war. The film is as impassive to their plight as the military is impervious to their plea.

Grave of the Fireflies is an uncompromising portrait of a Japanese psyche-in-a-mirror. It neither recoils in shock of itself, nor calls for cosmetic masking, and instead presents itself front-on for all to witness. But modulating this unforgiving address is the preciousness the film accords those living in the face of death. Setsuko and Seita suitably find peace in the magical glow of fireflies – glowing mirrors of their own spiritual energy that withers in the dark of war. Come the conclusion, the film enacts an impassive manoeuvre essential to wartime operations: it disregards people. With Setsuko and Seita having languished in their cave, the camera indifferently pans across the river following the strains of a record being played by a family who have returned now that the war has been declared over. The song is American: 'Home Sweet Home'.

Feature
Genre: Historical Drama
Dir/Scr: Isao Takahata; **Prod:** Toru Hara; **Chara:** Yoshifumi Kondo; **Score:** Michio Mamiya; **Sound:** Yasuo Urakami; **Novel:** *Hotaru no haka* (*Tombstone for Fireflies*); **Wr:** Akiyuki Nosaka.

Green Legend Ran (*Gurin rejendo ran*)
Japan, 1992
Satoshi Saga, Kengo Inagaki, Junichi Watanabe

In the opening of *Green Legend Ran* for no apparent reason, a set of
towering totemistic space-probes hovering in Earth's stratosphere
suddenly shoot down to penetrate the Earth and transform it into a
barren wasteland. Sentient sculptures, alien envoys, mystical instruments,
cosmic citadels – these are the Seibo. Their purpose is enigmatic, leading
to nations on Earth (Japan, specifically) rationalising the Seibo's existence
through an invented mystical signage from which an oppressive religious
regime is formed: the Lodoh. Greenery thrives only in the limited
perimeter of the embedded Seibo, and before long only the rich and
powerful occupy these zones, called Greens. Life is transformed under
these new planetary conditions, suddenly inverting all existing values.
Water becomes the most expensive elixir, the sweeping deserts become
the new oceans, and oil the primary fuel. The elemental interconnection
between them determines all commerce, trade and sustenance.

Green Legend Ran is not simply the regaling of this sci-fi fantasy, but
the unravelling of coded cosmological occurrences and the ways in which
they are misread, misinterpreted and mistreated. The domineering
religious group Lodoh becomes less a sect typical of Japanese religious
pluralism and more a nightmarish version of the Vatican and its maniacal
monotheism. The Bishops are gross mutations of power, a mix of
withered flesh and elongated appendages, signs of their mutated
amalgam of impotency and supremacy. Their reconstitution as genetic
aberrations comes from their being in such close proximity to the Seibo,
just as the Lodoh police seem afflicted with a lighter dose of this strange
malaise. The adjacent desert dwellers remain poor and exploited, but
retain a healthier human composition.

Class divisions, rebel undergrounds and government overthrows are
undying clichés of sci-fi and *anime*, but while they figure strongly in
Green Legend Ran, its primary story circulates the broader ecological

ramifications of how those social strata deal with issues and forces beyond their scope. The devastating impregnation of the Seibo is not simply a monumental quirk of planetary evolution, but a phase of planetary transition wherein flora is set to overcome all human life. The Bishops are advance warning of this with their random sprouting of thin vines from their veins; the Seibo have been positioned according to a cosmological acupuncture to neutralise human life and drain its toxic presence within Earth's eco-system.

As this becomes apparent, a metaphysical treatise on evolution replaces the originally perceived tale of revolution. Young Ran obsessed with hunting down the mysterious man who killed his mother, the fractured Hazard rebels led variously by Jiku and Kiba, and the mysteriously powered silver-haired Aira who is destined to sacrifice herself to the Lodoh – these characters formulate *Green Legend Ran*'s plot in subterfuge of the core revelation of the Seibo's organic master plan. Mind-bending merges between vegetable and human proliferate through the series, reworking humanity as the seeding of a new life cycle, and continually reinforcing how human life is wrapped within Earth's meta-canopy and hyper-roots in a dense jungle of co-existence.

OVA (3)

Genre: Eco Sci-Fi

Dir: Satoshi Saga, Kengo Inagaki, Junichi Watanabe; **Prod:** Taro Maki; **Scr:** Yu Yamamoto; **Anim:** Yoshimitsu Ohashi, Shuichi Shimamura; **Chara:** Yoshimitsu Ohashi; **Score:** Yoichiro Yoshikawa; **Sound:** Yasunori Honda.

Gunsmith Cats (*Gansumisu kyattsu*)
Japan, 1995
Takeshi Mori

The American video *Sexy Girls, Sexy Guns* (1995), is the marriage many (males, presumably) most want in their entertainment. Shot after shot, bouffanted, buffed and buxom women clad in thongs, bikinis and halter-tops shoot guns. Lots of them. And that's all they do. As their boobs jiggle to the cock-throb of the guns' mechanisms vibrating their bodies, they recite in an entirely distracted manner complete statistical data about each gun being fired. The video, of course, is a technical manual granting the viewer detailed info about the guns and their capabilities.

The charm of *Sexy Girls, Sexy Guns* is how unreal the tape is: the women can barely hold the guns; their bodies are purely there for titillation; the data is inconsequential despite its veracity. *Gunsmith Cats* is an animated mutation of American 'gun-erotica'. More so, it is a wholly serious importation of gun fetishisation into the hyper-iconic and meta-ideal realm of the animated image, where a babe can handle a gun like a goddess and be hyper-sexy at the same time. That's the outrageousness of *Gunsmith Cats* and its singular celebration of the phallic in ways beyond any of Freud's case studies.

Rally Vincent and Minnie May Hopkins are the *Gunsmith Cats*: a hodgepodge team of private detectives solving crimes bigger than both they and the police perceive. Their naiveté gets them into trouble well over their heads, but they pull through in a mix of teamwork, newly realised skill levels and absurdly providential circumstances. At the heart of their actions is their love of their guns. That's love in the most serious term, for it is through the respect that these girls have for their handguns that they eventually get the jump on criminals who use armoury as mere tools of force and coercion. In line with the Japanese observation of how the bind of within/without determines the energy of anything, Rally and Minnie equally fetishise their guns' objective aura, surface design and internal mechanics. It also doesn't take much to recognise strains of the

bushido and its doctrine of how the *samurai* must respect his blade.
Gunsmith Cats is thus a disconcerting mix of farcical violence and
mystical reverence, laced with heavy metal irony as these babes never get
a hair out of place or panty-creep as they somersault into action.

The most direct reference in *Gunsmith Cats* would be the *Lethal
Weapon* (1987) series. Its explosive spectacularisation of gun
embodiment is tellingly signified by the 'gun-becoming' of Mel Gibson's
Martin Riggs, who 'goes off like a loaded gun'. He is gun: metaphor and
metonym. The *Lethal Weapon* series can be viewed as a Hollywood

Gunsmith Cats: an animated mutation of American 'gun-erotica'

mystical series that idolises handguns, thereby contributing to an aspect of Americana cinerama that *anime* imports not merely as iconic quotation but as mystical citation. This is one of endless examples of how *anime* is less an act of translation and more a recontextualised mirroring of what already exists in the West.

OVA (3)

Genre: Crime Comedy

Dir: Takeshi Mori; **Prod:** Yoshimasa Mizo, Umeo Itoh, Hiroaki Takimoto, Toshiaki Okuno; **Scr:** Atsuji Kaneko; **Anim:** Kazuya Murata; **Chara:** Tokuhiro Matsubara, Kenichi Sonada; **Mecha:** Koji Sugiura; **Score:** Peter Erskine; **Sound:** Brian Risner; **Manga:** *Gansumisu kyattsu* (*Gunsmith Cats*); **Wr/Art:** Kenichi Sonada.

The Guyver – Bio Booster Armour (*Kyoshoku soko gaiba*)
Japan, 1989 and 1991
Koichi Ishiguro

The abject horror of becoming the Other is a theme central to existential horror. Within Western horror and sci-fi, losing one's body is as terrifying as losing one's mind. The 60s' revision of the super-hero in American comics created innocents who became infected to become 'super-human'. Conversely in *anime*, one's body has been perceived and presented as but the potential to be its Other – through possession, contamination, impregnation.

The Guyver – Bio Booster Armour can be postulated as a cyber-genetic remake of *I Was a Teenage Werewolf* (1957). The latter is now generally considered a corny B-grade travesty of horror symbolism, but at the subtextual level it withholds a disquietingly apt portrayal of the nightmare of male puberty within a repressive American 50s. *The Guyver* recognises that nightmare and treats it seriously and fearfully. High-schooler Sho unwittingly stumbles across a secret military device – a 'bio-booster armour' designed to create super-human soldiers by genetically altering their internal composition and neural-muscular capabilities. He unleashes its power and is transformed erratically and periodically into 'the Guyver' in which state he battles an unending horde of mis-transformed mutated prototype soldiers who could not contain the shape-shifting power of the bio-booster armour.

The Guyver places Sho's transformation scenes centre-stage. They are agonising, traumatising, exhausting. Each time he manages the transformation better, yet it is never easy. In contrast to the charming theatrical artifice of the 70s' *tokusatsu* TV series (where acts of transformation are a pyrotechnic quick-edit to the actor springing from a hidden trampoline in a lycra 'super-suit'), Sho screams, writhes, contorts. His body is literally overcome as it grows and reshapes itself into an erectile, engorged and enflamed corpus replete with the expected shift from latent to manifest sexuality. Sinewy muscular veins jump out from retracted cavities within his new mutant skin; deep growls rage forth from his genetically affected vocal chords; amplified psychic abilities sense things around him via his metallic third eye implanted in his forehead; and white hot beams of plasmatic energy shoot forth from his breasts as he rips open his pectoral muscles in a violent orgasm of polysexual aggression. Deep within the Guyver is Sho. Very deep within.

While armour is the conceptual design behind the bio-booster that covers Sho, it is less something to protect one from external force and more something to contain the power within the reformed body. Part sci-fi invention, part military historiography, the armour of *The Guyver* is a 'suit of the self' that Sho must commandeer despite being trapped within it. The legacy of controlling an additive energy – from the *samurai*'s sword to the *sumo*'s fat to Sho's suit – is central to the Japanese mind–body split, wherein the body is extended beyond its design to incorporate an alien, exterior and unnatural function. This is in marked contrast to the Chinese tradition of martial arts which treats the body as the sole and holistic source of energy, siting the human body as the machine to be mastered more than modified. *Anime* like *The Guyver* never veers from these notably Japanese distinctions of muscular arts.

OVA (12)

Genre: Mystical Power Suit

Dir: Koichi Ishiguro; **Prod:** Nagateru Kato; **Scr:** Atsushi Sanjo; **Anim:** Sumio Watanabe; **Chara:** Hide Omori; **Score:** Reijiro Komku, Toshi Otsuki; **Sound:** Koji Suyama; **Manga:** *Kyoshoku soko gaiba* (*Multiplying Power Armour Guyver*); **Wr/Art:** Yoshiki Takaya.

Hades Project Zeorymer
(*Meio keikaku Zeoraima*)
Japan, 1988/90
Toshihiro Hirano

There is something fascinatingly hysterical about *Hades Project Zeorymer*. It starts abruptly with the kidnapping of young Masato by a group of mysterious government-type henchmen. All he is told is that Zeorymer will awaken. The who/what/why of the unexplained becomes a major force within *Hades Project Zeorymer*, as its central queries about existence deduce that answers will never be found.

But the series does not start so philosophically. *Hades Project Zeorymer* is mostly a mecha-battle saga of psychic mobile suits. The Hau Dragon (headed by the spiteful spittle-spraying Chinese dragon lady, Yuratei) has been formed around eight giant mecha-mobile suits designed by Masaki Kihara. But after he rebels and steals the last suit – the mega-powerful Zeorymer – the Hau Dragon plan to rule the world has been foiled. Now, all seven suits are ready and raring to avenge the betrayal by Masaki, and one by one they engage in almighty war with the Zeorymer mecha – now powered by the unknowing Masato and Miku, the only two beings whose linked psycho-genetic make-up can mobilise the mecha.

After being subjected to mental torture by government officials preparing him for psycho-tactical warfare in the Zeorymer, Masato is thrown into the cockpit and instinctively takes control. In the process, he is gradually traumatised by what appears to be an overpowering split personality – which is revealed to be the genetic imprinting of Zeorymer's designer Masaki within Masato's psyche. To even mention the notion of 'self' here is futile. As Masato is churned not only inside-out, but reconstituted into a boiling foam of multiplied identity within which he is imprisoned, he, Miku, the government and the Hau Dragon are all confounded by their attempts to separate Masato from Masaki, and the Zeorymer from their human operators. This is a war waged in an identity-less dark.

Hades Project Zeorymer is tersely elliptical in its structure. Scenes are rushed into headlong; battles are kicked into high gear instantly; aftermaths are swallowed up in preparations for the next engagement. The logic and design to the Hau Dragon mechas are shown in fragments across the series. Seven ruthlessly fixated fighters operate the original seven mecha, representing an elemental force within Chinese mythology: Burstone (mountain), Briest (fire), Gallowin (water), Dinodilos (earth), Lanster (wind), Rose C'est La Vie (moon) and Omzack (thunder). Their pilots smoulder with unrepentant rage, forming a septet of seriously unbalanced psyches seeking retribution, revenge and redemption. Their battle powers and tactical manoeuvres are like a Taoist nightmare of possessed energies locked in mortal conflict and a collective consuming rage. Amazingly abstracted lines of energy created by the Hau Dragon mechas simulate wind, fire, rock, water to figuratively evidence the Earth itself being harnessed to destroy the Zeorymer.

More than another assertion of war's vainglorious spectacle, *Hades Project Zeorymer* hums with a disconcertingly futile tone, as these split personalities, shell-shocked avengers and genetically predestined minds are engaged in a multitude of deceptive determinants which are only revealed at the height of crisis.

OVA (2)

Genre: Mystical Sci-Fi

Dir: Toshihiro Hirano; **Prod:** Toru Miura; **Scr:** Noboru Aikawa; **Chara:** Michitaka Kikuchi; **Mecha:** Hideki Kakinuma, Kimitoshi Yamane, Yasuhiro Moriki; **Score:** Eiji Kawamura; **Manga:** *Meio keikaku Zeoraima* (*Hades Project Zeorymer*); **Wr/Art:** Morio Chimi.

Iczer-One (Tatakae! Ikusaa-1)
Japan, 1985
Toshihiro Hirano

You're in high school doing well. You don't cause trouble, you respect your parents, and you're just trying to do your best. Suddenly out of the blue you have to command and control some unearthly psycho-techno machine and battle insurmountable foes from alien and evil dimensions. Such is the lot of the average high-schooler in so much *anime* and *Iczer-One* particularly.

The absurdity yet familiarity of such a scenario is an elemental principle in *anime,* involving characters who have power thrust upon them as a power they must nonetheless earn to bear and learn to wear. Like any sensible high-schooler, Nagisa in *Iczer-One* wants none of this power, but now 'betrothed' to it, she must work out how it can absorb her and she subsume it. The acceptance of such outrageous circumstance in *anime* is a given. It can arise from hereditary possession and transference, random Buddhist reincarnation, or broader cosmological maps of balance drawn by universal energies well beyond the scope of a single human. In the expanded self-enveloping stratification of *anime*, the nuclear individual has no place. 'Heroics' then have little to do with high principles and noble values, and everything to do with cosmic balance.

In *Iczer-One*, the main recourse to balance – the much touted *wa* of Japanese harmony – is through synchronisation. Nagisa must psychically synchronise with her meta-suit: a self-contained quasi-robotic giant entity of navigational and directional capability. Only by being on the same wavelength as the alien battler Iczer-One can she become her destined self through becoming one with his life force to form the giant Iczer-Robo. In a sense, as an innocent kid struck by lightning out of the blue, Nagisa had been up to that point unknowingly out-of-sync with herself, just as the Earth is out of sync with its own past that comes to haunt it in the form of the invading alien Cthuwulf forces. 'Balance' is an expedient metaphor rudimentally applied in broad social and dramatic form, but 'synchronism' is a more affecting embrace of temporal, spatial, psychic and dimensional issues which reach well beyond the egocentric templates of classical fiction.

In an unexpectedly erotic twist, Nagisa's operation of the Iczer mechanoid is achieved by her floating within an ethereal amniotic womb, placing her at once within and without the Iczer-Robo. In this fantastic 'Ohm gel' she is suspended, divorced from her ego in a shock-absorbent space for focus and contemplation. Just as fluid mechanics and self-contained floating planes allow for complex mechanical components to synchronously respond to each other's movements, Nagisa's lube-space affords her similar connection to the Iczer-One and the Iczer-Robo. Surrounded by plasmic neutralising buoyancy, her being becomes the oil for the gears that mobilise and activate her mechanised self: a joint philosophical pursuit and robotic vision epicentral to the machinations of modern Japanese culture.

OVA (3)

Genre: Psychic Power Suit
Dir: Toshihiro Hirano; **Prod:** Toru Miura; **Scr:** Toshihiro Hirano; **Anim:** Toshihiro Hirano;
Chara: Toshihiro Hirano, Junichi Watanabe; **Mecha:** Masami Obari, Nobushi Aramaki;
Score: Michiaki Watanabe; **Manga:** *Tatakae! Ikusaa-1* (*Fight! Iczer-1*); **Wr/Art:** Rei Aran,
Rantama Akutsu.

Interstellar 5555 – The 5tory of the 5ecret 5tar 5ystem
Japan, 2002 – 67 mins
Kazuhisa Takenouchi, Reiji Matsumoto

For decades, many a distraught Nippophile has bemoaned the American influence on Japan – particularly following the early 80s' explosion of Harajuku's boutiques fetishising anything to do with classic 50s' Americana. Supposedly, one merely had to look down the streets of any such district and see nothing but images of the US flag, the Statue of Liberty, Cadillac bumpers, James Dean's quiff and Marilyn's lips. Dumb Nippophiles express great fondness for Japanese style, but are illiterate when it comes to reading its post-colonial signage and its semiotic veneer. For if there is any East–West compaction navigating the cultural twists and trends of contemporary Japan, it grows from its attraction to France, not America.

The mythologised refinement of French culture has for over a century posed a mirror for Japan's own obsession with the decorative. Both cultures are well aware of the other's arts and crafts and their foregrounding of visual detail. A bizarre psychic resonance between the two art histories creates a web of references many Nippophiles would perceive as transparent filamentules of no substance. Yet this webbing is precisely what makes *Interstellar 5555 – The 5tory of the 5ecret 5tar 5ystem* a cross-cultural post-modern phenomenon. In place of creating a set of video clips to promote their album 'Discovery' (2001), French duo Daft Punk sought 70s' *anime* legend Reiji Matsumoto to produce a featurette based on the story 'implied' by the sequence of songs that comprise the album. Indelibly supervised by Matsumoto, the outcome is *Interstellar 5555*: at once a potent elixir of Matsumoto's classic themes and iconography, and a dynamic and vertiginous 'retro-futro' audiovisual amalgam courtesy of Daft Punk's music.

Daft Punk are part of the late 90s' French ironic retro sweep that professed a particular fondness for the sumptuous decline of late 70s' disco – a period everyone else was characterising as deader than dead. But Daft Punk – in typical French perversity – were one of a number of bands that revived this period and breathed new mechanoid cyber-rhythmic life into its electric corpus. Combined with pitch-corrected digitised vocals that sound human yet robotic, theirs was a project reaching out to *anime*. The cyborg nature of the songs perfectly fit Matsumoto's legacy of cybernetic dreaming and the soulfulness encoded within the cyborg and its yearning connection to humans. *Interstellar 5555* thus tells a tale of a super-band loved by the people, but who are manipulated by a corporate evil force to control the masses, and thereby drain the true soulful energy of the band.

Matsumoto's sincerity and Daft Punk's perversity make *Interstellar 5555* a wonderfully problematised work, as it simultaneously embraces rapture and falsity in its dizzying ornate portrayal of the band in faux-retro 70s' style: streaming locks of hair and androgynous hip-hugging mega-flares on men and women alike, plus an arsenal of futuristic stage equipment as if imagined by a 70s' animated version of the Partridge Family in outer space in the year 2000. Hollywood right now continues to lose sleep figuring how to exploit the futuristic headiness of *anime* (from the 80s specifically). *Interstellar 5555* is about five hundred and fifty-five light years ahead.

Feature

Genre: Musical Sci-Fi

Dir: Kazuhisa Takenouchi, Reiji Matsumoto; **Prod:** Shinji Shimizu; **Scr:** Thomas Bangalter, Guy-Manuel de Homem-Christo; **Anim:** Fumio Hirokawa, Haruhiko Ishikawa; **Chara:** Hiroshi Kato; **Mecha:** Reiji Matsumoto; **Songs:** Daft Punk.

Kekko Kamen
Japan, 1991
Nobuhiro Kondo, Tomo Akiyama

The marriage between absurdity and irreverence has long been a binding principle in *manga*, creating cultural parodies, social satires and hilarious travesties of anything held high and sacred. The 70s is a particularly fertile period for establishing these counter-cultural voices in *manga*; correlations in *anime* and cinema explode more fully in the 80s.

Kekko Kamen is an interesting 'time-warp' that relates to the post-war relations between deliberately tasteless comedy in *manga* – a form with a wide audience demographic and related markets – and its later embrace within *anime* – a comparatively narrow field due to its ties to televisual corporations and their emphasis on child/teen markets. The *anime* of *Kekko Kamen* comes some thirty years after the original *manga*, serving less as a celebration of retro and more as a statement of *manga*'s legacy to *anime*.

The story of *Kekko Kamen* takes place in a high school, outrageously named the Toenail of Satan's Institute of Higher Education. Its staff includes a salivating perverted gym instructor and a maniacal sociopath principal, and the students range from monstrous clans to dispossessed outsiders – not one of them portraying any signs of being fit for society (suggesting yet again that the oppressive Japanese school system is inept in sculpting the social). Within this moral mire, a mysterious heroine takes it upon herself to return decency and fair dealing to the ruthless and vicious feudal dimension of the school, sealed in social darkness and needing the light of true justice. All good and well, but this heroine decides that to be pure in her pursuit, she must be naked – a classical Japanese mythological symbol of purity – and wear a mask to efface herself so as to spiritually guide her do-gooder direction. Thus she becomes Kekko Kamen – the masked one.

And so, she periodically appears naked and masked, spurred to right wrongs right at the moment when all seems lost. In a twist of

Superman's iconic voice of the people ('Look! Up in the sky!'), Kekko Kamen is a skilled gymnast who soars through the air at full gatherings at the school to publicly humiliate any staff or student of corrupt disposition. But Kekko is blind to the horde of drooling mouths and popped eyes that stare up at her private parts as she flies spreadeagled above them. A classic of hilarious *hentai* (perverse) *manga*, the *anime* series extends the core perversity of Kekko being masked yet 'unmasked' below.

Combined with this low-level humour, the over-arching comic tone of *Kekko Kamen* is its mockery of wartime militaristic *banzai* spirit and the myopic mindlessness of the supporters of such ideals. While under the American Occupation, this crypto-fascist spirit of 'youth-moulding' by teachers in the education system was superficially suppressed, students for decades after could read its intonation in their seething psychotic teachers, irrepressible vessels of that spirit. *Kekko Kamen* is a riotous payback in *anime* form for the continuation of such controlling mechanisms that make school hell. That's the deeper message under Kekko's mask.

OVA (2)

Genre: Teen Comedy

Dir: Nobuhiro Kondo, Tomo Akiyama; **Prod:** Kenji Nagai, Yoshinaga Minami, Masaharu Takayama; **Scr:** Masashi Sogo; **Anim:** Masaaki Sudo, Hironobu Masudo; **Chara:** Tomo Hirayama; **Score:** Keiju Ishikawa; **Sound:** Yoshikazu Iwanami; **Manga:** *Kekko Kamen* (*Awesome! Masked*); **Wr/Art:** Go Nagai.

Kiki's Delivery Service (Majo no takkyubin)
Japan, 1989 – 102 mins
Hayao Miyazaki

Kiki's Delivery Service is an allegorical tale of the joy and sadness of puberty told via young witch Kiki as she comes of age. According to witch customs, Kiki must leave her home and spend a period training as a witch while living with humans under their conditions. The premise cannily symbolises Japan's relation to the world – forcing itself out of isolationist traditions to connect with Others – but this theme's execution in the film is multi-faceted, soulful, and never didactic.

An especially humane witch, Kiki is not simply engaged in acts of flight and levitation through her empowered broom: she rises above various debilitating situations she encounters in the human realm, and

Kiki's Delivery Service: symbolising the 'last witch' in a vanishing eco-system

thereby learns as much about her own verve as she does of human foibles. In face of Japan's often-criticised inequality to women in the social sphere, Kiki is a statement of the dormant power women hold for Japan, and symbolises hope for the greater realisation of that power. This unique meld of social critique and mystical tale-spinning forms a peculiarly Japanese narrational analogue derived less from binaries of real-versus-fantasy and more connected to customs, contracts and consequences. Marking this clearly, Kiki encounters an 'outsider' from the city: the artist Ursula, secluded in the forest, enriched by its immersive fertility. Only far away from the social can this woman truly be herself.

This is possibly a determining factor in *Kiki's Delivery Service*'s fused settings and polyglottic production design, for how does one advance radical social change for a society steeped in tradition? Endemic to *anime*'s visual staging, scenic reality is not presented as 'plausible'. In fact, its implausibility is accentuated to direct symbolic reading well beyond mimetic codes. Thus, the town Kiki arrives at is a fanciful fusion of Naples, Lisbon, Paris, San Francisco and Stockholm. Japanese pop culture consistently privileges the imagined over the authenticated (while exhaustively authenticating any imagining), and *Kiki's Delivery Service* will certainly confound those who seek clear references to where and when the story is set. Of course the setting is fantastic, but this is to provide a staged contrast to the characterisation of Kiki and the people she meets – all of whom are grounded and believable.

The ornate 'Europeanesque' past of *Kiki's Delivery Service* can be superficially read as 'retro', but its slant on the past echoes two central themes. First, the film's neo-Europe sites witchcraft and its wicca craft origins as a global movement that has been progressively suppressed by emerging, enlightened and modern cultures. Wicca craft's respect of the forest in particular is often cited as the last vestige of a fulsome social embrace of the environmental and ecological, and Kiki symbolises the 'last witch' in a vanishing eco-system. Second, the era evoked by the film's settings is man's eighteenth-century triumph of flight. The wry implication is that while new-fangled machines capture the public's imagination in large-scale displays of prowess, witches had been achieving the same feats unnoticed by using the instruments of their forced domesticity: straw brooms.

Feature

Genre: Mystical Drama

Dir/Scr: Hayao Miyazaki; **Prod:** Hayao Miyazaki, Toshio Suzuki; **Anim:** Katsuya Kondo, Yoshifumi Kondo, Shinji Otsuka; **Chara:** Katsuya Kondo; **Score:** Joe Hisaishi; **Sound:** Shuji Inoue; **Book:** *Majo no takkyubin* (*Witch's Delivery Service*); **Wr:** Eiko Kadono.

Kimba the White Lion (Junguru taitei)
Japan, 1965
Eiichi Yamamoto

One way of viewing childhood entertainment is as deceitful, duplicitous and dangerous in its manifold fancies and falsehoods. This is enforced by a chief means of tale-spinning that employs animals to represent human thought and action. In real life, animals are enslaved, demonised, neutered and eaten. What a child is meant to learn from a cuddly desexed future-hamburger can only be confusion.

Kimba the White Lion is an openly self-reflexive query as to how animals can be used in this way. The originating epic *manga* series has generated two TV series and two feature films, with the first TV series – Japan's first colour *anime* series – being the definitive version of the *manga*. It exudes a noticeable harshness and sadness atypical of *anime* then and still now. Quoting a Zen notion of the greatness of nature and how 'the great fish must eat the small', many episodes capture death and injustice as the brutality of man is starkly aligned with the survival codes of jungle animals. Part mythological saga, part nature documentary, *Kimba the White Lion* never shies away from issues of balance: ethical, karmic, ecological and environmental. In essence, it is a Buddhist tract, transposed to a then-popular last terrain of natural laws of life in operation on the savannah plains of Africa.

This ideological deep-veined rift is layered deftly into the story's narrative mould through fantastic devices. The familial, social and genetic complexities of a lion family (Kimba and his father Leo), who learn to speak English and introduce vegetarian diets to carnivores, are amazing flights of the imagination. The hypothetical is always at the heart of *Kimba the White Lion* in the way it collides the human domain, the natural realm and the animal kingdom – a triumvirate that also populates much fantastical *anime*. *Kimba the White Lion* accordingly generates many exciting scenarios based around transgression, incursion, abuse and usurpation as these three key planes of existence jostle for supremacy.

And never far removed is the bizarrely adorable Kimba: ferociously cute, disturbingly humanist, and eternally committed to mediating between these irresolvable sides of planetary life.

Today, *Kimba the White Lion* can't be discussed without mentioning the *The Lion King* (1994) controversy. With a jungle saga crudely traced not only from the original Japanese story (translated as *The Jungle Emperor*) but also from the visual framing and momentum of the *manga* and *anime*, its similarities impress like a *déjà vu* slap in the face. The imperial gall of American entertainment was upheld by the Disney corporation's denial of any semblance between the two countries' cited works. Highly offensive to the Japanese at the time, Disney was telling the truth. Hallmark of great globalising entertainment – ineffectual at its own enterprises, bolstering its hollow might to outsiders, and bereft of any original ideas outside of the most cloying homilies – Disney's reductive faux-universalising in *The Lion King* is a galaxy away from the expansive unchildish world view of *Kimba the White Lion*.

TV
Genre: Eco Melodrama
Dir: Eiichi Yamamoto; **Prod:** Osamu Tezuka; **Scr:** Osamu Tezuka, Shin'ichi Yukimuro, Masaki Tsuji, Eiichi Yamamoto; **Anim:** Chikao Katsui; **Chara:** Eiichi Yamamoto; **Score:** Isao Tomita; **Sound:** Atsumi Tashiro; **Manga:** *Junguru taitei* (*Jungle Emperor*); **Wr/Art:** Osamu Tezuka.

Laputa – Castle in the Sky (Tenku no shiro laputa)
Japan, 1986 – 124 mins
Hayao Miyazaki

The balance of energies – how they lock into and against one another – is a fragile system. While we may intellectually appreciate the relations between microcosms and macrocosms, *anime* is notable for its reverence and respect of the same. Every energy source has its own threshold, its own location, its own environment of manifestation. One slight touch and everything is put out of balance. This is the core message of *Laputa – Castle in the Sky*.

Centred on young Pazu's drive to follow the path set by his lost father, and Sheeta's discovery of a secret internal power she has housed for mysterious reasons, *Laputa* follows the children as they weave their way above and beyond the clouds to eventually encounter the mythical sky castle. The visualisation of the flight sequences is poetic and memorable; the staging of the action sequences is truly awesome. The film's evocation of the coalition of creative and destructive forces is done with an intensity imaginable only in *anime*.

The apocalyptic finale to *Laputa* imagines this well. The monstrous, archaic construct of the floating sky castle suggests an unworldly presence of power, due to the gravity-defying spectacle of a solid rock castle floating in the air. When Sheeta and Pazu utter in unison the 'charm of ruin', they dislodge the sky castle's mystical power core, causing the whole energy system of the massive hovering rock to collapse. But what seems destructive is simply a return to natural equilibrium. Unshackled of its granite cover, the sky castle is revealed to be a marvellous organic root system which drew life and sustenance from the ground surrounding its core – the mystical 'levi stone'.

As the sky castle falls apart, the inner core of energy – a bright blue spherical apparition – is revealed to attract all surface material of the island (stone, ground, trees, roots, etc.). Just as the slight alteration of an

Laputa: the balance of energies as a fragile system

underground tectonic plate can effect a major earthquake, so does uttering the 'charm of ruin' cause the sky castle to collapse. Each creates a sonic vibration that unsettles a previously still surface, like the stone thrown in a pond creates concentric ripples. The sky castle's destruction is a visual rendering of the apocalyptic finality under which many pan-Pacific islands exist: any island enjoys stasis and equilibrium until sonic, tectonic and oceanic waves disturb it.

The levi stone of *Laputa* is a succinct visual symbol of macrocosmic eco-geological energies which hold the earth in place: planetary gravity, physical density, oceanic currents, migratory winds. Sheeta's levi stone pendant is a miniature version of the sky castle's huge levi stone. This stone not only allows bodies to levitate; it also gravitationally binds bodies to it. The core levi stone of Laputa is an energy ball that inverts energy waves to create a self-contained gravitational force for the floating island. Its invisible energy determines the visual landscape of its environment. And when that energy is rendered visible, destructive forces flow forth.

Feature

Genre: Psychic Eco Drama

Dir/Scr/Chara: Hayao Miyazaki; **Prod:** Isao Takahata; **Anim:** Tsukasa Tannai; **Score:** Joe Hisaishi; **Sound:** Shigeharu Shiba.

Macross – Do You Remember Love? (Makurosu – Ai Oboete Masuka?)
Japan, 1984 – 115 mins
Noboru Ishiguro, Shoji Kawamori

The term 'idol singer' (idoru) appears to be just another Japanese importation of a Western model. This has led to erroneous readings suggesting Japanese 'idol singers' are mere copies of everyone from Fabian to Britney. While the term etymologically stems from 'idolatry' and sardonically reflects fans who 'idolise' singers, in Japan the term means precisely 'idol': a figurine in human form which symbolically and iconically signifies the existence of a god. Idoru is only 'mortally' connected to the pop music industry.

The god and goddess evocation through idoru's self-idolised (i.e. transformed) vessels defines them as 'dolls of harmony'. They sing-speak a kind of 'truth' felt by their worshippers, with music symbolising the pre-language transmission of lyrical content in pure form. This ability is enabled in the most famous instance of idoru in anime: the singer Minmei in Macross – Do You Remember Love?. This is a seminal anime in the development of the 'mecha-melodrama' of space opera sagas defined by the Macross series of films and OVAs. Minmei is labelled as an idoru within this Macross instalment, singing to a unified adoring mass on an enormous interstellar polis. A complete city, its design is not unlike a mobile reconstruction of Japan's created cities on reclaimed land around Japan's epidermal coast line. The spaceship is so unending in its utopian shopping mall sprawl it even contains a concert stadium within which Minmei performs.

Within the exaggerated design of Macross, the idoru of Minmei is hyper-idolised. Her anorexic frailty and avarian femininity picture her as an extruded doll of malleable form. She appears – like most idoru irrespective of their gender – incapable of holding an audience in rapture. This is extended in a later Macross instalment, Macross Plus, with the virtual idoru, Sharon Apple. The economic wet dream of any record company executive, she is the computer-intelligent programmed response to the culture-effected programmed response of her audience, creating the ultimate synergistic looping of consumption and production. In *Macross Plus*, Sharon is a virtual star in a virtual space for a virtual industry with a virtual audience.

The femininity of Minmei evidences a typically contradictory trope of the *idoru*: her mix of vocalised vim and virginal virtue stage her simultaneously as a woman with power in her voice yet a bird in a gilded cage. Her mystical outreach through singing is algorithmically matched to her vocal and bodily objectification, just as her spiritually uplifting lilt is silently modulated by her erotically uplifting titillation. While this is a commonplace effect in the global history of the industrialised female singing voice, in *anime* it illuminates a peculiar power of the medium. *Anime* voice actors in the real world can sometimes be as famous or popular as the characters they voice. In the artificial, virtual and iconic interlocking realms of *anime*, human sound overrides inhuman image. Human sound also overrides unhuman force: in *Macross*, the deadly Zentraedi forces waging war against Earth renege their campaign when they hear the pure beauty of Minmei's anti-war song.

Feature
Genre: Sci-Fi Melodrama
Dir: Noboru Ishiguro, Shoji Kawamori; **Prod:** Tsuneyuki Enomoto, Akira Inoue, Hitoshi Iwata; **Scr:** Sukehiro Tomita; **Anim:** Haruhiko Mikimoto, Ichiro Itano, Toshihiro Hirano; **Chara:** Haruhiko Mikimoto; **Mecha:** Kazutaka Miyatake, Shoji Kawamori; **Score:** Kentaro Haneda; **Sound:** Noriyoshi Honda; **Story:** Shoji Kawamori.

Maison Ikkoku (Mezon Ikkoku)
Japan, 1986
Tomomichi Mochizuki, Kazuo Yamazaki

In a world far, far away in a time long before the sensory overloads harbingered by futuristic *anime*, there sits a soap opera about the tenants of a small rooming house run by a young widow, Kyoko. This low-key melodrama is known as *Maison Ikkoku*, a TV series based on the *manga* of the same name. Its attention to earthy elemental detail (milk circling in a cup of coffee, trains passing in the distance, a shirt flapping on a clothes line) displays an affinity with the mannered rhythms of *haiku* poetry and the cinema of Ozu.

Despite being a single TV series, *Maison Ikkoku* nonetheless serves as a distillation of the serial form endemic to *anime* that runs for many episodes, many seasons and many sequels. Central to the 'soap opera effect' in both Western and Eastern entertainment is not simply the extenuation of the pleasure principle derived from viewing, but the gradual growth the viewer experiences with the developing characters. While conservative dogma dictates that this should be the aim of all dramatic form, the reality of the industrialised ninety-minute movie overwhelmingly runs counter to such aspirations. Soap operas can then be viewed as delivering what so many feature films do not: a lingering, free-flowing, organic shaping of how characters interact with each other. *Anime* serials in general realise this in heightened form, thus contributing largely to the saga-obsessed and series-addicted world of Western fandom that supports such *anime*.

Maison Ikkoku is notable in its achievement of characterisation at particularly small-scale nuanced levels. Humour, pathos, absurdity and tragedy slowly unfurl throughout the series as university student Godai takes up tenancy at Maison Ikkoku. In painstakingly small steps he becomes attracted to the inner beauty of his landlord, the calming widow Kyoko. A broad range of characters inhabit Maison Ikkoku's cramped domus, allowing for numerous side-stories to develop, but the

Godai/Kyoko connection constitutes a ground hum to the series. Multiple symbolic ties bind their mutual yet unspoken attraction – mother/son; landlord/tenant; woman/man; master/student – but unspeakable love dynamises their silence.

The poetry of *Maison Ikkoku* occurs within surprisingly contracted spaces: a corridor, a kitchen, a pathway, an entrance. Its reliance on the essential detailing of domesticity grants it a familiarity just this side of banality. This is so much so that the distinctiveness of *Maison Ikkoku* comes from its refusal to brocade its scenarios. A decoloured drainage of setting typifies the *anime*'s style, both in painted background, restricted colour palette and graphic execution. The bareness of staging complements the minimal yet evocatively mimetic character design based closely on the *manga*. The series thus resembles an archly theatrical staging – something closer to *Noh* than *kabuki* – in that the *anime* surface serves as an emotionless mask through which amplified emotional tenor is expressed. This mix of impassivity, repression and control forms the crux of *giri* (social duty) and *ninjo* (personal emotional pursuit) which erotically stalls the relationship between Godai and Kyoko – and makes it so impactful when they finally move towards consummation.

TV

Genre: Urban Melodrama

Dir: Tomomichi Mochizuki, Kazuo Yamazaki; **Scr:** Rumiko Takahashi, Kazunori Ito, Shimada Michiru; **Anim:** Tsukasa Dokite; **Chara:** Yuji Moriyama, Akemi Takada; **Score:** Kenji Kawai; **Manga:** *Mezon Ikkoku*; **Wr/Art:** Rumiko Takahashi.

Marvellous Melmo (*Fushigina merumo*)
Japan, 1971
Osamu Tezuka, Tsunehito Nagaki

Marvellous Melmo follows the exploits of seven-year-old Melmo, who has been given a bottle of transformative growth pills by the spirit of her recently deceased mother. A red pill allows one to grow up; a blue one to grow down. These magical pills allow Melmo to do things like grow a human embryo of her baby brother in a bowl of water, and transform herself to a sexy teenager. The latter she does often, spending most of her stop-and-start teenagerhood wearing her kiddie clothes, now a very short dress and absurdly tight top. Through her trials and tribulations with those of the opposite age (adults) and those of the opposite sex (boys and men), morals, ethics, biology and sex education abound in the marvellously crazy series.

But despite the seemingly absurd premise of a story unthinkable in Western children's entertainment, *Marvellous Melmo* embodies many interesting observations of Japanese life. Melmo's mother, who dies in the first episode, is herself a widowed mother of two young children. Melmo then becomes in actuality what her mother symbolised: a single mother – something rarely depicted in Japanese cultural representations. Throughout the series, a broad-stroked panorama of Japan's treatment of women is presented, as Melmo is a single woman being forced into dealing with all levels of society, thereby revealing to her innocent mind the ways in which society treats women. This dynamic of thrusting the harsh adult reality of gender discrimination into the face of an innocent child makes *Marvellous Melmo* a rare *anime* indeed.

Marvellous Melmo though does fit a mould that is endemic to Japanese historical folklore and contemporary custom. Children in Japan are treated in a comparatively more adult way than they are in the West. Many critics have linked this to Japan's 'loss of childhood' through its regimented school training and related social controls, but this is tempered by the willingness with which responsibility is granted children.

Based on a *manga* written well after Japan's neo-fascistic conformity of children and adults alike, *Marvellous Melmo* also carries distant echoes of the post-war waif. Many a now-elderly person in Japan experienced hardships as children supporting their siblings following their parents' deaths.

But central to *Marvellous Melmo* is the role metamorphosis plays in the social imagination. More than in most other cultures, the act of 'becoming' in Japan represents the pathway to awareness of self. This suggests that no person is in fact whole, and that everyone has to become something or someone else to truly become themselves. The road to this discovery is represented as a wholly physical act, and though the scenes of metamorphosis in *Marvellous Melmo* can appear literal and absurd, their material nature is the foundation to their psychological and/or spiritual realisation. Melmo always remains a seven-year-old child and never chooses to ultimately 'be' other than what she is: a charmingly innocent waif struggling in a world that cares little for her situation. As such, Melmo learns about herself through observing others: her self-discovery is refreshingly free of the ego drives that spur most manuals for self-improvement.

TV

Genre: Gender Melodrama

Dir: Osamu Tezuka, Tsunehito Nagaki; **Prod:** Norio Suzuki; **Scr/Chara:** Osamu Tezuka; **Anim:** Osamu Tezuka, Shigeru Yamamoto; **Score:** Seichiro Uno; **Sound:** Susumu Aketagawa; **Manga:** *Fushigina merumo* (*Marvellous Melmo*); **Wr/Art:** Osamu Tezuka.

Mermaid Forest (*Rumic World: Ningyo no mori*)
Japan, 1991
Takaya Mizutani

Based on Japanese coastal folklore concerning the belief that if you eat the flesh of a mermaid you will become immortal, the two-part *anime* *Mermaid Forest* spins an eerie speculative tale around those who have been fatally lured by this mermaid myth. The first part revolves around a beautiful but sick woman, Towa, who has partaken of mermaid flesh in an attempt to avert her terminal illness. She survives through her unrequited lover (now an impotent old man) sawing off arms from fresh morgue bodies to replace her contaminated arm which resembles the limb of a hideous monster. The second story is centred on Masato, a boy no older than ten who has been infected by eating mermaid flesh also. His childlike demeanour becomes a proto-form of evil. His immaturity has prevented him from learning to deal with his immortality, making him an unstoppable child of the most dangerous kind.

Full of thrilling twists and fateful arcs, *Mermaid Forest* quietly resonates with a deeper tone. What sounds like a Gothic-tinged horror luridly raking over the coals of folklore to heat up the narrative is in fact a beautifully subdued and poetic *anime*. Recalling the delicate *shojo* nuances in the *manga* on which it is based, *Mermaid Forest* temporally and figuratively 'draws itself out' in a style akin to the *kabuki* performer's mannered theatrics (a mode of portraiture much *shojo manga* quotes). The result is *anime* sited in *manga*, thoroughly acknowledging its calligraphic legacy in a display of swirling lines, floating forms and patterned sheets which overlap, dissolve and merge across the moving pictorial plane. Flower petals, strands of hair, ocean spray and illuminated particles are repeatedly depicted in decorous slow-motion – as if the *anime* is trying to become still. This is because those afflicted with immortality once wanted time to never end; now they want it to come to a standstill.

The desire for stillness is expressed through the young man Yuta and the younger girl Mana, both of who feature in each part of *Mermaid Forest*. Yuta has eaten mermaid flesh many years ago, and is now an itinerant, aimlessly wandering the country. He befriends Mana and ends up giving her some of his blood in order to resurrect her after she has been thrown off a cliff: she thus becomes a fellow immortal. *Mermaid Forest* reveals itself as a tale of two bonded by an unforgiving immortality: Yuta and Mana are teenagers slowly coming to the realisation of the burden of forever remaining young.

Initially, the idea of a 'mermaid forest' seems an awkward metaphor in its mix of the sea with the land. But *Mermaid Forest*'s portrayal of life as an unending fatality paints Japan as a forest governed by an invisible terrain mapped by those who are its disaffected, existing like a psychic sub-root system within a strangling overgrowth. The foregrounded poetics of *Mermaid Forest* at the very least allow the possibility of such a humid reading.

OVA (2)
Genre: Mystical Folklore
Dir: Takaya Mizutani; **Scr:** Masaichiro Okubo; **Anim:** Sayuri Ikkoku; **Chara:** Sayuri Ikkoku; **Score:** Kenji Kawai; **Sound:** Yasunori Honda; **Manga:** *Ningyo no mori*; **Wr/Art:** Rumiko Takahashi.

Metal Fighters Miku (Metaru faitaa Miku)
Japan, 1994
Akiyuki Shinbo

In an era fixated on obesity as a 'problem' and plastic surgery as 'unnatural', defining the body in *sumo* wrestling becomes complicated. The *sumo* wrestler is the ultimate artificially grown body. He is fed to disproportion in order to become a body-machine within which the *sumo* wrestler exerts pressure and applies skill to force another similarly grown body out of the competitive territory for ritual combat. No one in Japan claims the *sumo* 'abuses' his body, or that his becoming *sumo* is a 'health risk'. This acceptance of the *sumo*'s physique is one of many veins which throb within the defining corpus of how bodies work in Japanese culture.

Metal Fighters Miku might appear to have nothing to do with *sumo* – but it does. Centred on Miku and her admittance into rookie wrestling tag-team the Pretty Four under irritable coach Eiichi, the series projects a hi-tech redefinition of competitive wrestling onto sumo. Competing in Women's Neo Pro Wrestling in 2061, the Pretty Four wear special metal suits that hug tight and look good. Their functionality lies in the way they become a second skin, granting a voyeuristic thrill for those attracted to the body garbed this way. However, much of the series is devoted to how the girls 'man' these suits. Miku's training is dedicated towards becoming one with her second skin: the suits weigh a considerable amount, plus they need to be controlled to extend their capabilities and exploit their energy levels. As per many suit-centred *anime*, the suit is a self to be tamed and managed, symbolising the notion of the self being an obstacle rather than a pursuit. It is only when one can confront the self and have a dialogue with it can one re-subsume that self into an expanded notion of 'self'. Suits in *anime* are the perfect device for dramatising these philosophical issues and grounding them in tactile, physical aspects of human life.

In *Metal Fighters Miku*, control over one's suit defines skill level when the team is engaged in combat with rival teams. Referencing both sports statistical mania and computer-game engagement, the screen often shows read-outs of the suits' depleting energy levels. The matches peppering *Metal Fighters Miku* are not only dramatic peaks in both individual and team goal-seeking, but also displays of how each character has progressed in their training. In extension, the traditional reading of team-oriented *anime* like *Metal Fighters Miku* as a sociological narrative of Japanese customs of *gambaru* (striving to overcome and succeed) and *wa* (the group working towards collective resolution and harmony) is simplistic and obvious. This approach never registers the deeper cultural resonances that inform the mechanisms – fictive and actual – that technologically and corporeally define the group. *Metal Fighters Miku* is full of *gambaru* and *wa* – and a cumbersome swag of conventions that define the subgeneric lines of team *anime* – but it is ultimately a celebration of 'suit-becoming': of how one ascends to a post-human state and bears the legacy of power inherited through achieving 'suitdom'. And that's something so Japanese there's no manual for translating it into a mere custom.

OVA (7)

Genre: Urban Power Suit

Dir: Akiyuki Shinbo; **Prod:** Yoji Kamei, Sigeaki Komatsu, Hiroyuki Orugawa; **Scr:** Hirano Yasushi; **Anim:** Sakamaki Arihiko; **Chara:** Susumu Honda; **Score:** Kenji Kawai; **Sound:** Jun Watanabe; **Story:** Daisaku Ogawa.

Metropolis (*Metoroporisu*)
Japan, 2001 – 107 mins
Rin Taro

A view of an American city skyline witnessed by an arriving German film director in 1924, made into a German movie in 1926 set around 2000, from which a still is seen by a Japanese *manga* artist in 1943, who produces a *manga* in 1949 set around 2000, from which an *anime* is made in 2002. *Metropolis* is the title of this trans-global post-modern time-shifted chart. The *anime* at the end of the line accrues this chart's directional flux, making the *Metropolis anime* a dimensionally dense text of futuristic inscription.

Any determining relationship between the German silent movie and the original *manga* is obtuse if at all evident: the latter employs the movie still of the famous Maria robot as part palimpsest for overwriting, part doorway to a re-imagined world. While the Germanic history of robotics leads back to the Golem myth, the Japanese embrace of robotics shoots forward to general principles of industrialisation. This cultural schism between the dual *Metropolis* texts platforms the best vantage to perceive the energy at work within the *Metropolis anime*.

Centred on Michi – an ethereally created robotic being whose presence in Earth's future transpires to be a mystic visitation of sorts – *Metropolis* employs her as a vehicle for traversing the crumbling city of Metropolis, a vainglorious repository of all the city once achieved. Michi is oblivious to both the wonderment and elegy expressed by the current town from its imposing heights to its tattered depths. Likewise, she is innocently exposed to the social stratification and powers that are held by mysteriously cloaked sectors of control. In some senses, Michi is the spirit of what the city of Metropolis could have been. Encountering the foreboding city like a disenfranchised itinerant, she recognises neither it nor herself in it. When her place within the city – and the city's symbolic reunification within her proto-angelic metropolitan essence – are realised, the city can return to growing rather than decaying.

The imaging of the city is one of the most seductive and spectacular aspects of *Metropolis*. Most action occurs at street level or underground. Outside, the upper reaches of the city's towers are visible as decimated monuments, their girding and exposed infrastructures bent into a forest of melted minarets. Yet no burning or ashen texture is evident. The sky is always bright blue during the day, and the colours of the buildings retain a rich tonal range of primary and secondary colours. The only other signs of deterioration are delicate streaks of rust. This is a strange destructive zone indeed. It is almost as if buildings in the future might be painted bright colours that no form of destruction can mar or fade. Or, bizarre smart bombs have been developed which can select discrete areas of a skyscraper to destroy. There is something hauntingly 'unfinished' in the destruction of Metropolis, rendering its scenography like a giant theme park whose dismantling has been halted and frozen in time. A world away from the Gothic light-versus-dark of the silent film version's expressionist tenor, the *Metropolis anime* looks forward in archetypical style to a post-dystopian dimension.

Feature

Genre: Robot Sci-Fi

Dir: Rin Taro; **Prod:** Yutaka Maseba; **Scr:** Katsuhiro Otomo; **Anim/Chara:** Yasuhiro Nakamura; **Score:** Toshiyuki Honda; **Sound:** Masafumi Mima; **Manga:** *Metoroporisu* (*Metropolis*); **Wr/Art:** Osamu Tezuka.

Moldiver (*Morudaiba*)
Japan, 1993
Hiroyuki Kitazume

Super-hero histrionics are mercilessly satirised in *Moldiver*. Yet the parodic tone of the *anime* is not its prime purpose despite the many hilarious attacks on the self-important posture of the super-hero and his supposedly selfless saving of the world. Through its humour, *Moldiver* posits that the super-hero is but a gross electro-magnification of the powerless frustrated by their lack.

Hiroshi is a mildly dysfunctional nerd inventor who dreams of designing a 'dream super suit'. He eventually develops one through a bizarrely concocted application of molecular restructuring, creating a suit composed of 'pseudo-molecules' that completely cover the body to create an immersive realm for the human within. The mobile suit concept is here reworked to place the 'wearer' in perfectly harmonised insulation and ionised isolation: the mental head space of nerdy types like Hiroshi. In as much as his suit is symbolic of Japanese psychological withdrawal, the public's name for his super-hero status is Mr Tokyo. Their patriotic fervour is sardonically portrayed by their response to the ridiculousness of this super-hero, dedicated as it is not to noble values but to Hiroshi's own repressed needs.

But Hiroshi's sister Mirai wants in on the suit. She steals the transforming tape and its code and uses it for her own ends: to get closer to Masaki with whom she is infatuated. When Mirai first uses the suit, it doesn't sync with her molecular data and leaves her fixed within Hiroshi's design – a stud-masculine body that he has based on his friend Masaki, the very guy Mirai is after. Mirai eventually syncs her data to the suit to become her own hyper-feminine super-heroine in a dream idol singer outfit. She names her transformation Moldiver, replete with her rally-call 'Metamorforce!' (one of numerous Japlish puns throughout the series). The suit truly is a 'mould of diversity' due to its capability to be programmed to match the siblings' psychotic desires. In ensuing

Moldiver: super-hero histrionics mercilessly satirised

episodes, Mirai and Hiroshi get their suits mixed up in a hysterical collapse of gender: Mirai's squeak from within the macho form of Mr Tokyo and Ozaru's bark from within the spunky form of Moldiver render them more laughable than fearful.

The 'evil villain' Mr Tokyo/Moldiver battle is Hiroshi's ex-teacher, Professor Amagi. But Amagi's inventions and genius are dedicated to finding ways to steal everything from F-1 cars to NASA space shuttles purely for his collection of 'archaic' techology from the 80s. His thieving alter ego is Machinegal, a super-greedy old man who heads a squad of buxom assistants dedicated to helping him complete his retro-tech collection. Super-villains and super-heroes/heroines alike are depicted as solipsistic crusaders for their private antisocial obsessions. In the mega-mall shoppers' dimension that characterises *Moldiver*'s futuristic Tokyo, the audience to the outrageously destructive battles between Machinegal and either Mr Tokyo or Moldiver is indifferent to the battling super-powers. Wryly, Japan of the future is depicted super-numbed and encased in its own self-obsessed insular worlds. If the super-hero is an exaggeration of the common person, *Moldiver*'s sibling heroes fit the mould perfectly.

OVA (6)
Genre: Robot Sci-Fi
Dir: Hiroyuki Kitazume; **Prod:** Hiroaki Inoue, Hiroshi Kakoi, Hisao Yamada, Kazuaki Morijiri; **Scr:** Manabu Nakamura, Ryoei Tsukimura; **Anim:** Hiroyuki Kitazume, Jun Okuda, Sadafumi Hiramatsu; **Chara:** Hiroyuki Kitazume; **Score:** Kei Wakakusa; **Sound:** Hiroki Matsuoka, Fusanabo Fujiyama; **Story:** Hiroyuki Kitazume.

MS Gundam 0083 – Stardust Memory (*Kido Senshi Gandamu 0083 - Sutaa dasuto memori*)

Japan, 1990

Takashi Imanishi, Mitsuko Kase

Belittling the notion of 'saga', the *Gundam* phenomenon has sprawled numerous TV and OVA series and feature films over the last two decades. Each has its special features, coloured by new characterisation modes and new technological visions. *MS Gundam 0083 – Stardust Memory* is possibly the most focused on drama created by the intermeshing of its multitude of characters, giving rise to a distinctive reading of how the mobile suits relate to those who man them.

Like the sword in *chambara* (swordplay) movies, the mobile suit in *MS Gundam 0083* is the instrument through which its owner attains power, becomes empowered, and overpowers external forces. In doing so, he becomes one with the instrument as the two fuse each other's mechanics, materiality and memory. The mobile suits are monstrously enlarged exo-skeletons, human in form, clothed in metallic jet armour, shaped like feudal lord finery, and possessing mecha-swords of tremendous energy. More important than this exterior appearance and its iconic heritage is the internal construction of the suits and their meta-mechanical extensions of the motor mechanisms of the human inside them. Again like the sword, the mobility of these suits is controlled by the user/rider/fighter within, whose own bodily control and prowess determines the suit's amplified analogues of human mechanics. This grants the mobile suits an incongruous agility, just as the humans inside become virtual machines. Such fluid interchangeability and fused duality are both a tenet of the *bushido* code of the *samurai* and a prime design factor in the manual of mobile suit operation.

MS Gundam 0083's central 'inner humans' are Uraki and his friend Keith. Conforming to the heroic template of the *Gundam* cycle, they are young, naive, eager. Each goes through stages of learning and being taught by Lt Burning (and the crucial software techs Mora and Nina) to eventually control his mobile suit and become a key player in interstellar combat that leads to an Earth-shattering climax. Uraki and Keith's team, crew, officers, commanders and generals stratify their place within the Albion space ship hierarchy, creating the chart of duties and debts they must service as part of their growth to 'mobile-manhood'. Yet the mobile suit remains the macro-stage for the self, encapsulating one's emotional turmoil, existential angst and euphoric rise. Often alone within the mobile suit's psychological cockpit, Uraki and Keith voice inner fears and doubts, making the suit an apt 'dramatic vehicle' for their development.

Scale is never short of astounding throughout *MS Gundam 0083*. From the size of the mobile suits, to the mammoth ships that house them, to the sprawling war waged throughout the Sea of Solomon and its endless space junk, to the final reveal of the Shower GM Canon mega-gun aimed at Earth – scale is beyond any sense of human form. No mere glorification of might, *MS Gundam 0083*'s embrace of towering terror strategically reveals the role mere humans play in shaping and deploying these mega-powers. Encased within gigantic suits and gargantuan ships, Uraki, the Federation army and its opposed Delaz Fleet demonstrate how they deal with the gravity of decision and the weight of responsibility.

OVA (13)

Genre: Power-Suit Sci-Fi

Dir: Takashi Imanishi, Mitsuko Kase; **Prod:** Masuo Ueda, Minoru Takanashi; **Scr:** Akinori Endo, Fuyushi Gobu, Asahide Ohkuma, Ryosuke Takahashi; **Anim:** Toshihiro Kawamoto, Hiroki Kanno, Hiroshi Osaka; **Chara:** Toshihiro Kawamoto; **Mecha:** Hajime Katoki, Mika Akitaka, Shoji Kawamori, Yasushi Ishizu; **Score:** Mitsuo Hagita; **Sound:** Yasuo Uragami; **Original Creators:** Hajime Yatate, Yoshiyuki Tomino.

My Neighbor Totoro (*Tonari no totoro*)
Japan, 1988 – 86 mins
Hayao Miyazaki

Most advanced, modernised and progressive cultures voice some regret over the transformations that effectively erased their pre-industrial, pre-urban and pre-modern times. Emblematic of the most drastic changes between these epochs, Japan has often been cited as a culture (predominantly by Western writers) that had a rich past, yet now lacks soul and identity. Dewy-eyed and romantic despite there being substance in some of these sociological arguments, the cry of a 'lost Japan' is testy and colonial.

Japan critiques itself in more complex ways. *My Neighbor Totoro* on the one hand subscribes to a yearning for that 'lost Japan', detailing with great charm and warmth the deepening awareness experienced by an urban family (Tora and his two children, Mei and Satsuki) once they relocate to an old country home and sense the beauty and power of nature around them. Mixing social observation with folkloric wonderment, five-year-old Mei is especially sensitive to the woodland spirits. Her open-eyed innocence expresses the film's desire for Japan to perceive nature similarly and re-connect to its elemental manifestation.

On the other hand, *My Neighbor Totoro* promotes a pragmatic yet macrocosmic view of nature. Just as the family is coming to terms with their absent mother interred in hospital with a pre-modern disease (tuberculosis) so do they accept the cyclical connectedness of nature and its own non-human charting of life, energy and spirituality. In this sense, *My Neighbor Totoro* is a tale of spiritual ecology within which humans are not central.

In one key scene, Mei and Satsuki are privy to the workings of nature unseen by humans. Late at night under a full moon, King Totoro wills a tree to grow from a seedling patch. As the tree grows, we witness an animated simulation of time-lapse photography which portrays the invisible time line of the tree's life force. This serves as a reminder of how little we perceive of nature, for the moment of our perception (the 'image' of the tree) is ultimately a mere intersection in another continuum (the 'life' of the tree). The tree is greater than us: this is the secret Mei and Satsuki witness from Totoro's demonstration, and the lesson the film advances to its human audience.

Comprehending the continuum of nature, the apparently visual world around us can be surmised as the recordings of past and dormant energy fields. The most forceful demonstration of this relationship between the latent/invisible/hidden energy of the ground and the manifest/visible/exposed energy of the tree lies in the haunting resemblance the sprouting form bears to the infamous 'mushroom cloud' of atomic bomb blasts. Consequently, such an image can cast the tree as violently rupturing the earth, or cast a bomb blast as being part of a life–death cycle for a city. Each are exemplars of a bi-polar energy flow that is – philosophically, at least – accepted as the nature of life more by the East than by the West. As with most of *My Neighbor Totoro*, this scene is poignant and elegiac, yet it does not shy away from the power of metaphor it employs.

Feature

Genre: Eco Drama

Dir/Scr/Anim/Chara: Hayao Miyazaki; **Prod:** Toru Hara; **Score:** Joe Hisaishi;
Sound: Shigeharu Shiba.

Nausicaa of the Valley of the Wind (*Kaze no tani no Naushika*)
Japan, 1984 – 116 mins
Hayao Miyazaki

Inspired by a medieval folk tale about a princess who could commune with insects, *Nausicaa of the Valley of the Wind* transports that idea of a human's hyper-sensitivity to the natural order of life into a futuristic world ravaged by ecological disorder. The future of *Nausicaa* is one where deadly, microscopic spore (housed in a massive, decayed forest belt, the Sea of Corruption) could at any point be carried by winds to devastate further land mass. Downwind from the Sea of Corruption lies the Valley of the Wind. Nausicaa is the warrior princess of the valley, a territory whose frail existence is largely based around wind technologies. Nausicaa knows well that the decayed state of the world is due to mankind upsetting nature's order. As a leader of humans, she embodies ethical and political clashes with a maturity, awareness and reserve that out-stretches her years. Her consequent decisions and actions make for a thrilling and engrossing drama of human conflict and global resolution.

Nausicaa proceeds along epic lines: complete civilisations are known to have been decimated by mysterious archaic forces; formidable and ancient gods surveyed terrains now inhabited by humans; and geography rests at the precipice of momentous change. Nausicaa represents but one of many territories, societies, lineages and political alliances, involving opposed values, technologies and even species. Yet the epic veneer of *Nausicaa* is gradually revealed to not be an aspect of dramatic scale as modelled on historical studies, but a reflection of the all-encompassing power of nature.

Nausicaa is a military saga that subverts the narrative binary of warring sides and their principles, and in place introduces a far greater force for them to combat: the very Earth which they contest and attempt to possess. The gods to which these human armies lay claim are in fact not deities for human glorification but pure elemental forces which are eventually awakened to repel human presence, as if nature is allergic to mankind. The breath-taking sweep by which *Nausicaa* symbolises this is superbly orchestrated. When the massed Ohmu giant bugs are mobilised they are like a complete desert surging forth like an unstoppable crustaceous tsunami; when a god warrior Kyoshinhei is revived as a melting gargantuan of breathing acidic death he can decimate a complete army in one exhale.

The ecological bent of *Nausicaa* is impossible to miss – though it is hard to perceive its precise orientation. This is no mere humanist hand-wringing wish to 'save the Earth': this is a redefinition of 'ecology' to be the advent of how nature is problematised by human existence. Couched within an Eastern sense of balance, *Nausicaa* poses that humans and the Earth can co-exist under great pressure and harmful impact – but at a certain point the Earth will reveal the true extent of its power. Nausicaa's respect for the smallest spore prepares her to comprehend the vastness of this earthly power, casting her as an ecological ruler of people – something entirely absent from human history, but possible in *anime*.

Feature

Genre: Eco Sci-Fi

Dir/Scr/Chara: Hayao Miyazaki; **Prod:** Isao Takahata; **Anim/Chara:** Kazuo Komatsubara; **Score:** Joe Hisaishi; **Sound:** Shigeharu Shiba; **Manga:** *Kaze no tani no Naushika* (*Nausicaa of the Valley of the Wind*); **Wr/Art:** Hayao Miyazaki.

Neon Genesis Evangelion (*Shinseiki evangerion*)
Japan, 1995
Hideaki Anno

It's obviously post-apocalyptic. It's noticeably post-human. And it's possibly 'post-*anime*'. How can *Neon Genesis Evangelion* be all this? By redefining the audiovisual precepts of human space, monstrous invasion and psychic machines.

First, human space. Humans inhabit the city of Tokyo-3 (a spread of 'armament buildings' which retract underground when the Angel invasions occur) and the headquarters of NERV (based underground in a 'geo-front' complete with artificially maintained land, water, light and air). All preconceptions of difference between inside and outside, between stasis and motion, between base and apex, between form and ambience no longer operate in such a city of the future. Second, monstrous invasion. Each of the Angels (the diabolical threat to Earth) has their own look and an equally distinctive sound. They range from morphic mutations to those who resemble modernist and ancient archetypes of biomorphic form - from Aztec wall paintings to Miro's murals to Donald Judd cubes. And third, psychic machines. The gifted 'children' Shinji, Rei and Asuka operate their Evas (giant robots) by being inserted into them via a liquid-oxygenated capsule which psychically links their nervous system with the Eva's sophisticated robotics. Sight, space and sound are bound to behave differently under such conditions, and an awareness of this governs much of *Evangelion*'s design.

The future in *Evangelion* – like the post-apocalyptic continuum which paves the way for Japan's unsettling existence – is on the brink of destruction, and all that is calm is merely the potential for radical destabilisation. Spatio-temporal rupture rages throughout this *anime*. Often we are caught in the claustrophobic mind of young Shinji as he grapples with an aching existential dilemma of how to live alone, divorced from social and human contact. The screen will go black, white, or assault the eye with *Pokemon*-style strobe-cutting. Silence screams

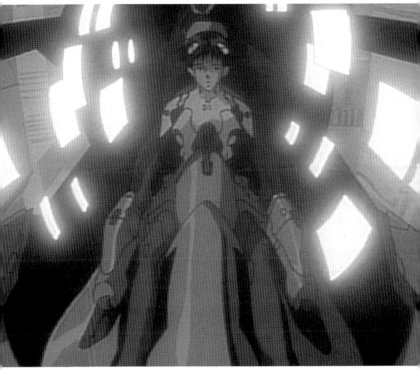

Neon Genesis Evangelion: shimmering and shifting apparitions of emotional complexity

and pierces the soundtrack; detonations capitulate to a soft roar; all energies are continually inverted and reversed to complement and counterpoint their dramatic weight. Sometimes complete sections of plot disappear to convey Shinji's loss of consciousness inside an Eva. Sometimes his psychic sensitivity teleports him unexpectedly to ill-defined locales.

In the West, we will crudely designate the hero, the buffoon, the cynic, the sage; in the East, characters are founded upon their schizophrenia, established through their multiplicity and defined by their inability to be grounded. *Evangelion*'s characters – especially the three 'children' who complexly represent Japan's own problematised Generation-X – are formed by means of emotional compaction. Joy harmonises grief; suffering prompts laughter; compassion folds violence; hatred suppresses innocence. *Evangelion*'s characters are quintessentially good, bad and ugly. Their visage and voice dance in intricately orchestrated lines that map out these characters not as containers or vessels of emotion, but shimmering and shifting apparitions of emotional complexity – not 'rounded out' by authorial conceit, but unrefined as befits the prickly irrationality which dictates our everyday exchanges.

Evangelion is a complete and rigorous excavation of *anime* up to this point. It queries identity to the point of catatonia; it pulls asunder all familial frameworks; it compounds desire as a debilitating mechanism; and it ultimately suggests that *anime* is but the synaptic short-circuiting that occurs within the mind under pressure. Entertaining it might be, but entertainment it is not.

TV

Genre: Power-Suit Sci-Fi

Dir/Scr: Hideaki Anno; **Prod:** Noriko Kobayashi, Yutaka Sugiyama; **Anim:** Shunji Suzuki, Hiroaki Anno; **Chara:** Yoshiyuki Sadamoto, Mahiro Maeda (Angels); **Mecha:** Hideaki Anno, Ikuto Yamashita; **Score:** Shiro Sagisu; **Sound:** Hideyuki Tanaka.

Night on the Galactic Railroad
(*Ginga tetsudo no yoru*)
Japan, 1985 – 105 mins
Gisaburo Sugii

A popular and persistent way of 'reading movies' has been through reconstituting any film into pulped myth. This has created unconscious support for a fictive 'uniting church' of human drama that attributes the mere impulse of storytelling to grand narratives, global archetypes and universal truths. Of the varied practices of cinema around the world that do not conform to this literary straight-jacketing, *anime* is a most perplexing form for those who attempt to apply Judeo-Christian templates.

Night on the Galactic Railroad is a perfect example of how *anime* proceeds in polite ignorance of myths, heroes and their journeys. Centred on the cat Giovanni who lives in a small village tending his ill mother, the story opens with him distractedly imagining the frightening expansiveness of the galaxy. His teacher is attempting to tell the class about the Milky Way, but Giovanni imagines himself floating through its myriad constellations. Giovanni is a dreamer and somewhat ostracised by the rest of the class. His only friend – a distanced one at that – is Campanella. The astronomy class symbolically outlines the map across which a hero would then journey, befitting the grand heroic narratives of the European tradition. But Giovanni undertakes a far different journey.

With Campanella, he travels on a train that has suddenly appeared to take them through the Milky Way. It's a highly poetic journey: measured, detailed, lingering. No rings of Hades, stations of the cross or wonders of the world. In place, a widening cosmological understanding of the swirling intangibility of life. Transportation as a metaphor for transcendence – in trains particularly – has appeared in many modern Japanese narratives, of which the original *Night on the Galactic Railroad* novel is seminal. For the 'quest' as such in this film is the coming to terms with suicide – something that rarely if ever appears in the catalogue of tasks for 'the hero'. Campanella's 'drowning' remains mysterious to Giovanni. The motivation behind those who commit suicide suicide is both enigma and emblem of Japanese society, and *Night on the Galactic Railroad* is ultimately a pondering on the Japanese psyche.

The Japanese 'face' of *Night on the Galactic Railroad* is there for those who can read through it. Masks have often been used in theories of mythology to suggest that cultural difference is simply a mask that discloses the essential 'human' face of all endeavour and its dramatisation. *Night on the Galactic Railroad* has a far more complex conception of masks. First, the act of masking is highly foregrounded and not something to be 'uncovered' as per mythological analysis. The story's use of cats anthropomorphised into European human attire is accepted as a mutative importation of styles and codes, highlighted by the cats' relation to milk – a quintessentially non-Japanese food. Second – and in wry self-contradiction of the first point – the cat mask references Japanese children's role-playing during traditional festivals (*matsuri*), such as the moon/star festival centred within the story. Third, the notion of the mask in Japan relates to complex socio-cultural mores where the expressive face is avoided in both social exchanges as well as in dramatic forms like *Noh*. Rather than be a dupe to 'the real story', *Night on the Galactic Railroad*'s use of masks and masking is in itself the declaration of its cultural essence.

Feature

Genre: Mystical Allegory

Dir: Gisaburo Sugii; **Prod:** Masato Hara, Atsumi Tashiro; **Scr:** Minoru Betsuyaku; **Anim:** Marisuke Eguchi; **Chara:** Takao Kodama; **Score:** Haruomi Hosono; **Sound:** Atsumi Tashiro; **Novel:** *Ginga tetsudo no yoru* (*Night on the Galactic Railroad*); **Wr:** Kenji Miyazawa; **Manga:** *Ginga tetsudo no yoru* (*Night on the Galactic Railroad*); **Art:** Hiroshi Masumura.

Ninja Scroll (Jubei ninpucho)
Japan, 1993 – 94 mins
Yoshiaki Kawajiri

Near the opening of *Ninja Scroll*, a woman walks through a ravaged village in a zombie-like state. She speaks in a stilted monotone and moves with strained co-ordination. Elsewhere, evil lord Urimaru mouths the words which synchronously motorise the lips of this catatonic corpus. Once finished with her as his rotting messenger, she falls down dead like a lifeless puppet detached from the master's control.

She is/was a being whose voice is owned elsewhere, whose words are controlled by remote. Imaging the 'voiceless' commoners in feudal Japan, she evidences the wrath of power the *daimyo* lords originally held over their people. Urimaru's ultimate power is this type of voice which is

Ninja Scroll: characters who speak and 'are spoken' across dimensions

a mystical constant in Japanese folklore and *anime*. He uses similar communication to whisper commands to his *ninja* army from afar. In a method akin to children's telephonic string tied between two tin cans, a glistening trail of fleetingly visible thread streams through the forest and is attached to others' lips.

Curiously, the para-mystical vocalisation of puppets, the possessed and other proxies figures strongly in much Japanese fantasy *anime*, with characters who can speak – and in a sense 'are spoken' – across dimensions, call beyond states, and communicate through realities. In *Ninja Scroll* this voicing is a sign of the super-human control Urimaru maintains over his subjects. Shrouded in darkness and layers of ornate fabric, cloistered in an indistinct corner of his domain, this glistening thread lingers within the folds of his adorned personage. It sparkles like spider webbing; it can entrap similarly. When he is angered by someone he spits forth his thread and can strangle – this is how he controls the beautiful Benisato. This thread is the deadly strings of the puppet-master, here materialising the dread induced by hearing his voice and the power his words hold over his listener.

Ninja Scroll can be accepted as a modern update of the ubiquitous seventeenth-century legend of Yagyu Jubei that has fuelled many tales since. But it also is a scintillating audiovisualisation through *anime* of how tremendous power could control so many people in a bygone era. *Ninja Scroll* literally animates an ancient dimension where energies and forces are clearly sited not in the elemental or natural, but in the social and the cultural. The way the *ninja* jump through the trees is fantastic for its demonstration of the level of commitment and control they bring to their actions. This army springs to action and propels itself forward with dogged myopic force, embodying a mythology of group energy in Japan that stretches through epochs to the present and beyond, qualifying the Japanese blend of obedience and engagement. Similarly, when Tessai hurls through the forest carving flora and *ninja* into lifeless splinters and slivers, his dynamo of death pictures a grossly controlled unit – a self-reincarnating post-human *kamikaze* made of molten rock that can use his bodily mass and compaction to kill all in his path. *Ninja Scroll* is gloriously 'ancient' in its story, but eerily modern in its characterisation.

Feature

Genre: Mystical Folklore

Dir/Scr: Yoshiaki Kawajiri; **Prod:** Komatsu Shigeaki, Haruo Sai, Masaki Sawanobori; **Anim/Chara:** Yutaka Minowa; **Score:** Kaoru Wada; **Sound:** Yasunori Honda; **Manga:** *Jubei ninpucho* (*Ninja Wind Scroll of Jubei*); **Wr/Art:** Yoshiaki Kawajiri.

Only Yesterday (*Omohide poro poro*)
Japan, 1991 – 119 mins
Isao Takahata

In a hangover of agrarian life, contemporary Japanese society still likens an unmarried woman over twenty-five years old to a Christmas cake left uneaten by the New Year. Many an *OL* (office lady) has had to bear this stigma of 'being stale' in order to forge whatever career and education were affordable to her. While the existential plight of the salary man has been exhaustively treated in Japanese cinema, *manga* has been the medium that interprets this effect upon the individualist aspirations of the maturing working woman. One such *manga* is *Omohide poro poro* (translatable as 'tear drops of memory'), made into the *anime Only Yesterday*.

A semi-autobiographical story tinged with memories both cherished and enlightening, *Only Yesterday* follows *OL* Taeko as she returns to where she grew up, the rural community of Yamagata. The *anime* is fibrillated by its induction of memory, folding baby-boomer nostalgia into an affection for retro detailing. The quietude of the country and its self-sustaining existence provide a bowl into which Taeko's memories uncontrollably pour. She becomes full of her past, exposed to how much it makes her who she is, and conscious of how much her urban life had temporarily clouded her past. The film embraces a duality of temporal existence: Taeko is depicted as being simultaneously twenty-six and ten years old as she is caught reconciling the remembrance of her past desires with the consideration of her present actualities. This tale of two Taekos is tiled in mosaic fashion as the young adult Taeko reflects on her present and past, while the child Taeko contemplates her present and future. At key moments her younger self co-exists with her like an imaginary friend. It's a wonderful use of *anime*'s capacity for fantasy, here put to a very worldly and subtly personal purpose.

The rural return may appear clichéd – and it certainly has been abused by selling the country as antidote to urban congestion – but the medium of *anime* in *Only Yesterday* paints the country as a mental space of clear running water and fresh air that allows perspective to attain a soft consciousness. This is a tradition in centuries of folding screen paintings in Japan that frame the rural environment as a phenomenological poem. A beautiful and telling moment of this avoidance of cliché in *Only Yesterday* is when Taeko is working in the field early one morning. Suddenly she notices that all the elder women have stopped and are looking in one direction – at the sun coming over the mountain. It's a near-still image, devoid of movement bar the slow illumination of the field being coloured with intense vibrancy. The women bow their heads in a silent prayer of thanks. Being out-of-sync with this attunement to nature, Taeko realises precisely at this moment that this is who she is and where she must be. She too bows her head towards the sun in brilliant silence: she is not a Christmas cake in the New Year, but a fuller woman on a new day.

Feature

Genre: Urban Drama

Dir/Scr: Isao Takahata; **Prod:** Ritsuo Isobe, Yasuyoshi Tokuma, Yoshio Sasaki, Toru Hara; **Anim:** Yoshifumi Kondo, Katsuya Kondo, Yoshiharu Sato; **Chara:** Yoshifumi Kondo; **Score:** Katsu Hoshi; **Sound:** Naoko Asari; **Manga:** *Omohide poro poro* (*Falling Tears of Memory*); **Wr:** Hotaru Okamoto; **Art:** Yuko Tone.

Patlabor – Mobile Police (*Kido keisatsu Patoreiba*)
Japan, 1989/92
Mamoru Oshii

A dumb question to be asked of any of the innumerable *anime* dealing with giant robots driven by humans is 'but how could a single person operate something so big?' Yet that is the serious question posed by the *Patlabor – Mobile Police* series. The prompting is not due to any incredulousness – for many para-mystical, metaphysical and psycho-mechanical factors determine the man-machine mould of giant transforming robot vehicles in *anime* – but because *Patlabor – Mobile Police* brings the future to bear weight on the present.

The 'mobile police force' in the series is precisely that: trained officers who operate giant Shinohara bi-ped exo-skeletons. Robotics is eschewed in place of computerised control of pumps, hydraulics and gears, making the Shinoharas enlarged 'wearable' bulldozers supported by precision maintenance normally reserved for Formula 1 racing engines. The job of the Patlabor unit is to patrol labors – 'labors' being the common term for all forms of automated or manned robotic engines and devices – whose circuitry is the persistent target, presumably, of urban terrorists attempting to destabilise the city and destroy its reliance on robotics. This places the Patlabor unit in an awkward position: many people hate robots, yet the Patlabor unit uses them to fight renegade labors, plus the police end up destroying as much as their opponents in the process. This no-win situation provides the ongoing backdrop for the series' skilful and measured study of the team, centred around rookie Noa who has great respect for the Shinoharas.

Patlabor – Mobile Police is the inverse of any of the *Gundam* series: it is based on land alone, hamstrung by bureaucratic process, devoid of any grand heroics, rooted in pedestrian daily work, and restricted by council ordinances and department budgets. Welcome to modern-day Japan, the series wryly intones as it follows the frustrations and achievements of the

Patlabor: bringing the future to bear weight on the present

Patlabor unit. Yet in perverse contrast to the realist nuances of the everyday depicted in the script and the characterisations of Noa and her unit, *Patlabor – Mobile Police* is an exhausting consideration of every possible facet of affording a man control of such huge exo-skeletons. The physics of mass, force, weight and gravity are obsessively detailed in every episode as Noa has to learn how to operate her Shinohara. From learning to stand up without falling down, to charging full speed with sabre-gun raised, the series self-reflexively reverses the magic of the animated medium by showing us how difficult it is to move something with a human inside.

Patlabor – Mobile Police extends this definition of the human into a socialised diagram of the urban city and how individuals and groups work with and against each other as well as the machines they employ, utilise and abuse. The man-machine mould is here recast to shape issues of territory, occupation, congestion and growth as the metropolis is not a frozen cartography but a fluid machine that requires continual lubrication. Welcome to the modern-day Japan that is *Patlabor – Mobile Police*.

OVA (16)

Genre: Urban Power-Suit Melodrama

Dir: Mamoru Oshii; **Prod:** Shin Unosawa, Taro Maki, Makoto Kubo; **Scr:** Kazunori Ito; **Anim:** Kazuya Kise, Masahiro Kitazaki, Takuya Wada, Naoto Takahashi; **Chara:** Akemi Takada; **Mecha:** Yutaka Izubuchi; **Score:** Kenji Kawai; **Sound:** Shigeharu Shiba; **Manga:** *Kido keisatsu Patoreiba* (*Patlabor Mobile Police*); **Wr/Art:** Masami Yuuki.

Patlabor III – Wasted XIII (*Patoreiba III – Wasted XIII*)
Japan, 2002 – 105 mins
Fumihiko Takayama

Mostly, sequels and additional OVAs released as part of an *anime* title will extend definable characteristics that made the originating *anime* popular. *Patlabor III* almost denies that the Patlabor universe existed prior to this film. The Patlabor unit and their Shinohara labors appear two thirds into the film and play a noticeably small role. This generates an interesting textual effect that positions most of the action as decontextualised, prepared as you might be to tie in the Shinohara labors. This refusal of expected narrative grounding imbues *Patlabor III*'s *mise en scène* with unexpected pregnancy.

Additionally, the story is a convoluted concatenation of seemingly disconnected events that thread a near-incomprehensible through-line, gathering the master/pupil detective duo of Kusuri/Hata in its forward momentum. Investigating a spate of deaths, they uncover the possibility of a mutant underwater beast terrorising Tokyo Bay. Their investigation leads them to infer military and scientific ties behind the creation of this prototype chimera, especially as Hata pursues with deepening attraction the beautiful geneticist Misaki Saeko. Yet this description could fit so many sci-fi mystery *anime*. *Patlabor III* is fixated on the narrative suspension that dynamises such generic templates; it savours the incidences that float like forensic fluff in front of the detectives. On numerous occasions, Kusuri and Hata are in isolation, pondering and considering the ramifications and coincidences of their collected data. In true Japanese thinking mode, they contemplate the bigger picture. The *anime* is toned with this sense of contemplation, especially as they draw close to uncovering the reasons why a woman scientist would desire to create such a 'monster'.

In a slight yet profoundly intricate orchestration of light, colour, sound and movement, *Patlabor III* outlays a 'pure' *anime* that only superficially shapes itself to contain characters and plot. A heady sensory ambience pervades as any scene is articulated more through its poetic denouement than its plot mechanics. A perplexing experience only if you impose prose on its evocative shimmering surface, *Patlabor III* delights in obtusely staging a scene and gradually opening out to reveal the interconnection between aural and visual details. While this might appear counter to the urban fundamentality of the preceding *Patlabor* series, OVAs and films, *Patlabor III* essentially remains true to the registration of a familiar landscape – but chooses to tune in to the psychological vibrations of its characters, their motivations and their feelings. The score in particular signposts this approach, choosing not to outwardly dictate melodic lines, but instead murmur, intone and exhale timbrel shivers of its rich instrumentation.

In keeping with this accent on audiovisual orchestration, synaesthetic exploration and frequency sensitivity within the more action-oriented conventions of its sci-fi form, an important detail of *Patlabor III*'s mystery notes how the mutant beast is attuned to the upper frequency range of recorded music only recordable on vinyl and not on DAT or CD media. Echoing the fact that Kusuri is a vinyl purist with a large collection of classical records and a high-end valve amplifier system, this lends a delightful touch to a film predicated on nuance, presence and invisible sense.

Feature

Genre: Mutant Sci-Fi

Dir: Fumihiko Takayama; **Prod:** Atsushi Sugita, Masahiro Fukushima; **Scr:** Miki Tori; **Anim:** Takuji Endo; **Chara:** Hiroki Takagi; **Mecha:** Hajime Katoki, Shoji Kawamori, Yataka Izubuchi; **Score:** Kenji Kawai; **Sound:** Toshiki Kameyama.

Perfect Blue
Japan, 1997 – 82 mins
Satsoshi Kon

The *idoru* (pop music idol) industry is lauded and levelled for its ability to replicate and simulate singing stars whose sameness can be either appealing or appalling. The *idoru* fan worships the star for its microcosmic uniqueness, just as the *idoru* critic damns the star for its macrocosmic undifferentiation. Locked between these opposed trajectories, *Perfect Blue* frames a chilling portrait of how the *idoru* industry functions for those within and without its fabrication.

After Mina has announced her retirement from the trio Cham, she prepares for her upcoming role in the TV movie 'Double Bind'. She is

Perfect Blue: doubled and troubled in a maddening hall of mirrors

committed to this image change despite one of her managers, Rumi, and many of her fans not being happy. Mina's status within the *idoru* industry and its heavily annotated reportage of its 'product' posits her as someone whom even fans think they can mould and control: they feel they are shaping and even advising Mina through their supportive worship of her. Yet Mina is grounded in knowing that her real life has nothing to do with the fantasies and falsehoods promoted through the *idoru* machinery: her shopping chores are uneventful; her cramped apartment is no palace; her fish garner her most attention.

It is in Mina's private space that she stumbles across the website 'Mina's Room' which amuses her in its fictional reportage of her own diary. But due to its accuracy, Mina soon realises that someone is shadowing her every move as an invisible stalker – not harassing her, but becoming her. The pressure Mina suffers in working on her character for 'Double Bind' takes it toll and she experiences identity conflict in trying to separate the stalker's Mina from her own self. Further complications arise from Mina trying to separate her already problematised self from the character in 'Double Bind' – especially once the producers rewrite her character as a stripper raped in a club who then goes on a rampage killing men. The TV promotion of her rising star in television also creates personality schisms in the transition from cutie-pie idol to soft-porn seductress. And once people involved in changing her image start dying violent deaths, Mina becomes a mess of multiples.

Perfect Blue exploits *anime*'s ability to 'double' characters in mind-bending ways. Replicating Mina's state, we experience how the difference between the physical Mina standing next to a poster image of Mina becomes unperceivable. Shops, plazas and subways covered with advertising imagery promoting stars, models and celebrities, create a disorienting diorama of real and non-real figures. As Mina sinks into a pool of widening schizophrenic waves, she sees herself reflected everywhere in mirrors, glass and chrome. This 'other' Mina is the repository of mediarised and desired Minas, taunting her for discarding her 'true' role as pop *idoru*. Doubled and troubled in a maddening hall of mirrors, she starts believing not her own hype, but the negative image overlaid on her by ex-fans and worshippers dissatisfied with this tarnished Tinkerbell. Already submerged in a swamp of adopted role-plays, she battles to 'unbecome' their Mina – and become her own Mina.

Feature

Genre: Psychic Crime

Dir: Satsoshi Kon; **Prod:** Hiroaki Inoue, Masao Maruyama, Takeshi Washitani; **Scr:** Sadayuki Murai; **Anim:** Hideki Hamazu; **Chara:** Hideki Hamazu, Hisashi Eguchi, Satsoshi Kon; **Score:** Masahiro Ikumi; **Sound:** Shizuo Kurahashi; **Novel:** *Perfect Blue*; **Wr:** Yoshikazu Takeuchi; **Manga.** *Perfect Blue*, Art. Satsoshi Kon.

Plastic Little (Purasitikku Ritoru)
Japan, 1994
Kinji Yoshimoto

Being in Japan can be likened to being in an episode of *The Twilight Zone* where you discover that Disneyland is the real world and everything you thought was real is actually a theme park. A cheap journalistic metaphor in some respects, such a comparative device is employed by many *anime* to visualise a future setting for their stories. In doing so, they ultimately reflect their present condition, revealing that the dichotomy between artifice and actuality operable in the West is but a wound-down machine of no further use. *Plastic Little* is set in one such world.

In an amalgamated mutation of Earthly references, the planet Yietta is a Nihonesque Disneyland of a world. Land and water are evident – as are massive expanses of gaseous clouds in which 'swim' giant whales and other creatures of similar proportion. Teen Tita is captain of a gigantic 'ship' which sails these clouds to capture whales to sell to pet shops. Chance connects her to the younger Elysee who is on the run from government agents. Tita and the crew of her ship end up protecting Elysee and unleashing a civil war of sorts as they fight mounting government forces. Standard space-saga heroics, but here portrayed by – literally – babes in swimsuits. The ship is more like an aquatic playground complete with water slides, hotel lobbies, restaurants and recreational sites. These settings are incongruous – especially when the battles take on a decidedly violent tone – but they reflect a studied decision to portray a certain 'reality' of Japan: theme parks.

Much ridicule and consternation has been levelled at Japan's undying love of theme parks. These critiques ignore how deeply ingrained ritual, gesture and interaction are within Japanese society as artificial and mannered modes of exchange. From temples to castles to museums to carnivals to parks, these public edifices and grounds are accepted as entirely unnatural monuments of form and space. This otherworldliness of detached simulation liberates its participants from connecting to anything real – the precise charm and attraction of Disneyland. *Plastic Little*'s 'world design' is one where all modes of social, commercial and even military engagement are aligned to this principle of 'worldisation'. Sidestepping architectural orthodoxy and industrial design dogma, the world of Yietta is one that dreams that there is no real world: no pre-existing realm within which humans and society could build and shape things. As *anime*, *Plastic Little* visualises such heightened flights of fancy as a futuristic vision not of 'the world' but how we might design worlds in the future.

In this respect *Plastic Little* is surprisingly accurate in its capture of contemporary design, creating mutant historical panoramas which are no more outrageously divorced from reality than the average American shopping mall. Additionally, the 'other planet' location of Yietta is never pictured as belonging to the cosmos, but always sited on planetary ground, giving us a cavalcade of interior design, urban façades and spectacular venues which typify the extremes of Japanese post-modern architecture. For some Westerners, this is a vision of a consumer Hades. For Tita and her crew, it's home.

OVA (1)

Genre: Sci-Fi Melodrama

Dir: Kinji Yoshimoto; **Prod:** Hideaki Fujii, Kazuhiko Ikeguchi; **Scr:** Masayori Sekimoto; **Anim/Chara:** Satoshi Urushihara; **Score:** Tamio Terashima; **Sound:** Fusanabo Fujiyama; **Manga:** *Purasitikku Ritoru* (*Plastic Little*); **Wr:** Satoshi Urushihara, Kinji Yoshimoto; **Art:** Satoshi Urushihara.

Please Save My Earth
(*Boku no chikyu o mamotte*)
Japan, 1993
Kazuo Yamazaki

If the world is a stage and we are players in its human drama, it would be logical that 'realism' and 'naturalism' remain in the wings of theatre and off-screen in cinema. It would also be logical that as *anime* specialises in cyclic enveloping narratives of reincarnation to define continuity of multiple characters in different bodies in shifted dimensions, it should jettison causal, plausible narrative structures. This is exactly what *Please Save My Earth* does.

Please Save My Earth is a planetary narrative, occupying spatial and temporal expanses of such scale. Eons ago on moon base KK-101, a team of scientists conducting observational duties for their distant solar system are stranded when interplanetary war destroys their home planet. Isolated, the team devolves into frayed emotional shells of their former selves. The main attraction between Mokuren and Gyokuran is upset by manoeuvres by the unbalanced Shion. Disease breaks out and Gyokuran directs the only sample antidote to be given to Shion, so that Gyokuran and Mokuren can die together. Shion lingers alive and alone for much longer. Present-day Earth: the two lovers have been reincarnated into teenagers Alice and Jinpachi; the psychopath into Rin. These parallel dramas co-exist, the former intervening the other. The moon base story is revealed in fragmented disjointed fashion, replicating the state of confusion these Earth kids are experiencing through realising their place in the karmic cycle.

But as Alice, Jinpachi and Rin develop a sense of their current interconnectedness and their continuation of karmic lines from their previous existence, the 'revolving stage' for this human drama becomes

(Opposite page) *Please Save My Earth*: redefining 'attraction' and 'motivation' in its love triangle

planetary in scale. They proceed conscious of their roles and status as players in their own partially pre-shaped 'human drama'. This intertextual playfulness is something freely achievable and exploited by *anime*'s reliance on fantastical mapping of reincarnative consequences. *Please Save My Earth*'s characters 'play destiny' just as the *anime* 'stages destiny'. In *anime*'s post-modern modality, reincarnation is not simply a karmic/Eastern principle, but the means for the realignment of individuality to greater arcs beyond the social and the familial (which are essentially costumes for the self in these scenarios).

Please Save My Earth redefines notions of 'attraction' and 'motivation' in its love triangle, creating a contraction of narrative due to the magnetisation and implosion of reincarnative 'love-pulls' that reach across space and time. The more Alice/Jinpachi/Rin become the rebirthed totalities of Mokuren/Gyokuran/Shion, the more the means by which we recognise their 'characters' becomes problematised, though nonetheless engaging. While the story may appear convoluted, it develops into a 'meta-story' that traces and outlines the paths of emotional energies that circulate unleashed by their cosmic connections. The score and its ethereal vocal beauty is crucial in underscoring this shift from plot mechanics into a trans-generational aura of the lovers' bind. The replayable refrains of the score symbolise everyone's unification across time and space and the repeatable tropes of their amorous engagement. Melody becomes a distant memory floating across the stage of *Please Save My Earth*, heard by its players who seem locked in pondering 'Where have I heard that before?'.

OVA (6)

Genre: Mystical Drama

Dir: Kazuo Yamazaki; **Prod:** Mitshuhisa Ishikawa, Tetsuya Maeda, Yuko Sakurai; **Scr:** Kazuo Yamazaki; **Anim/Chara:** Takayuki Goto; **Score:** Yoko Kanno, Hajime Mizoguchi; **Sound:** Yasuo Uragami, Katsuyoshi Kobayashi; **Manga:** *Boku no chikyu o mamotte* (*Please Save My Earth*); **Wr/Art:** Saki Hiwatari.

Poltergeist Report (Yu Yu Hakusho)
Japan, 1992
Akiyuki Shinbo, Noriyuki Abe

The representation of action is best conveyed through violence. The momentum between cause and effect is ruthlessly translated into the link between impact and pain, and the time-based capture of cinema is well suited to depicting violence. Bemoaning the state of violence in cinema is predicated on a fear of the photographic – on its supposed nightmare of the real rather than its dream of the image – to such an extent that other visual modes of rendering and effecting violence seem impossible.

Yet when *anime* is violent, it surpasses cinema's desperate grip of the real. *Anime* actively disbelieves the power of the photographic and in place intensifies violence more than the photographic image could maintain. An exhaustive example of unending violence in *anime* is the TV series of *Poltergeist Report*. Young streetwise troublemaker Yuusuke dies in the opening episode as he tries to save a small kid from being run over. This inexplicable act of kindness and self-sacrifice sets off a karmic imbalance which grips him between the spirit world (Rei Kei) and the human world (Ningenkai).

The team of *Poltergeist Report* that gather around Yuusuke as he returns to Ningenkai to protect it from invading demons is a gaggle of personae: cute guide Botan, stern master Genkai, sprightly Yoko, fiery Hiei, effete Shuichi, brutish Kuwabara. Pertinent to the physicality of *Poltergeist Report*, they each reveal their inner selves through outward displays of physical force. Yuusuke is central to this through his chosen martial arts. At any given moment he instantaneously unleashes a rain of power punches and kinetic kicks upon an endless stream of monstrous demon fighters conjured forth from a hellish version of federation wrestling. Yuusuke's might is ferociously earthy in its bloody expulsion and frighteningly cosmic in its post-corporeal manifestation. He might be a spirit, but this does not prevent him from coughing up blood, sweating profusely, and nearly popping veins as he musters all the strength he possesses.

Yuusuke is birthed from a long lineage of fighters in Japanese pop culture generally, and *manga* specifically. A significant number of *shonen manga* are centred on pugilistic pulp heroes ranging from professional boxers to high-school delinquents whose whole life across serialised antics require they be beaten to the edge of death only to miraculously find a hidden reserve of strength to overcome their enemies. Physically impossible on all fronts, these street-level hunks are disallowed the respectable crowned glories of the *sumo*, and instead are conferred a humbling 'personal best' which either stills their inner turmoil or tightens the bonds with their friends or gang. After many a gut-hammering bout in *Poltergeist Report*, Yuusuke and the others become a tighter unit, physically, emotionally and spiritually. Just like the Japanese kid who is expected to immediately stand up straight ready for more beating once he has initially been struck by a superior, the unbroken beings and unbending bones in *Poltergeist Report* are a testament to the impermanence of pain and the fundamentality of violence which characterises life for some.

TV

Genre: Mystical Action

Dir: Akiyuki Shinbo, Noriyuki Abe; **Prod:** Ken Hagino, Kenji Shimizu, Koji Kaneda, Kyotaro Kimura; **Scr:** Shikichi Ohashi; **Anim:** Noriyuki Abe; **Chara:** Minoru Yamazawa; **Score:** Yusuke Honma; **Sound:** Kan Fukushima; **Manga:** *Yu Yu Hakusho* (*Playful Ghost White Paper Report*); **Wr:/Art:** Yoshihiro Togashi.

Pompoko (Heisei tanuki gassen pompoko)
Japan, 1994 – 119 mins
Isao Takahata

Using the rich folklore of the indigenous *tanuki* (the fat happy 'raccoon' that welcomes you outside Japanese restaurants – now dwindling in numbers), *Pompoko* maps out a socio-political scenario to question the effectiveness of certain strategies in bringing attention to ecological issues. The message in this film is not simply 'save the forest' but a question as to how one saves the forest. The answers posed at the film's conclusion provide much food for thought.

The story of *Pompoko* is densely 'Eastern', making it a film for the adventurous *gaijin* (foreigner) – due not to the film's innumerable cultural references, but because of the means by which its animation characterises the *tanuki*. According to folklore, *tanuki* are capable of transformative powers and can metamorphose into anything. In short, they are ideal beings for animation. Throughout *Pompoko*, they undergo shape-shifts while switching between three primary modes of depiction: realistic, comic and iconic. When and where this occurs relates to their state of mind and reactions to a current situation. Yet despite this multiplicity of apparition, the personalities of the various *tanuki* and their clans are sharply defined. Individual character is further refined through the story's social dynamics, as numerous debates and conflicts ensue when the *tanuki* try to solve the problem of the encroaching suburban sprawl of Tama New Town.

Pompoko is startling in its exploration of things as viewed by the *tanuki* without resorting to overt 'humanising' of these creatures. The key inventiveness to *Pompoko* is the way it perversely reverses the anthropomorphism at the base of Western cartooning. *Pompoko*'s *tanuki* are rendered in this animation by humans purely because humans have rendered the *tanuki*'s existence in danger. Then the *tanuki* are granted human characteristics to demonstrate how humans can be engaged in the fight to save the *tanuki* – who themselves are engaged in pursuing an effective path of co-habitation with humans. At the end of the day, the *tanuki* are being forced to use their mystical powers of transformation to undertake an entirely human endeavour: assimilation.

This interloping narration and mimetic contortion are responsible for the difficulty in reading *Pompoko* from a solely Western viewpoint. As per calligraphy, *Pompoko*'s meaning is contained in the act of rendering as well as what is being expressed through the rendered. A musical correlation to these issues of rendering aids in orienting a fuller reading of the film. The score is a suite of songs and themes performed in the original folk style of *enka* called *minyo* – an indigenous minimal sing-songy folk music derived from rural and costal villages. The arrangements though are performed by a modern ensemble who radically shift from brash electric versions to quiet acoustic renditions to instrumental melodic interpretations of the distinctive *minyo* modal. No 'true' voice of *minyo* is claimed for musicological veracity, just as 'nature' can no longer be named as an essential given. For Japan's modern society, nature is a process engaged by the social, and in the human realm requires a dialogue where each must listen to the other carefully.

Feature
Genre: Eco Drama
Dir/Scr: Isao Takahata; **Prod:** Toshio Suzuki; **Anim/Chara:** Shinji Otsuka; **Score:** Koryu (Toshiaki Sakamoto); **Sound:** Hisanori Oshiro, Yasu Uragami.

Princess Knight (*Ribon no kishi*)
Japan, 1967
Chikao Katsui, Kanji Akabori

For a culture that consistently throws back to the West a reversed image of anything the West believes to be irreversible, it is not surprising that the binary fixture of gender is switched and swapped in Japan. From the all-male illusionism in *kabuki* to the all-female spectacularism of the Takarazuka Review, Japanese culture over the past 400 years has daringly treated gender as a gauntlet not a given.

Anime is rife with gender dissolution. One of its earliest manifestations of cultural cross-dressing is *Princess Knight*, based on a 1954 *manga*, largely responsible for birthing the *shojo* school of girls-only *manga*. Set in a lurid fantasy-Europe which makes Disney's penchant for European castles seem restrained, this is the story of Sapphire who cannot succeed to the throne of Goldland because she is a girl. She passes as a boy and attains power which she wields rationally and wisely, shattering the presumed idea that a woman could not govern a populace. But being forced to live a double life leads to all sorts of situations where her identity becomes enmeshed in layers of sexual subterfuge. One major sub-theme revolves around her 'returning' to be a woman, requiring her to re-disguise herself as a blonde girl for a journey to Silverland. There she smites Franz Charming, who thereafter pursues this mysterious blonde who captivated him. Shakespearean humour and circumstance is woven through many episodes, but ultimately brocaded in something far richer and less bound by moral resolution than the bard entertained.

Whereas the European lineage of gender-switching is narratively designed and never veers dangerously into true sexual confusion, *Princess Knight* is centred on the psychological, emotional and romantic (if not erotic) shudders which vibrate and reshape the princess's psyche through impulsive desires. Only alluded to in the TV series (and removed altogether from the American translation), these complications ultimately arise because when Sapphire was born, a mischievous angel (Tink in the original; Choppy in the American) pushed the heart of a boy into her mouth when Sapphire was being assigned her gender in the heavens: she actually has the 'hearts' of both sexes within her. The ramifications for reading *Princess Knight* lead to wildly sprouting possibilities counter to the supposed fixity of sexual identity and gender displacement. A pre-transsexual text, *Princess Knight* is a tale liberated from gender distinction not because it 'breaks the taboos' of the social clothing in which sex is dressed or the behavioural and societal constrictions placed on men and women, but because of the innate malleability of character and circumstance inscribed by gender typing.

This 'malleability' accounts for the sexual visage of not only *Princess Knight* but so much *anime* which to many Western eyes prompts confusion over who are the boys and who are the girls. While cute neotonic morphology in Western children's entertainment collapses gender through returning form to the barely sexed body of the baby, *anime* reverses this to portray adults as still linked to the wavering gender status of the pre-socialised baby. This is the deeper meaning of *kawaii* culture, brazenly paraded in *Princess Knight*: nothing is singularly gendered; everything is multi-sexed.

TV

Genre: Gender Melodrama
Dir: Chikao Katsui, Kanji Akabori; **Prod:** Kazuyuki Hirokawa, Tadayoshi Watanabe; **Scr:** Masaki Tsuji; **Anim/Chara:** Kazuko Nakamura, Sadao Miyamoto; **Score:** Isao Tomita; **Sound:** Susumu Aketagawa; **Manga:** *Ribon no kishi* (*The Ribbon Knight*); **Wr/Art:** Osamu Tezuka.

Princess Mononoke (*Mononoke hime*)
Japan, 1997 – 133 mins
Hayao Miyazaki

Princess Mononoke poses the most simple of questions: what is energy? Its story is an endoscopic exploration of the materiality of energy, divining its presence, following its spread, witnessing its effect and resounding its quake. It telescopes towards an infinitely expanding cosmos of energy fields within energy fields, tracing the ways that any form of existence both demarcates and subsumes itself and others. This sounds dizzyingly and forbiddingly philosophical, but *Princess Mononoke* grows an utterly captivating story from such a densely contemplative terrain.

The narrative fixes on Ashitaka who, after being ravaged by a wild boar poisoned by unknown means, is in turn cursed and infected with what a village elder terms 'hatred'. This *anime*'s visualisation of 'hatred' as an organic shape-shifting entity of worms covering the form of the boar is a landmark in imaginative realisation. Having regretfully shot the boar, the visceral veil of 'hatred' resides to reveal the dying boar – and a

Princess Mononoke: an endoscopic exploration of the materiality of energy

strange lump of metal. Standard mystical quests will start with something
shiny – a dazzling crystal, a gold ring – but *Princess Mononoke* starts
with a dirty malformed lump of metal. Expelled from his village for being
infected, Ashitaka embarks on what becomes less a mystery or journey
and more a tracing of how man makes things from and through nature.

The 'lump' is a proto-type bullet. It has been produced by the
Tataraba village, firmly under the control of Lady Eboshi. A vivid symbol
for the ancient industriousness which led Japan to heights of commerce
in ancient epochs, she is responsible for decimating entire forests in order
to burn enough wood to make the iron instruments upon which her
empire depends. With searing clarity, *Princess Mononoke* suggests that
this Iron Age is one of the first disastrous ecological transformations of
the planet.

The deforestation that concentrically expands from Tataraba is an
archaeological wasteland akin to the scarred planets which populate
futurist *anime*. *Princess Mononoke* though is a tale of the past, set in
Japan's Muromachi era (early 13th century to late 16th century) and
obliquely invoking the ancestry of the indigenous Ainu people. They
are symbolised through San – the Princess Mononoke – a human raised
in the barren woods by wolves. She is attuned to the spiritual realm of
animals, and does not even regard herself as human. This is possibly
the most sociologically comprehensive portrait of the 'post-human'
central to so much *anime*, for San is between-species, between-
consciousness, between-energies. Psychically attuned to human
incursion of her terrain, physically attuned to the aura of the earth, she
is a unique hybrid who alone holds the key to how humans and nature
might best co-exist.

There is no 'hero' in *Princess Mononoke*. At the film's closure, the
only 'heroes' are the land, its totality, and the way both can be enlivened
through the act of animating. In place of the magical movement of
articulated bodies, we are left with a series of morphs from scenes of
utter devastation to panoramas of earth-laden life. No humans appear in
these scenes. Indeed, no characters witness their totality. This is nature in

operation by itself – without you or I, without any heroes of narrative – simply the answer to the film's crucial question: earth.

Feature

Genre: Eco Gender Folklore

Dir/Scr/Chara: Hayao Miyazaki; **Prod:** Toshio Suzuki; **Anim:** Masashi Ando, Yoshifumi Kondo, Katsuya Kondo, Kitaro Kosaka; **Score:** Joe Hisaishi; **Sound:** Kazuhiro Wakabayashi.

RG Veda (*Seiden rg veda*)
Japan, 1991
Hiroyuki Ebata, Takamasa Ikegami

The influx of Hinduism into ancient Japan and its reformation as a form of Tantric Buddhism is symptomatic of how various theological doctrines have been subsumed into Japan's non-Judeo-Christian folklore. The aerated absence of dogma and the fluid swirling of mythology that arise from these importations and modifications constitute the contra-fundamentalist mystical narratives of many *anime*. The reworking of the Hindu saga 'Rig Veda' into the *anime RG Veda* is a great example in its transposition of Bodhisattva (deities) to *bishonen/bishojo* (beautiful boys/girls).

The attraction of *RG Veda* lies as much in its transcultural historiography as it does in its departure from its purported scriptural references. The *anime* extends and continues the tradition of improvised myth-annotation which is the basis of Japan's religious multiplicity, and shapes its heroic fantasy tale into a mandala of emotional, psychic and metaphysical encounters of a group on a spiritual quest. These six warriors (initially five, eventually six) constitute a foretold six-point star of energy, generated by the six who have received visions telling them they are destined to join forces and overcome the domination of the bloodthirsty General Taishakuten.

Each is a re-imagining of one of the Rig Veda's deities, collectively moulded into a meta-*manga* bi-gendered cross-section of heroic archetypes. This typographical characterisation is integral to the style of the originating *manga* and its *doujinshi* (*manga* fanzine) appeal. *RG Veda*'s characters are vehicles for this propulsion of over-heroicised over-romanticised figures, freezing, framing and favouring them as hyper-icons of super-beautiful beings. Yasha is impossibly stoic; Ashura is freakishly cute; Ryouh is heavily caricatured as impetuous; Karura is saintly in her quietude. Like the originating deities of the Bodhisattva, each is a statuesque compaction of traits, powers and moods. As in the *manga*, their differing drawing styles constitute a mode of 'figurining', providing a heterogeneous visuality that again reflects the cultural processing which shifts the Rig Veda into being *RG Veda*.

Strangely, *RG Veda* is virtually tantric in form, in that its depiction of the six warriors and their numerous nemeses is a meditation on their power, beauty and allure. In keeping with the heady patterning of *shojo* (girl) *manga*, their calligraphic decoration and detailing are akin to the overflowing of paraphernalia and costumery that adorns statues and altars in Buddhist shrines. Yasha and Ashura in particular are highlighted as abstracted figurines whose clothing, hair and eyes engulf their physical appearance and render them iconic in the spiritual sense. Their placement within the narrative generates a spectacular attraction to their visual beauty.

At a number of points, the story and plot of *RG Veda* dematerialises to centre a transformative display of the innocent Ashura suddenly discovering a new level to the multi-planed mandala of deified powers that gradually comprise her spiritual enlightenment. Bodies float upward, swords materialise in hand, eyes sense the beyond, spatial domains are inverted. Rather than represent an apocalyptic colliding of realms, *RG Veda* presents these moments as the tantric becoming the tactile: when mortals touch the energy of the gods.

OVA (2)

Genre: Mystical Sci-Fi

Dir: Hiroyuki Ebata, Takamasa Ikegami; **Prod:** Mokona Apapa; **Scr:** Nanase Ohkawa; **Anim:** Tetsuro Aoki; **Chara:** Mokona Apapa, Tetsuro Aoki, Kiichi Takaoka, Futoshi Fujikawa; **Score:** Nick Wood; **Manga:** *Seiden rg veda* (*Holy Legend Rg Veda*); **Wr/Art:** CLAMP.

Roujin-Z
Japan, 1991 – 80 mins
Hiroyuki Kitakubo

Technology going awry is such a deeply embedded desire in sci-fi that one suspects it will never occur on the apocalyptical scale imagined in modern dystopian cinema. *Roujin-Z* seems similarly imprinted, but – as with its originating manga – its critique is aimed at covert government agencies which allow technology to be applied sans scruples. Satirical in tone, *Roujin-Z* is free of moralistic finger-wagging, yet its grasp of how power, technology and society are interlocked like dense cabling and congested plumbing remains effectively sobering.

Old man (*roujin*) Kujiro is chosen as patient 'Z' to aid in testing then presenting to the press a new hi-tech self-monitoring computerised bed. A robot replacement for homestay nursing of elderly patients, the contraption is designed to address a major problem in Japanese demographics: the 'inverted pyramid' of a mass of old people who will drain the welfare system while a miniscule number of young people work to fund the programmes. Trainee nurse Haruko is attached to caring for Kujiro with a 'human touch'. Her sudden replacement by the Z-001 prototype robot mega-bed leads her to rally against this industrialised panacea designed not for the elderly but for their offspring who find tending their parents bothersome.

The mega-bed might seem absurdist, but toilets in Japan verge on the robotic with their temperature controls, bidet sprays and piped music. Waste management is a serious design task in Japan with its disarming lack of body-conscious reticence, so *Roujin-Z*'s mega-bed is a plausible transition from hi-tech toilet seats to total 'health-suits'. The fantastic projection beyond this lies in how the computerised controls of the Z-001 have been implanted for further development as military modules. Once this software is tampered with, real chaos ensues as the bed forms itself into a sentient mecha-body, encasing the frail and delirious Kujiro and fulfilling his idle wish to return to the seaside, site of the cherished memories he holds of his mother.

The 'inner energy' of the Z-001 is the thematic heart of *Roujin-Z*. When Haruko and fellow nurses steal Kujiro in his bed and are caught in the process, Kujiro's subconscious desire to escape aids in transforming the bed's capabilities, exposing how its neural design is ultimately one of a mobile suit for military use. Moving beyond standard cyber-punk premises, the Z-001 is a sponge for any surrounding energies. From Hakuro's hospital a gaggle of geriatric hackers network their computers to help the bed mobilise itself to escape incarceration. In order to communicate to the mega-bed, they feed Hakuro's voice into the networked connection they have made to the Z-001 – consequently creating a psychic presence within the bed of Hakuro's own grandmother who passed away in an elderly care home when Haruko was young. The final version of the bed is a veritable mountain of council infrastructure and technology it attracts to its corpus en route to the ocean. A multi-voiced social computer harbouring malicious purpose, possessed by restless spirits and propelled by idle desire, it is Japan's true 'ghost in the machine'.

Feature

Genre: Urban Sci-Fi

Dir: Hiroyuki Kitakubo; **Prod:** Yasuku Kazama, Yoshiaki Motoya, Yasuhito Nomura;
Scr: Katsuhiro Otomo; **Anim:** Fumio Iida; **Chara:** Hisashi Eguchi; **Mecha:** Katsuhiro Otomo, Mitsuo Iso; **Score:** Bun Itakura; **Sound:** Yasunori Honda; **Manga:** *Roujjin-Z* (*Old Man Z*);
Wr: Katsuhiro Otomo; **Art:** Tai Okada.

Rozen Maiden
Japan, 2004
Mamoru Matsuo, Moria Asaka

Japan breeds social syndromes like genetically modified plants. Some are journalistic creations, imported by the West and embellished through fruity decontexualised translation. Some are genuine, unique, inexplicable. *Hikikomori* is the pathological condition to 'stay at home'. Uncovered as a new-millennium condition, it appears as a generational 'social shrinking' effect where a late teen or older male denies all external contact and withdraws into a micro-world of computer games and other televisual/electronic succour. While this might appear to pay lip service to dated fears of 'mindless media control', *hikikomori* is more related to an acute aversion to the rigid codification of social behaviour within school and the workplace.

Rozen Maiden is an oblique response to *hikikomori*. Jun is a young boy who, in classic *otaku* overdrive, is totally avoiding school. He lives in a spacious mansion, but spends the bulk of his time in his bedroom. His 'friends' are three dolls: Shinku, Hinaichigo and Suiseiseki. While the quasi-fantasy setting of the tale evidences the dolls as part of a mystical network of drama and conflict (into which Jun has become ensnared by discovering the Rozen Maiden 'living doll' Shinku), that same fantasy works as a symbol of the social possibility that these dolls are in his mind, and that they are discrete sectors of his stressed imagination. The 'stay-at-home' syndrome as lived by Jun might then be an attempt to therapeutically rehearse his mind in the seclusion of a 'space of the self'. 'Stay-at-home' could be restated as 'stay-with-self', away from the noise of the crowd and the voice of society that incants to control the individualised self. Jun's isolation booth – like the pivotal bedroom used by those afflicted with *hikikomori* – is an important recuperation zone for this hyper-*otaku*.

Vehemently divorced from Japanese surroundings, the doll trio of *Rozen Maiden* are resolutely European in design, bearing nuances of

Gothic cuteness and *bishojo* abstraction. Their ornate wigs and multi-layered gowns present them as baroque explosions of silken curls and velvet folds that ornately envelop their delicate miniature heads. Their eyes convey a 'meta-dollness' in their conflation of *anime* conventions in rendering humans, and doll design's history of iconicising the same. Their identity is coded as much in their eyes as their attire: Shinku has the largest eyes that never change expression; Hinaichigo has two different-coloured eyes, indicating a history of repair (hence traumatisation); Suiseiseki's smaller eyes reflect her diminutive repose. Encased as they are within a contemporary Japanese suburban mansion, their ties to Europe imbue them with a tragic demeanour – something integral to the doll as archetypal figure looking for a maternal owner.

Through its deliriously emotional, psychological and mystical developments, *Rozen Maiden* reinvents a new family structure that bends the series more towards R. D. Laing than Japan. Jun bears great responsibility for the dolls – Shinku especially – in a way that recalculates standard familial relationships. This is a fantasy *anime* whose contra-family theme subtextually but cogently addresses the social plane that breeds conditions as haunting as *hikikomori*.

TV
Genre: Mystical Melodrama
Dir: Mamoru Matsuo, Moria Asaka; **Prod:** Hiroichi Kokago, Kozue Kana, Masaru Kitao, Shinichi Nakamura, Takashi Jinguuji; **Scr:** Jukki Hanada, Mari Okada, Tsuyoshi Tamai; **Anim:** Kumi Ishii, Akemi Kobayashi; **Chara:** Kumi Ishii; **Score:** Shinkichi Mitsume; **Sound:** Yoto Tsuruoka; **Manga:** *Rozen Maiden*; **Wr/Art:** Peach-Pit.

Sailor Moon (Bishojo senshi Seiraa Muun)
Japan, 1992
Junichi Sato

While the West has historically tended to produce kid-vid animation and live action aimed at co-ed groups of pre-teens and teens, Japan is abundant with gender-specific *manga* and *anime*. More so than in America especially, the Japanese gender markets have developed specific stylistic modes and image codes. The boy markets – rooted in the tradition of *shonen manga* for boys – are not far removed from the American super-hero style of comics: muscle-bound bodies hurtling through space expounding energy in dynamic lines connoting hyper-motion and kineticism. The girl markets – rooted in the tradition of *shojo manga* for girls – are totally different. Their *manga* pages verge on eroticised abstraction, with the frames, boxes and bubbles often blurring, disintegrating and dissolving into a full page awash with dimensional effects and sensational line-work and patterning.

In a sense, *Sailor Moon* is a neo-*shojo anime*, considering the form has been around in Japan since the mid-50s, and the way that *Sailor Moon*'s narrative draws upon a long line of *manga* and *anime* based on younger girls idolising older girls. The basic recurring plot revolves around Usagi, who is befriended by mystical black cat Luna who gives Usagi and her group of school friends reincarnated magic powers, each power being related to their astrological planet. To invoke their magic powers they cry out 'MAKE-UP!' and are transformed in a swirl of light and colour as trinkets and attire are zapped onto them. This is the same type of power fetishisation that repeatedly peaks in boy comics and cartoons (Eastern and Western), but in *Sailor Moon* every fetishistic element is of value only within a prescribed 'girl' world. The armoury of make-up thus becomes an artillery of feminine tokens to be imaginatively wielded by the young fans of the show.

Additionally, two features mark *Sailor Moon* as peculiarly Japanese in its narrative orientation. First, there is a clear split between Usagi romanticising older boys (even the mysterious young man, Chiba

Sailor Moon: pre-pubescent female hysteria as re-channelled energy

Mamoru aka Tuxedo Kamen) and other older girls at school. Her fixation on others is gender-unbiased and not solely at the service of male hero worship. Second, the various 'evil' beings in the recurring plot resemble mournful aliens who yearn for life like humans have on Earth. Under the matriarchal control of Queen Belasarius, they always are trying to invade the human realm and destroy Usagi and her friends. But they do so not because they are essentially evil but because they are motivated by desire – a theme atomised through all *shojo* entertainment.

In its 'neo' guise, *Sailor Moon* extols pre-pubescent female hysteria as a rechannelled form of energy. Rather than typecasting this energy as pre-sexual childish frenzy (as the West has portrayed 'crazed/obsessed' Bay City Rollers fans, for example) *Sailor Moon* takes that energy and shapes it into a dimension: a psycho-emotional reality which is meaningful essentially to those who throb with that energy: pre-teen girls.

TV

Genre: Mystical Melodrama
Dir: Junichi Sato; **Prod:** Toei Animation; **Scr:** Sukehiro Tomita; **Anim:** Hiromi Matsushita, Hisashi Kagawa, Ikuko Ito, Kazuko Tadano, Masahiro Ando; **Chara:** Ikuko Ito, Kazuko Tadanno; **Score:** Takanori Arisawa, Tetsuya Komoro, Kazuo Sato; **Manga:** *Sailor Moon*; **Wr/Art:** Naoko Takeuchi.

Samurai Champloo
Japan, 2004
Shinichiro Watanabe

'Retro' as a conceptual style is likely now to be retro. Design around the world has been in a post-retro warp for some time. The past and present are so inlaid with each other that history is not so much lost as it is rendered impossibly present. *Samurai Champloo* is set in the Edo era, but not at any moment does it attempt to return us to the past. The series' inventiveness lies in this enlivened anti-historiography.

The connections between neo-Nu Skool hip hop (imported into Japanese music as an ongoing current in the style tides of millennial Japan) and the social weave of Japan's Edo period (well documented and represented within Japan's national museography) are non-existent save for their artificial merger in *Samurai Champloo*. The incongruous connections are deliberate, flaunted consistently, and interlocked by a previously unimagined assemblage. Abstract graffiti patterns and neo-mod website layering are merged with Edo scroll colouring and printing techniques. Blaxploitation score interludes are laid over rural historical locations where a wah-wah would never have sounded. Vinyl scratching erupts on the soundtrack to sync to cross-cuts and scene transitions, forming the *anime* into a remix of itself. It's like a hip-hop crew has been warped back to Edo to tell the story of *Samurai Champloo* like a wildstyle *kamishibai* – traditional Japanese storytellers who rode bikes and narrated tales while showing painted pictures and making their own sound effects.

Yes, there is a story told through these stylistic effects – and it's as manic as one would not expect of the Edo period. Two penniless roamers – Mugen, a blunt Okinawan, and Jin, a mannered *ronin* – are contracted by the impish but volatile Fuu to find the love of her dreams:

(Next page) *Samurai Champloo*: incongruous connections and enlivened anti-historiography

a *samurai* who smells of sunflowers. Mugen and Jin also happen to be supreme swordsmen of unconventional technique and bold confidence. Fluctuating romance and eye-popping swordplay propel and rupture each other in the episodic tales of this trio, just as the past and present mottle the smooth veneer of each.

Although 'Champloo' refers to the Okinawan slang *camploo* that describes food prepared with a variety of mixed-up ingredients, *Samurai Champloo* is not an exercise in unfounded heterogeneity. Every facet of its style and every sliver of its narrative binds its parts in a manner akin to hip hop's sampledelic fusion of fragments to make musicalised wholes. Before long, the story is digestible as a measured dissection of Edo society. Celebrated as one of Japan's less brutal periods responsible for the blooming and booming of arts, crafts and customs of the *vox populi*, *Samurai Champloo* clings to the ragged edges of such idealised screens and scrolls of quintessential Edo. Mugen and Jin symbolise the outer limits of the period's social fraying, from Mugen's rough anti-metropolitan rejection of societal protocol to Jin's cynical and intellectualised rejection of those same conventions and their false manners. Together they stake the bi-polar extremes of humanity that frame the ongoing brutality often rendered pastel and ornate by Japanese history. *Samurai Champloo*'s deliberate overloading of decorative effects is a sharply sardonic inscription of the series' trans-retro historical remix revisionism.

TV
Genre: Samurai Action
Dir: Shinichiro Watanabe; **Prod:** Takatoshi Hamano, Takashi Kohchiyama, Tetsuro Satomi; **Scr:** Shinji Obara, Dai Sato; **Anim/Chara:** Kazuto Nakazawa; **Mecha:** Mahiro Maeda (weapons); **Score/Songs:** Tsutchi, Fat Jon, Nujabes, Force of Nature; **Sound:** Border Line, Techno Sound.

SD Gundam (Kido Senshi SD Gandamu)
Japan, 1988
Osamu Sekita

Poor, dumb Japan. Controlled by Hello Kitty and imprisoned by demons of 'cute', its brain-washed citizenry have no concept of how such vacuousness pervades their lives. So reads the standard edict of Western critique of Japanese 'cute'. These views would be laughable if they weren't so repetitive, offensive and imperceptive.

SD Gundam is a great place to start deprogramming those views. 'SD' is shorthand for 'Super Deformed', and 'Gundam' relates to one of the definitive if not longest running 80s' mobile suit *anime*. 'SD', *chibi* (small, childlike) and *kawaii* (cute) collectively morph into an image that Japan refracts of and to itself. Being a doll culture at base level – one that perceives the figurine as a free-floating iconic stand-in for human inscription – Japan's semiotic exchanges are open, casual and everyday. This means that any image of something is a stand-alone symbol of or index for either the ideal version of that thing, or a subset of variations that define that thing. In the case of dolls, they can represent various states of human existence, various levels of human physiology and various dimensions of human psychology. They do not represent 'a child's toy' as they would in the West. Extending this, anything in Japan that seems 'childlike', 'for children only' or even 'childish' is likely none of those categories.

While the West clings to the European Enlightenment as legacy to warrant intelligence as an upwardly mobile, progressivist or mature sign of perception, Japan's apparent reliance on so many seemingly 'unadult' manifestations causes a crisis of representation. Yet neotony as a psycho-genetic principle has become a potent strand of Japanese image consciousness. It has nothing to do with regression, immaturity or mindlessness. When *SD Gundam* portrays the socially serious and dramatically engaging exploits of the sprawling saga of the *Gundam* series, the result is part affection, part parody, and part underscoring of how any cultural iconography and signage can morph into a full embrace of its opposite. This is a post-textual process – one where the reader can accept all imaginary extensions of what has been written. This shapes freely reformed/deformed/super-deformed texts like *SD Gundam* to be anti-matter versions of the fundamentalism which guides Anglo-American literary, theological and legal dogma. No wonder the West is so scared of Hello Kitty: its hyper-logoistic transcendence of form is the ultimate escape from fundamentalism.

'Super Deformity' isn't cute at all. Japan experienced and underwent the ultimate state of 'transcendence of form' that still hovers darkly over the so-called modern world: genetic mutation through excessive radioactive exposure. Japan's unsettling subsumption of post-nuclear effects and their combination with neotony and psychic displacement – all key ingredients in *SD Gundam* – is possibly the most perplexing aspect of the SD/*chibi*/*kawaii* syndrome. While America – primary industrial producer of the atomic bomb – laughs nervously through the guilt-ridden parental anxiety of *Honey I Shrunk The Kids* (1989), *SD Gundam* is born by a culture that treats machines as pets, instruments as children, computers as lovers and mutants as people. It's a special type of humanism missed by those who have nightmares over Hello Kitty.

OVA (3)

Genre: Sci-Fi Comedy

Dir: Osamu Sekita; **Prod:** Hirotoshi Nakagawa; **Scr:** Hiroyuki Hoshiyama; **Anim:** Hiroshi Watanabe; **Mecha:** Kunio Okawara; **Score:** Norimasa Yamanaka; **Sound:** Koichi Chiba.

The Sensualist (*Ihara saikaku: Koshoku ichidai otoko*)
Japan, 1990
Yukio Abe

The Sensualist may be celebrated as a restrained and tasteful alternative to the swarming tentacled sex-o-ramas that unfold in erotic horror *anime*, but it is disserviced by being read as a direct reaction against those pornographic subgenres. Its inner strength is garnered from its portrayal of the erotic as something cherished and remembered.

Swilled and decanted from a seventeenth-century erotic novel, *The Sensualist* extemporises the fluctuating memories of Eros held by the merchant Yonosuke as he stands at the precipice of old age. Two narrative currents surge through the film. Over a series of visual panoramas and motion effects of swirling decorative elements from the Edo period, a narrator chronologically lists the amorous exploits of Yonosuke. Rapaciously addicted to the erotic, his desire for sexual thrills leads him to the brink of destitution before he manages to return to his merchant activities, only to again succumb to the lure of physical pleasures. From this vast catalogue of heady pursuits, one story is isolated and parlayed at a comparatively slow pace. The pathetic but endearing tailor Juzo has made a drunken bet with friends that he could engage the famous courtesan Komurasaki of the Yoshiwara pleasure district – the epicentral 'floating world' backdrop to Edo erotic illustration.

Juzo visits Yonosuke before departing for Yoshiwara, and Yonosuke advises him to wear a special sheaf for his phallus when he encounters Komurasaki. What neither we nor Juzo realise is that Yonosuke has shared many encounters with Komurasaki. She recognises the sheath on Juzo and, to everyone's surprise, beds him. The erotic crux of *The Sensualist* is the phantom sex-by-proxy in which Yonosuke and Komurasaki are engaged; his sending of the sheath activates his past memories of Komurasaki, just as hers are relit by having sex with Juzo.

Across time and space, a meta-sexual act is performed, with the Eros of this imaginary union directing *The Sensualist*'s erotic staging.

The gravitational pull Yonosuke and Komurasaki have on each other literally teases out and figuratively draws out their immersive psychological space. *The Sensualist*'s visual style is closely modelled on famous Edo portraiture (granting an immediate lesson in how post-war *manga* and *anime* are indebted to the calligraphic line-work and wood-block inking of Edo prints), but the Edo references are extended to a poetics of motion that enlivens the now-vicarious sensations Yonosuke feels in remembering his youth. The backgrounds of land, water and flora from the Edo prints, the vertiginous depths of kimono fabrics, the breath-taking sparseness of interior spatial design, and the interpolation of heraldic *kamon* crests are all folded into the head space and body heat of Yonosuke.

At the close of *The Sensualist*, Yonosuke stands before the ocean as ennui sets in following the come-down of his erotic reverie. Suddenly invigorated – as per his past vacillations between wild abandon and sensible composure – he rallies his crew to set sail and find an island of women where they can spend their last days in ecstasy. Physically impotent yet with enough fertile memories to believe his sexuality will outlive him, Yonosuke is an undying sensualist.

OVA (1)

Genre: Erotic Drama

Dir: Yukio Abe; **Prod:** Ren Usami, Tsunemasa Hatano, Zuza Hagiwara; **Scr:** Eiichi Yamamoto; **Anim:** Tomoko Ogawa, Masaharu Endo, Hiroyuki Kondo; **Score:** Keiju Ishikawa; **Sound:** Susumu Aketagawa; **Novel:** *Koshoku ichidai otoko* (*The Smartest Lady's Man of the Century*); **Wr:** Ihara Saikaku.

Silent Mobius (*Sairento mebiusu*)
Japan, 1991/2
Masanorei Ide, Michitaka Kikuchi, Kazuo Tomisawa

Silent Mobius is a good example from the 80s' OVA boom of the kind of generic hybrids which fuelled the seemingly endless production of sci-fi and fantasy titles during this hyperactive period. This hybridity, though, is not simply a case of eclectic post-modern conglomeration. That might explain the recipe and the ingredients, but not the flavour. *Silent Mobius* distils many themes from this era – evidenced in its view of technology; its weaving of mysticism; its concept of energy; its sense of dimensionality; and its diffusion and redistribution of sexual difference.

The story of *Silent Mobius* is centred on the Attack Mystification Police: a unit composed of and run by women, each of whom have special skills and/or powers. As per most mystical drama in *anime*, there is a dimension of the Other, this time called Lucifer Folk. Superficially a mix of *Hill Street Blues*, *Ghostbusters* (1984) and *The Omen* (1976), the secret method to *Silent Mobius's* hybrid recipe lies in colliding the hard legality of a law enforcement agency with the intangible machinations of something that breaks dimensional laws. *Silent Mobius's* metaphysical premise is treated in a straightforward urban manner, and the beauty of its drama is that no big deal is made about the generic fusion and mutation of the story: it's simply about cops who have to deal with deadly creatures who jump out of walls.

Much of the story depicts procedural details, like cordoning off a 'hot' alley where mystic detectives can feel beings from the other side attempting to find a harmonic break-point to come through to the human world. Even the major architectural feature of this particular Neo Tokyo is a huge spiral edifice built on the mystical site of an almost forgotten transgression by the human world upon a previous demonic realm. The city folk of *Silent Mobius* don't think much about the history of this site, but their ignorance and lack of caring about the past causes major problems when the past rears its ugly – and demonic – head.

Silent Mobius: fantasy erasure of the presence of men

Removed from the wider currents of *otaku* 'bikini babes with laser guns', *Silent Mobius* simply casts its characters in the female sex. Social issues of work ethics, familial respect, teamwork and individualism are carried on not in an overtly pro-feminist way, but in accordance with the milieu of the *OL* (office ladies – working women who battle it out with salary men). But whereas the West will stage this socialised environment of gender difference either as women-with-balls or girls-laughing-at-the-boys, *Silent Mobius* presents futuristic *OL*s Katsumi, Rally, Kiddy and Lebia first as workers, and only second as women, never framing them for us to either champion or sympathise with. They're not really doing 'a man's job' (there are no males except for the guttural voice of the Lucifer

Folk); and they suffer no gender-related discriminatory plight (once again because there are simply no men in their world). This is a crucial layer to the film's 'fantasy': its prime gender collision lies in its redefinition of sexual difference under the terms of erasing the presence of men.

OVA (2)

Genre: Mystical Future Crime

Dir: Masanorei Ide, Michitaka Kikuchi, Kazuo Tomisawa; **Prod:** Makoto Hasegawa, Haruki Kadokawa, Ryuichi Noda; **Scr:** Michitaka Kikuchi, Kei Shigema, Hiroyuki Kawasaki, Kenichi Kanemaki, Nami Narita, Katsuhiro Takayama; **Anim/Chara:** Michitaka Kikuchi; **Score:** Kaoru Wada; **Manga:** *Sairento mebiusu* (*Silent Mobius*); **Wr/Art:** Kia Asamiya.

Slight Fever Syndrome (*Binetsu Shokogun*)
Japan, 1996
Fuyuzo Shirakawa

As with any saturated form or genre, there are two basic ways to approach the critique of pornography: dive deep into its ocean and find a distinctive example, or scoop the foaming surface for its efferverscent quality. Using the second approach, *Slight Fever Syndrome* can demonstrate some fundamental characteristics of *anime* porn.

The term 'demonstrate' is ironic, as an incredible amount of *anime* porn demonstrates sexual techniques through stories where characters demonstrate those techniques to others. In *Slight Fever Syndrome*, Ms Mizuki has just started work as a school doctor. But the students and staff she services treat her more as sex therapist than an infirmary nurse. A range of problems are presented to her which she must solve through active demonstration, from showing young girls how to masturbate without a dildo to showing a fellow teacher how to be comfortable with anal penetration. In the process of these demonstrations, Ms Mizuki becomes aroused and experiences a range of uncontrollable passions.

The light comic tone and sexual daydream scenarios – not to mention their implausible denouement – are standard indicators of generic hetero porno. But how this obviousness is transposed and transfigured within the form of *anime* remains of interest. With *Slight Fever Syndrome* (and most post-90s' *anime* porn), it is not a simple matter of 'animating' the pornographic. With greater cultural specificity, *Slight Fever Syndrome* is a product of *doujinshi* culture: the sprawling network of amateur fan *anime* and *manga* that has become emblematic of late 90s' *otaku* (fan) culture. In some respects, the 90s witnessed a 'doujinshi-sation' of *anime*, as an inordinate amount of titles in *anime* and *manga* not only catered to the *otaku* sub-markets, but also appealed to them directly through appearing to be 'amateur' in tone.

This is not to say that these titles are rendered cheaply and ineffectively: the production value of many *doujinshi* works are far from inept or facile. Rather, a certain stylistic trend in depicting bodies, faces, hair and costumes has created a lexicon of 'body-typing' that defines *doujinshi*-style. The eyes are huge, the mouths infinitesimal, the breasts humongous, the thighs towering. But this is not simply an intensification of the exaggeration inherent in *anime*'s bodily depiction. The enlargement of selected parts of the body (especially eyes and breasts) reveals a psychological compulsion to be impossibly near to those parts. Like a psycho-sexual fish-eye lens, *anime* like *Slight Fever Syndrome* ogles prioritised body parts in expression of the desire to dive into those swimming pool eyes and *cumulus nimbus* breasts. This symbolises a healthy though hysterical hunger for proximity in place of intimacy: closeness is desired physically, not emotionally.

The disproportionate shaping of the body in *doujinshi* is very close to the SD and *chibi* syndromes of neotonic body design in *anime*, but in porn like *Slight Fever Syndrome*, a para-paedophiliac effect is neither deliberated nor desired. At face value, the staff and students are separable only through their uniforms, clothes and mannerisms, making them all appear like grossly exaggerated sex-toy-baby-dolls in sexual *kosupre* (costume role-playing). A closer inspection will evidence the *doujinshi* effect.

OVA (1)

Genre: Erotic Comedy

Dir: Fuyuzo Shirakawa; **Prod:** Shigeyuki Haseqawa, Noriko Nishino; **Scr:** Takashi Aoyama; **Anim:** Ichiro Ola; **Sound:** Hideyuki Tanaka; **Manga:** *Binetsu Shokogun* (*Slight Fever Syndrome*); **Wr/Art:** Rumi Miyamoto.

Sol Bianca (*Tai no Fune Soru Bianka*)
Japan, 1990/1
Katsuhito Akiyama, Hiroki Hayashi

Sol Bianca is a standard amalgam of futurism, heroics, technology, fantasy and action that tends to make 'space operas' wearing and numbing affairs. This *anime* follows the exploits of an all-women pirate crew on the spaceship Sol Bianca after they accidentally pick up a young stowaway, Rin. He persuades the crew of leader Feb, the fiery duo of Jan and April, the cutie May and the data fanatic June, to return Rin to his planet Uno, which is under the dictatorship of twin planet Tres led by Emporer Baltros. The narrative is costumed in tawdry attire, yet a closer look reveals a strange inner corpus to this swash-buckling pantomine.

The first noticeable schism is the depiction of lust and greed within the women as pirates. More feminine reconstructions of 'gold-diggers' and 'bargain hunters' than macho rummies of the high seas, they roam the galaxies not to rape and pillage, but to satiate their longing for the glittering beauty of treasures. Even the strong-willed Feb is reduced to giddiness when she spies the treasure hold on planet Tres, as she is transformed into a modern-day shopper at a mall mega-sale. Elsewhere, the crew are shown fetishising their booty of armaments, holding them in their hands like women holding up dresses against their torsos to see if they suit them.

The Sol Bianca crew's main objective in going to Tres is not to aid Rin and the resistance of his people, but to acquire the Golden Box, purportedly containing the 'knowledge of the gods'. Where the male figure of compulsion, power and greed recalls the psychoses of Captain Ahab and Blackbeard, Sol Bianca's crew are devoid of such self-destructive drives. In place, they are motivated by desire in its purest form. Feb warns April at one point not to make decisions when she is emotionally reacting to her situation, demonstrating that the crew are fuelled by desire beyond the binary of 'rational' and 'emotional' controls. When they recover the Golden Box, they realise it is a time-capsule message sent to the cosmos centuries ago by a once-flourishing Earth. Rather than be outraged by the uselessness of this treasure, the crew are heartened by its repository of hopes from a lost race.

But the most overt 'femasculation' of *Sol Bianca*'s buccaneering lies in the Sol Bianca's design. More organic in its crustaceous formation than other ships, it has the capability to 'submerge' into deep-space, figuring its oneness with the voluminous spatial void as a feminine symbol of power. When Baltros engages his hyper-phallic Citadel gun to decimate the planet Uno, the Sol Bianca 'erects' its limbs, shafts and plates to reveal inner components that interlink to form an energy dome. It fires a neutralising power ball to the Citadel gun that reverses its force into a self-destructive explosion. Obliquely though uncannily, this recalls a long line of women in Japanese cinema – mostly *geisha*, courtesans, 'comfort women' and prostitutes – who invert and void themselves in order to overcome their male nemesis. At the climax of *Sol Bianca* it's an unexpected twist that refreshingly disarms the pirate mythology the *anime* mimics.

OVA (2)

Genre: Mystical Sci-Fi

Dir: Katsuhito Akiyama, Hiroki Hayashi; **Prod:** Kazuaki Morijiri; **Scr:** Mayori Sekijima, Hidemi Kamata; **Anim/Chara:** Naoyuki Onda; **Mecha:** Atsushi Takeuchi; **Score:** Toru Hirano, Kohsei Kenjoh, Seiko Nagaoka; **Sound:** Haruo Ushio.

Space Adventure Cobra
(Supesu Adobencha Kobura)
Japan, 1982 – 99 mins
Osamu Dezaki

Many of the major futuristic *anime* of the 80s collectively assemble their
scenarios from the spectacularly destructive debris scattered across the
Hollywoodised terrain of *Alien* (1979), *Mad Max* (1979), *The Thing*
(1982), *Bladerunner* (1982), *Blue Thunder* (1982), *Ghostbusters* (1984),
The Terminator (1984) and *Aliens* (1986). These are key Western films
which feature a metropolis, outpost or facility exploding due to some
sort of technological, extraterrestrial or cybernetic force brought to bear
on its domain – a key theme which post-war Japanese entertainment has
embraced and recodified under post-apocalyptic terms.

　　Both the original *manga* and the film *Space Adventure Cobra* draw a
line that bypasses this fertile zone of influence. Perpendicularly, the
smarmy but jovial bounty hunter Cobra realigns a less urban and more
urbane line of figures: from Sean Connery's James Bond to Clint
Eastwood's Man with No Name to Jean-Paul Belmondo's many
professional criminal portrayals. And just as the orgy of destruction in
big-budget Hollywood action movies can be viewed as complex impulses
traceable to the final solution America employed by using atomic warfare
against Japan, so Cobra's cool and self-mocking heroics remind us of the
wry isolationist *samurai* figure in Japanese cinema – particularly the
internationally renowned work of Akira Kurosawa. While Kurosawa often
based his *samurai* sagas on Shakespearean epics, Italian director Sergio
Leone was moved to cast his 'man with no name' character in the same
mould from which came Kurosawa's *Yojimbo* (1961). *Space Adventure
Cobra* extends this transnational referencing as a means of defining a
'Nihonoise' European figure in Cobra.

　　Space Adventure Cobra comes in the midst of a glut of post-*Star
Wars* space sagas and robot dioramas, and stakes a clear claim for a
Japanese–European dialogue of style. While the original *manga* is a

quirky mix of Tezukian wonder and *Playboy* magazine illustration, the film is quite different. The Tezuka sensibility is stronger and the women are rendered in a more overtly *bishojo* style of eroticism, with swirling landscapes of colour and abstracted shapes. It is this fusion between Japanese and European aesthetics that makes *Space Adventure Cobra* visually scintillating and formally distinctive. However, beyond affording an appreciation of the decorative, a fascinating gender map covers the expanse of the film's saga.

A bounty hunter by trade, Cobra is hired by Jane to find her two sisters, Kathleen and Dominique. Once reunited, they will form a cosmic trio of powerful energies, and are being tracked by Crystal Boy, a pathological villain driven to possess that same power. Cobra undertakes the job – seduced by the siren-like beauty of Jane – and is typically unaware of how difficult it will be due to his cocky machismo. A true 'man's man', Cobra's weak spot is beautiful women. The trio of Jane, Kathleen and Dominique float throughout the film like an enchanted perfume – hence the overt stylisation of their presence. Furthermore, these three sirens are psychically linked to each other, extending their feminine allure and sexual power into a network of erotic energy. Cobra is often depicted ensnared by their immersive power, intoxicated by their erotic aura. So despite the film bearing a European legacy in its heroics, its uniquely Japanese presence of woman makes *Space Adventure Cobra* a particularly rich tale of gender.

Feature

Genre: Mystical Sci-Fi

Dir: Osamu Dezaki; **Prod:** Tatsuo Ikeuchi; **Scr:** Buichi Terasawa, Haruya Yamazaki; **Anim:** Akio Sugino; **Chara:** Buichi Terasawa; **Score:** Osamu Tokaibayashi; **Sound:** Satoshi Kato; **Manga:** *Kobura* (*Cobra*); **Wr/Art:** Buichi Terasawa.

Space Firebird 2772
(*Hi no tori 2772: ai no kosumozon*)
Japan, 1980 – 122 mins
Taku Sugiyama

Space Firebird 2772 is loosely based on the futuristic aspects of the sprawling *Hi no tori* (*Phoenix*) *manga* series, regarded by many as being among the most sophisticated *manga* produced in Japan. *Space Firebird 2772* is a similarly long saga which may appear confused and patchy at times, but is nonetheless an ambitious *anime* created from infusing Buddhist, Shinto and Zen concepts with standard sci-fi pondering. As such, it serves as a potent dose of a non-Western view on life and the cosmos, achieving something that *anime* sci-fi specialises in but Western sci-fi lacks: a post-human consciousness.

As if to demonstrate this difference and pinpoint its origins, the opening sequence of *Space Firebird 2772* shows the creation and birthing of a test tube human male. Far from being hamstrung by the circular ethics which persist worldwide over genetic modification, IVF and cloning, the environment for this 'birth' is bereft of all human presence, depicting the child as a cell from the mechanoid gods delivered in a gleaming clinical hi-tech space station to the strains of 'beautiful' orchestral music. Many might find theses scenes laughable, but they constitute a profoundly Oriental contemplation of scientific progress far removed from the romantic angst still cast by Frankenstein's shadow.

The baby – Godoh - is attended by a sexy maternal robot, Olga, who can also change herself into an amazing array of sexy machines and appliances at the service of the developing child. Olga is like a convertible cartography of American post-war consumer design, where everything from car fins to stove knobs was eroticised in praise of seductive metallia. Like a subservient sex-doll, she bends and struts tirelessly to shape the growing child, giving us a disconcerting image of the Mother in Japan. Only in *anime* could such a child-rearing environment be presented in such a sexually coded yet utopian way.

Godoh grows up in this environment until he is a late-teenager, after which he goes out into the world for a series of adventures. He is ultimately an individual unit who has to develop his social interaction skills by instinct rather than programmed design. As a Japanese 'loner' figure, his character is conveyed less through heroic action and more through personal maturation. Godoh reflects not only ways in which the individual functions in the seemingly controlled Japanese social world, but also how the individual develops a sense of self voided from the social mass to which he must belong.

Much sociological analysis has been accorded these identity-forming dynamics in Japan, but in *Space Firebird 2772* (as with the originating *Hi no tori manga*) we are granted an internal perspective looking outwards from the self to the group. Godoh's expanded post-human consciousness arises from his being raised by the robot Olga. He has developed a closeness to the machinic and the mechanoid that allows him to offer more rounded judgments when dealing with conflicts between humans and machines. The main point voiced is that oppressive conditioning can push the individual to a higher plane of awareness of those conditioning forces – a possibility rarely considered in Western condemnations of Japanese social structures.

Feature

Genre: Mystical Sci-Fi

Dir: Taku Sugiyama; **Prod:** Yoshikaz Ichikawa, Susumu Aketagawa; **Scr:** Taku Sugiyama, Osamu Tezuka; **Anim:** Noboru Ishiguro, Kazuko Nakamura; **Chara:** Osamu Tezuka; **Mecha:** Satomi Ozu; **Score:** Yasuo Higuchi; **Sound:** Susumu Aketagawa; **Manga:** *Hi no tori* (*Phoenix*); **Wr/Art:** Osamu Tezuka.

Spirited Away (*Sen to chihiro no kamikakushi*)
Japan, 2001 –125 mins
Hayao Miyazaki

Anime is often celebrated for its acts of levitation, and how their degravitised gestures embody the 'flights of fancy' crucial to *anime*'s fantasia. *Spirited Away* certainly has its share of uplifting, transporting and soaring moments, but its sublime capture of motion in animated form is the body of Chihiro.

On the verge of puberty, childish in mind and manner but sprouting into an ungainly and awkward physique before blossoming into womanhood, Chihiro moves throughout *Spirited Away* like a puppet of unbelievable realism. Her complete being is expressed more by mime than mimetics. This is animation in an unadulterated state: showing how things move rather than merely moving them. Spoilt, clinging, weak willed and sullen (a deliberately harsh critique of pre-teens in contemporary mid-affluent Japan), Chihiro is suddenly thrust into a strange world of phantasmagorical allegory. Her parents become pigs, leaving her to become a menial worker in a giant bath house where gods and spirits of all kinds come to cleanse and rest. Chihiro must navigate this new alienating world without any of her emotional or social props from her complacent privileged life in the 'real world' before. Thus, her mobility is rendered frail, unsure, traumatised. When she moves down treacherous steps to the workhouse of Kamaji to apply for work, the elongated scene is a miniature 'rite of passage' through bodily control, lingering over every move no matter how slight. Chihiro can barely take a first step – yet that she must do, and with no help whatsoever.

The strengths Chihiro develops come from her being left totally on her own. She must learn to walk again in the psychological sense, without emotional crutches and freed of her familial callipers. *Spirited Away* is an argument to become separate from the family – to be spirited away from their clutches, like a bird pushed from the nest to learn flight. The spiritual journey on which Chihiro embarks is this type of solitary

Spirited Away: Chihiro moving like a puppet of unbelievable realism

step-taking. It figuratively stands in contrast to the bulk of *anime* which expresses similar ideals but through acts of levitation. *Spirited Away* reverses this to show that basic control of motor mechanisms of one's corporeal body within the spiritual world can be just as taxing and rewarding. Eventually, Chihiro matures through her perception of those around her and how she connects to them. Freed of family conditioning, she maps out her own social space and traverses it through emotional exploration – such as when she finds unexpected empathy for the tragic No Face. It is through the dehumanising spirit world (that is, the erasure of human conditioning and perspectival framing) that Chihiro can shape herself free from social constrictions.

In the global context, *Spirited Away* shoots us into a microcosm of bodily physics just as Western animation touts simulative digital technologies as being able to animate things 'limited only by our imagination'. Then how dull must the imaginations be of so many supposed visionaries of CGI who amount to doing not much more than playing with franchised toys in a cine-digital sand-pit. *Spirited Away*'s focus on the frailty of a living individual spirits us far away from such mundanities.

Feature

Genre: Mystical Folklore

Dir: Hayao Miyazaki; **Prod:** Toshio Suzuki; **Scr:** Hayao Miyazaki; **Anim:** Masashi Ando; **Score:** Joe Hisaishi; **Sound:** Shuji Inoue, Toru Noguchi.

Steamboy (Sutyimu boi)
Japan, 2004 – 126 mins
Katsuhiro Otomo

In a saturated art form like *anime* where binaries of archaic/futuristic, traditional/post-modern, and Eurocentric/Nihoncentric are deck-shuffled to ensure an evenly random distribution of possibilities, *Steamboy* manages to be an amazing testament to the fluidity of Japanese narrative symbolism. Thoroughly rooted not in a historical sediment of solid archetypes but in a dimensional transparency of floating analogues, it imagines through vivid demonstrative connections how future and past can be encoded in each other.

The title 'Manchester 1886' is a proscenium device to announce all that is historically stretched by the story. Ray's father Eddy and grandfather Lloyd are inventors who have been developing radical new steam technology for the powerful O'Hara Foundation. Following Lloyd's defection and his attempt to send their key invention – the steam ball energy unit – to Ray, complex double-crosses swallow up Ray as he is kidnapped by the O'Hara Foundation to retrieve the steam ball. He discovers the organisation to be hidden within a huge manor in England, readying its technological outcomes for the Crystal Palace World Exposition, where they will be promoted for purchase by any interested countries in the lead-up to what will become World War I. Lloyd and Eddy have come to an ideological stalemate on their roles as scientists, and now Ray is caught between their views, trying to develop his own position while marvelling at the progress his father and grandfather have made.

A holistic perception of energy contextualises *Steamboy*'s dissertation on steam technology. From Eddy controlling the Steam City like an antique automaton-cyborg embedded within its clocks, gears and pressure gauges, to the 'fly-swat-simulation' of the Self-Defence Mechanism that tries to thwart Ray's attempts to neutralise the Steam City's core, the power of technology is breath-takingly evinced not as elemental but as compounded and harnessed by man. The bulk of the film is in fact a real-time charting of the gigantic orbed Steam City rising from the ground only to slowly descend and decimate the British metropolis. Through this old world apocalypse, a complete cycle of the Steam City's techno-system is actioned like a self-contained eco-system: the industrial black smoke it belches generates the white steam it gushes which transforms the city into an icy landscape which melts into a winter wonderland of delicate snow flakes. This uniquely Japanese 'techno-nature' is celebrated for its spectacular destructiveness in a series of panoramas which evoke the Hindenburg, Hiroshima and Space Shuttle Challenger, conflated through their conjoined collapse of design and disaster.

No retro-futro assignment, *Steamboy* is symptomatic of how the future and the past have not simply contracted in an accelerated era or become fearfully insignificant in a depoliticised era, but how they mirror each other in their ultimate non-existence. Long gone is the idea that the future will ever be arrived at, or that the past can ever be recouped. *Steamboy* expresses the traditionally speculative impulse of sci-fi, but forwards no chrono-linear direction for figurative debate. It is an anti-rhetorical *anime* that metaphorically and self-reflexively melts, fuses and welds discursive directions and lines into a ball of steam: the key source of energy of its story.

Feature

Genre: Robot Sci-Fi

Dir/Chara/Mecha: Katsuhiro Otomo; **Prod:** Shigeru Watanabe, Hideyuki Tomioka, Shinji Komori; **Scr:** Katsuhiro Otomo, Sadayuki Murai; **Anim:** Shinji Takagi; **Score:** Steve Jablonsky; **Sound:** Keiichi Momose.

The Tale of Genji
(*Murasaki shikibu genji monogatari*)
Japan, 1987 – 110 mins
Gisaburo Sugii

A traditional way to read the *anime* of *The Tale of Genji*, based on the tenth-century Heian-era novel, would be to read it as if it were the book. This would not only be blind and deaf to the *anime*'s aura, but it would also ignore the contemporary conditions under which the *anime* repositions the erotic text of the original novel.

The Tale of Genji intensifies the sexual psyche of youthful court retainer Lord Genji, employing shifts in audiovisual depiction to mark the contrast between Genji's sexual dreaming and social duties. His social world is largely absented in the *anime*, appearing fleetingly via passing retinues who cryptically gossip, quote aphorisms and discharge political barbs. Genji, his wife Aoi and his various lovers float through these veils of societal decorum. Genji especially is impervious to their attempts to pull him into line: he exists as a transfigured lord, living a nocturnal life of clandestine encounters opposed to the daily routines of the court.

Genji's displacement provides the poetic materiality to *The Tale of Genji*. His composure, appearance, gestures and movements embody an eroticised make-up that declares and hides his operations. A modern way to read this *anime* would be to note the predatory nature of Genji: a serial sex offender who despite articulating his attractions and compulsions in condensed poetic phrases is nonetheless a sexual being beyond control. The restrictive court protocol and its theatrical façade pressurises and amplifies Genji's actions, atomising the taboo-ridden tone of the novel's erotic detailing.

As *anime*, *The Tale of Genji* 'revises' the novel by viscerally and sensually transforming its poetic mental reveries into heady synaesthetic dances. Its visualisation references scroll paintings from the Heian period, and with remarkable precision 'animates' those forms without breaking the implied continuity of their design. The movement of the characters is as stylised and mannered as the original paintings – especially in the returning motif of Genji performing a perfectly composed dance, which symbolises his self-awareness of loss within. The backgrounds against which Genji and others are placed do not so directly connect to the scroll paintings, and instead construct a series of *kabuki*-like panoramas which play upon the deliberate artificiality of the court environs, designed as they were to formalise and theatricalise all social encounters. Throughout *The Tale of Genji*, people are arranged in relation to screens, scrims, walls and even the fans they hold. All space is staged, just as all facial expressions are frozen into masks of repression and all verbal exchange is expressed through multi-coded allusions.

Ultimately it is the stillness of *The Tale of Genji* that is most memorable. Numerous scenes are abstracted in their denouement, structured as if camera-tracking past a *tableau vivant* of frozen life. This not only echoes the displacement of Genji within the Heinan court culture, but also choreographs the audiovisual voids that stretch space, halt time and transform depth in a series of metaphysical poems. Genji's dreams of clutching his dying mother's kimono, exploring the pre-Freudian tree hole, and riding his erotic death-wish trips through blinding blue light illuminate the psycho-sexual cavern of his mind.

Feature

Genre: Historical Drama

Dir: Gisaburo Sugii; **Prod:** Atsumi Tashiro, Masato Hara; **Scr:** Tomomi Tsutsui; **Anim:** Yasuo Maeda; **Chara:** Nashiro Yakura; **Score:** Haruomi Hosono; **Novel:** *Genji monogatari* (*The Tale of Genji*); **Wr:** Murasaki Shikibu.

Tamala 2010 – A Punk Cat in Space (*Tamala 2010*)

Japan, 2002 – 92 mins

t.o.L

For the past five years or more, 'cute' in Japan has undergone numerous ironic make-overs. Most 'cute' things now are vicious, neurotic, aberrant, antisocial. *Tamala 2010 – A Punk Cat in Space* is not only a sign of this shift from the cuddly to the confronting, but also a comprehensive study in iconic refraction. Cannily attuned to the punk ethos and its self-debasement through subcultural coding, *Tamala 2010* is a multi-layered package of over-prepared and over-wrapped style, excessively labelled with 'neo', 'retro' and 'anti' labels – just like a punk jacket from 1977.

The story could be described as a dream had by a punk chick living on New York's lower East Side in the late 70s in a lifestyle straight out of the infamous *Punk* magazine of the time. In this dream – possibly aided by an excessive intake of speed and alcohol – she dreams she is a cat living in an *anime* made over thirty years in the future. This really isn't what 'happens' in *Tamala 2010*, but it is an apt way to describe the positioning of the *anime* in line with its declared affection towards another era from another culture. The 'story' action is superficially one of Tamala – a 'punk cat' with attitude who is unknowingly the reincarnation of Tatla, an Amazonian cyborg within which is housed the spirit of the Goddess Minerva from 3000 BC. Tatla, through Tamala, seems destined to be reborn on Planet Q to restore balance in a world controlled by the corporate mind-bending of Catty & Co.

But this 'story' floats in a free-form distracted fashion, rarely connecting events with precision and instead preferring to sail through its scenarios as if in a drug-induced numbness. It's not a lazy project, though: this haziness perfectly captures Tamala's punkish detachment from the world. With Blank Generation affectation, she is indifferent to the corporate miasma within which she and her fellow punks swim, marking it symptomatic of much pop culture effluvia which alarm those who seek authorial critique in such works. *Tamala 2010* is a subcultural inflection of attitudinal response to its broadcast environment: the saturated state of *anime* and other media in Japan. The veneer of *Tamala 2010* is thus a consistent style mash-up, resembling the televisual meld of CMs on Japanese TV which veer wildly from one heightened emotional state to the next within seconds. The resulting effect is like watching a number of programmes simultaneously, generating a distinctive audiovisual 'noise' despite the surface cuteness and its contrived kid-vid simplicity in detailing and movement.

Wrapped in bandages, puffing a cigarette, wearing black thigh-high boots, Tamala's cuteness is her fucked-up indifference to everything, including her boyfriend Michelangelo. Her fixed demeanour resembles a punk chick's doll, staring back at its imbalanced owner who gazes into her doll's big eyes and sees her own inner emotional flux. Savagery, desperation and nihilism are thus confronted in this face-off, making *Tamala 2010* less a 'story' and more an unexpectedly powerful psychological portrait of the disaffection integral to youth no matter where or when they reside.

Feature

Dir/Scr: t.o.L; **Prod:** Kazuko Mio, Seichi Tsukada, t.o.L; **Anim:** Kentaro Nemoto, Michiro Tsutsumoto; **Chara:** t.o.L, Kentaro Nemoto; **Mecha:** Kenji Okada; **Score:** t.o.L; **Sound:** Houmei Tanabe.

Tokyo Babylon (Tokyo Babiron)
Japan, 1992
Koichi Chigara

Issues of translation at script, dramatic and cultural levels constitute the major impediment to the greater proliferation of *anime* outside Japan. Yet while this is gradually being surmounted, the base tongue of Japan proves to be its untransformable power. How fitting when so many *anime* scenarios are predicated on the essential and undilutable state of any and all energies. The title of one *anime*, *Tokyo Babylon*, is an apt moniker for the greater reserve of untranslatable *anime* (not to mention the far greater bulk of *manga*) that towers in the alternative universe of
~n.

Bu...   is central to the first part of *Tokyo Babylon*. Subaru is a spiritual meu.   ᵓoable of setting lost souls to rest and breaking the shields that negative ⁺ᶜ hold over persecuted living beings. A psychic spirit-breaker for hire, he is ⸱ ᵗⁿually caught in fanciful poses of deep concentration, chanting scriptural ᵢ.   ᵗᵗs in a babble of karmic redistribution. Subaru's commune with the ᶦᵗual side also uncovers the Babylon of dimensions that exist within the rᵢ ᶦ realm: multiple languages exist because multiple planes and schisms of ɛ. ᶰce are woven within and without the physical domain.

Subaru's greatest challenge in *Tokyo Babylon* is sited at the construction of the Babylon Project – a thinly veiled quotation of Shinjuku's business district. The architects of this monstrous edifice and the town planners who are responsible for allowing its development have conspired to cover up insidious operations which are now becoming manifest as deadly paranormal activities. Upon the haunted building site, Subaru must work blindly, not privy to the double-dealings which have upset the karmic balance and created a hothouse of disaffected spirits. Symbolising the ruthless urban development of Japan that cares naught for context and placement of most of its monumental constructions, the Babylon Project becomes a beacon for dispossessed entities. Their collective energy and their impenetrable babble mirrors the 'noise' induced by the visual and spatial pollution caused by so many mega-buildings. This is the war zone which Subaru enters, armed only with soothing words to set things at ease.

In the chauvinistic world of greedy developers, egotistical architects and maniacal engineers, Subaru strikes a distinctly feminine figure. He is notably hyper-sensitive to the vibrations produced by the disturbed. His voice is calm, controlled and absent of any vein-throbbing aggression. His attire is so androgynous you could be excused for watching the whole *anime* and mistaking him for a woman. His lean physique paints him as a toned ballet dancer capable of careening within these dimensional multiplicities. A *bishonen* (beautiful boy) figurine (in both the *anime* and the originating *manga*), his displacement from the clear-spoken language of sexual difference locates him within the polysexual multi-voiced babble that escapes sexual coding. Appropriately, his spiritual nemesis at the construction site takes the form of energised blood growling and howling forth in a wolf-like frottage of deadly force. This is the spiritual world speaking beyond language, directly from the body, vomiting forth its vented energy. Only by calling forth incantations from the deepest recesses of his post-gendered being can Subaru vocally repel such an attack.

OVA (1)

Genre: Mystical Future Crime

Dir: Koichi Chigara; **Prod:** Yumiko Masujima, Kasuhiko Ikeguchi; **Scr:** Tatsuhiko Urahata; **Chara:** Kumikko Takahashi; **Anim:** Hideji Ito, Kazuo Shimizu, Michiko Hayashi, Osamu Kobayashi; **Score:** Toshiyuki Honda; **Sound:** Daisuke Jinbo; **Manga:** *Tokyo Babiron* (*Tokyo Babylon*); **Wr/Art:** CLAMP.

U-Jin Brand
Japan, 1991
Osamu Okada

An unsettling ambivalence towards gender roles and their correlation to positions of power in Japanese society hangs thick over *U-Jin Brand*. A series of humorous vignettes that gyrate around a 'battle-of-the-sexes' central plaza, this soft-porn comedy *anime* based on the numerous *manga* anthologies of the same name is comprised of three discrete stories. Seemingly light in tone, they collectively assemble the social psyche of the male sexual predator in contemporary Japan.

In 'When Idols Fall Prey to Luck', Kazama is a renowned composer beseeched by record companies to compose the first song for their debut idols. But Kazama must bed them first in order to 'know' them – a ruse which everyone including the idols treats as a mere machination of the industry. The double irony is that Kazama is a complete hack churning out crud, making most of his creative decisions according to a roll of his pencil. Reprehensible to the nth degree, he is depicted in a world defined by equal disaffection. His playboy delusion, the industry of his art, its supposed innocents, its indifferent consuming audience – all are planed into a horizontal emptiness which brings *U-Jin Brand* closer to Kafka than Heffner.

The two other episodes – 'When a Virgin Steals a Man' and 'When a Superior Takes Your Girl' – are centred around a major business company headed by Mr Toyama. In each, salary men and office ladies are engaged in power struggles either to express and attain affection, or to climb up the corporate ladder. Parody is put into destructive overdrive when Mr Toyama is revealed to be a rapist for hire, seducing women who have been lying to men so that he can then show them up for being impure and manipulative. These scenarios are far from comforting. The women are odious, the men spineless, and Mr Toyama is no valiant crusader, but just another perverter of power as head of the company.

A numbing pornographic air is expressed without respite in all three episodes; men particularly are instated as sexual predators, devoid of desire yet compelled to copulate. But despite the ham-fisted comedy-drama and blunt desperation of its sexcapades, *U-Jin Brand* charts how the pervasive and persuasive spread of sexual subterfuge and erotic duplicity affects everyday economics and social exchanges like a cold through air conditioning in a crowded business complex. The subliminal message is that sex is the city at its most banal and cursory. Far from the gaudy neon din of hostesses, scout men and *yakuza* is the rest of Japan's metropolis – and it is just as sexually problematised as any social domain pressurised by the binaries of work and pleasure. Most interesting – though not necessarily pleasurable – is the deliberate complication of sex with power. This is in marked contrast to Western symbolic codes that would 'tastefully' refuse such casual and non-judgmental depiction of men outrightly abusing their power for sexual gratification. A certain threadbare coarseness just covers *U-Jin Brand*, making it a stinging yet refreshing aeration of the gendered power plays lying deep within the dark folds of Western drama's modern cloak.

OVA (1)

Genre: Erotic Comedy

Dir: Osamu Okada; **Prod:** Yumiko Masujima, Yutaka Takahashi; **Scr:** Satoru Akahori, U-Jin; **Anim/Chara:** Yumi Nakayama; **Score:** Nobuo Ito; **Manga:** *U-Jin Brand*; **Wr/Art:** U-Jin.

Urotsukidoji (Chojin densetsu urotsukidoji)
Japan, 1987
Hideki Takayama

The apocalypse is a recurring figure in the mythology of many and varied cultures. The guise of the apocalypse – or total devastation of a world – can be viewed in a variety of ways: theological, elemental, mystical, political, egocentric, scientific, moral. In the Eurocentric domain, the end of the world is viewed in terms of fundamentalist finality, peppered with ethical reservations of progressivist scientific inquiry. In earthquake-dogged Japan – as in numerous pan-Pacific island cultures – the apocalypse is part of an ecological cycle, one that is momentous in scale yet inevitable and part of a certain organic/mystical logic.

The *Urotsuki Doji* OVA series was compiled into the *Overfiend* trilogy: *Legend of the Overfiend*, *Legend of the Demon Womb* and *Return of the Overfiend*. It is a good example of how the Japanese freely mix high-iconic symbols of sex and violence into a post-apocalyptic scenario which equally feeds off technological and mystical pondering (images of which have appeared with increasingly graphic content in *manga* since the late 70s). The *Urotsuki Doji* series fuses an epic tale of three dimensions converging (the human, the animal and the monster) which precipitates a series of apocalypses. As with much *anime*, the end of the world is yet again the beginning of a 'neo' era (or simply another OVA series). By mixing the mystical premise into an urbanised/technologicalised environment, interesting and confounding (and for some, offensive) symbolic and textual moments arise, wherein power and energy are represented.

In the Eastern sense, power is both the potential and the manifestation of energy. Following the premise that energy can never be destroyed only transformed, energy in the *Urotsuki Doji* series lurks within any scene – be it in characters' physical abilities and their suppressed memories; in spiritual locations and sacred sites; in hidden laboratories and clandestine operations; in corporate muscle and militarised government. In *anime*, the main task is often how to visualise and represent energy and power when it occurs. In this sense, the 'invisible' concept of power is always made visible. Throughout *Urotsuki Doji*, sheets of light engulf the screen; abstract dimensions open up and swallow the representational world; beams and lasers emit from every possible body part; psychic presences swirl before one's eyes.

Working within the operative generic codes of Japanese erotic horror, *Urotsuki Doji* manifests sexual energy through swirling penile tentacles which hold bodies in bondage; demonic energy is materialised through bodies randomly turning inside-out and mutating with each other in an orgy of limbs and viscera; and corporate power is represented by huge architectural edifices collapsing and showering the city. In short, symbolic sites of power and control – phallic momentum, personal sanity, urban architecture – are possessed by energy: the latent becomes manifest as the dormant, hidden or disguised energy of anything is suddenly cast loose in an uncontrollable event of destruction. Frighteningly puerile entertainment in some respects, the *Urotsuki Doji* series reveals an essential channelling of sexual energy and its coalition with social and cultural power.

OVA (5)

Genre: Erotic Horror

Dir: Hideki Takayama; **Prod:** Yoshinobu Nishizaki, Yasuhito Yamaki; **Scr:** Noboru Aikawa; **Anim:** Shiro Kasami, Mari Mizuta; **Chara:** Dan Kongoji, Eitaro Tono, Akihiko Yamashita; **Score:** Masamichi Amano; **Sound:** Yasunori Honda; **Manga:** *Chojin densetsu urotsukidoji (Legend of the Overfiend–Walkabout Kid)*; **Wr./Art:** Toshio Maeda.

Urusei Yatsura – Beautiful Dreamer (*Urusei yatsura 2– Beautiful Dreamer*)
Japan, 1984
Mamoru Oshii

There is something not quite right about *Urusei Yatsura*'s second film *Beautiful Dreamer*. It has all the key characters from the hilarious long-running *manga* and TV series, circling them around the central duo of alien princess Lum and her lecherous but likeable love-object Ataru. But from the outset, a different tone carries this film: it is not quite right because the world of Lum, Ataru and the others is 'not quite right'. *Beautiful Dreamer* is a dream that ponders whether it is a film that had a dream, or a dream that has been made into a film. This metaphysical mirroring of form and perception is the principal cause of its disconcerting yet captivating 'a-comedic' tone.

Beautiful Dreamer is a fascinating example of how far one can explore narrative schisms once the televisual continuity of a title is established. This is an approach peculiar to extended series of popular *anime* wherein characters are defined through their deviation from type, norm and behaviour. It also accounts for why many *anime* series are so long running: they are inexhaustible because they mostly seek to rewrite their characters in order to deepen and complicate their emotional and psychological composure. The anarchism of *Urusei Yatsura* is frequently modulated by touching and softening moments, and these 'mood swings' are more accepted in *anime* than in most Western televisual serialisations and their focus on finalising their characters' mythic traits.

Beautiful Dreamer is the most extreme of all the *Urusei Yatsura* catalogue due to its story being hermetically controlled by the dream-state and sense of reality of the alien princess Lum. The apparent surface of the Tomobiki High School is familiar yet strange, due to it being composed by Lum's reading of the human world. With giddy self-reflexivity, the world of Ataru that has been turned upside-down by Lum's appearance on Earth is now reconstituted through Lum's 'normalising' of her presence on Earth by imagining and desiring how she can fit in and be happy with Ataru, his parents and friends.

Yet throughout *Beautiful Dreamer* a subtle but pervasive tone rings like a distant wind chime in a world without wind. Lum's version of the world is laced with a melancholia which hints at the long-running co-dependency of Lum and Ataru shaped by their eternally unrequited love. It's an engaging yet disquieting relationship central to the series. Numerous poetic moments and passages are placed throughout *Beautiful Dreamer*'s unravelling story, scattered like breadcrumbs left to allow one to retrace this soft sadness that winds around the world of Lum and Ataru. Images of clouds and people reflected in pools of water reinforce the 'through-the-looking-glass' sheen of Lum's dream world; Escher-like architecture suddenly appears and disappears without destabilising the narrative; and endless roads that lead back to where people start are traversed in deep silence. Disorienting to us, the world as viewed by Lum is oriented by her desire to delineate an amorous time–space continuum for Ataru, giving us the beautiful dream which Lum lives.

Feature

Genre: Mystical Teen Comedy

Dir: Mamoru Oshii; **Prod:** Hidenori Taga; **Scr:** Mamoru Oshii; **Anim:** Yuji Moriyama; **Chara:** Kazuo Yamazaki; **Mecha:** Kenichi Maeda; **Score:** Katsu Hoshi; **Sound:** Shigeharu Shiba; **Manga:** *Urusei yatsura* (*Noisy Guys*); **Wr/Art:** Rumiko Takahashi.

Vampire Hunter D (*Bampaia Hanta D*)
Japan, 1985 – 80 mins
Toyoo Ashida

While European and Occidental Gothic expressions are the result of importation, the Gothic in Japanese guise is the result of direct injection and a consequent inability to digest. The spectre of Japan's unnerving isolationism governs Japanese aesthetics to such an extent that transcultural occurrences such as the Gothic are never subsumed, fused or blended: they curdle, pock and mar their reflecting surfaces into micro-terrains of cultural mutation. From the burst of *yokai* (ghost) cinema in the 60s to the current *gosurori* ('Gothic Lolita') fashion subculture, these are the conditions under which the Gothic lives.

Vampire Hunter D is as multi-seeded and cross-fertilised as one would expect from Japanese Gothic. Tracing the exploits of its eponymous avenger, it invents a quasi-European landscape culled from memories of British horror movies shot in former-Yugoslavia and Italian Westerns shot in Spain. Across these decaying panoramas, D walks and stalks, bearing the standard mix of lean loner and lost lover, toning his story as a tragic one: his conviction to hunt all vampires back to their final grave is an affliction akin to vampiric possession. His monocular quest to truly kill his nemesis Count Magnus Lee characterises him less as a rational planner and more as a cool yet compulsive killer of those who haunt him.

It is not surprising that in the gene-splicing that generates the generic aberration of Japanese Gothic, *Vampire Hunter D* aerates the sexual repressiveness of Gothic literature (not only in the *anime*, but in the series of novels from which the *anime* is derived). In place of the sensationalised feminine figure in her virginal yet see-through nightgown carrying a single candle and venturing into dark labyrinths in the middle of the night, D is a masculinised titillation of this same figure. Tall, handsome, sensual, he is also an echo of the thin androgynous figurines that populate *shonen ai manga* (boy-love comics) centred on the para-gay hyper-romantic and occasionally necrophiliac ties between men in love. This erotic aura of the leather-clad Latin-lover cowboy Goth god that is D centralises all the drama of *Vampire Hunter D* and conducts it like a sexualised symphony in keeping with the sexiness inherit in the vampire figure.

While this collapse of gender within a sexual hall of mirrors where the masculine and feminine mimic each other's guise is a distinctively Japanese formulation, the Eastern affectations pressed into the Gothic surface of *Vampire Hunter D* return us again to the wandering lordless *ronin* – that morose ex-*samurai* set afloat with no allegiance and left to form new alliances. D's living-dead quality as someone actually alive but who has 'died within' is a conflation of vampire with *ronin*. His skills are concentrated on disempowering the vampiric forces which have now divorced him from normal social intercourse, marking him as a *ronin* who unspeakably curses the lords who made him what he is.

Feature

Genre: Gothic Action

Dir: Toyoo Ashida; **Prod:** Hiroshi Kato, Mitsuhisa Koeda, Yuko Nagasaki; **Scr:** Yasushi Hirano; **Anim:** Yutaka Minowa; **Chara:** Yoshitaku Amano; **Score:** Noriyoshi Matsuura; **Sound:** Tetsuya Komuro; **Novel:** *Banpaia Hanta D* (*Vampire Hunter D*); **Wr:** Hideyuki Kikuchi.

Vampire Princess Miyu (Kyuketsuki miyu)
Japan, 1988
Toshihiro Hirano

Pervading *Vampire Princess Miyu* is a primordial pool of possessed, dispossessed and repossessed voices. Based on both the phantasmagoria of *bunraku* puppet theatre and its oriental *deus ex machina* (the use of men clothed in black set against a black backdrop while they manipulate intricate, down-scaled, fully articulated mannequins), Miyu is a young girl who has been summoned to connect with her *shinma*: a tall, skeletal, dark figure, Larvae. He even resembles a *bunraku* puppeteer, hovering over Miyu and performing identical synchronous actions with her in a display of control. The relationship between the two is partly that of the vampire and his undead victim, but more, a

Vampire Princess Miyu: vocal cords as visceral strings for the puppeteer

mirroring of the condition of *shinma*: loosely, the originating state wherein deity and evil spirit were in ancient time conjoined and inhabited a single plane of existence. Capable of traversing corporeal and spiritual worlds, Miyu navigates a dimensionally warping expanse devoid of Western binary morals and strewn with collapsed psychotic figures.

In the second instalment of the series, Miyu encounters Ran-Ca, a delicate dolllike schoolgirl who has been uncontrollably killing her lovers as she attempts to consummate a relationship. Through the act of her love, she transforms them into life-size *bunraku* figures, partly through a denial of her own status as a cursed human who must exist as a puppet in human form. Miyu uncovers this after a young man to whom Miyu is attracted (Yuzuki Kei) is seduced by Ran-Ca. Following a complex psychic battle, Miyu witnesses the now-dead Kei speak through the voice of Ran-Ca as the latter holds his body like a puppeteer. Clothing falls from both their bodies to reveal the *bunraku* form of chained and linked muscular armatures; they then depart into another dimension as doomed lovers at strange peace with their non-human form.

By this stage of the tale, the ownership of voice – not to mention the territorialisation of vocal cords as visceral strings for the puppeteer – is presented as a shifting occurrence of oral real estate. Miyu often operates as a medium for others, and her 'self' is intricately bound with the mute Larvae. Through the alternating current of her vocal reflux, she demonstrates how voice is dispersed and diffused across psychic and psychological landscapes: no one solely owns their own voice, but everyone can have potential purchase of the voices of all others. The fantastic scenarios of *Vampire Princess Miyu* re-evaluate the strained measures by which the human voice is treated as a localised, stabilised point of origin. While classical European drama valiantly strains to shape its message through centralised voices, *Vampire Princess Miyu* in its unleashing of the fantastic ponders the problems produced by the functioning of proxies. The staging of the voice as a vocal field – a locatable space of the vocal event – is transformed into a vocal matrix: an expandable network of vocal lines which creates the space for vocal multiplicity, within which vocal ownership is a questionable investment.

OVA (4)

Genre: Mystical Horror

Dir: Toshihiro Hirano; **Prod:** Toru Miura, Kazufumi Nomura; **Scr:** Aikawa Noboru;
Anim: Narumi Kakinouchi, Nashii Masahiro; **Chara:** Narumi Kakinouchi; **Score:** Kenji Kawai;
Sound: Junichi Sasaki, Etsushi Yamada; **Manga:** *Kyuketsuki miyu* (*Blood-sucking Miyu*);
Wr/Art: Toshihiro Hirano.

Violence Jack (*Baiorensu jyakku jigokugai*)
Japan, 1989
Ichiro Itano, Takuya Wada

The rubric of 'post-apocalyptica' which announces the general dystopian position of much futuristic *anime* is a wide chapter heading. Two polarities define this width. To one extreme is an impossibly projected future – one that might be eons ahead, even incorporating Earth's recolonisation of some distant planet. At the other extreme is 'the day after': a fresh, fetid dystopia where social and cultural frameworks have been wrenched from all fixture. This second type of post-apocalypse provides the setting for *Violence Jack*.

Following an earthquake that has decimated Tokyo, life has reverted to primitive existence. Three groups live in districts carved out from the rubble underground: the chauvinist bureaucrats of District A, the mad bikers in District B and a group of gorgeous fashion models in District C. With unrepentant separatism, *Violence Jack* shows that when society is razed, males become reconditioned as morally feral and psycho-sexually primed. At this level, *Violence Jack* is not futuristic at all, but a thinly disguised return to the famine, pestilence and pillaging which governed the land, resources and people of Japan through centuries of abusive rule during its feudal era. Starved into submission and moulded by terror, these remnants of civilisation are animalistic. No karmic, spiritual and/or mystical facets of life come to the surface in such a desperately pragmatic environment. Direct physical existence is the only operable paradigm for living.

Enter Jack: a pillar of frightening force, he is a stoic statue of compressed energy born under these post-apocalyptic conditions. In a world of ruthless physicality where gender war ensues, he is a throbbing life force of hyper-energised asceticism, capable of brute strength while all others have withered and wilted. This focus on post-sexual physicality is epicentral to *Violence Jack*'s visceral narrative. Jack is a mystical being of sorts due to his retaining of physical strength and sexual control, positing him as a reservoir of energy that the earthquake did not replete. His corpus is a reminder of how much vitality has been erased in the new world; his mute being is the consciousness of this abuse of life, figuring him in line with many a mythological mute or blind monk whose memory and consciousness 'silences' them to the world they traverse.

But Jack isn't always silent. When pushed, his rage erupts in a hyper-physical revisitation of the violence that governs Tokyo in its current form. In this regard, *Violence Jack* is refreshingly true to its moniker: the scenes are agreeably violent, and do not employ fey metaphors. Jack's entire being is beyond physical limits: he is the personification of martial arts doctrines that recast the body as a container of invisible meta-forces. Yet this also provides another layer to the Otherness of Jack. His inner force is essentially the abjection of violence: while his consciousness controls it, it nonetheless exists as a reminder of the power invoked in destroyed worlds, monopolised societies and militarised spreads. Typically tragic, he is displaced by the post-apocalypse – born of it but ostracised from growing within it.

OVA (5)

Genre: Urban Sci-Fi

Dir: Ichiro Itano, Takuya Wada; **Prod:** Yasushi Nomura; **Scr:** Noboru Egawa; **Anim/Chara:** Takuya Wada; **Score:** Hiroshi Ogasawara; **Sound:** Yasunori Honda; **Manga:** *Baiorensu jyakku* (*Violence Jack*); **Wr/Art:** Go Nagai.

Wicked City (*Yojou toshi*)
Japan, 1987 – 80 mins
Yoshiaki Kawajiri

Freudian analyses of cinema are often laughable because of their rote application of psychoanalytic theory to films in presumption of the texts being ignorant or repressive of their own psycho-sexual mechanisms. This is particularly telling when psychoanalytic theory is applied to the erotic horror subgenres of *anime*. When a beautiful vampish woman contorts into a four-legged 'arachno-domme' replete with a teeth-lined vaginal gash between her thighs in *Wicked City*, one does not need to 'reveal' a symbolic *vagina dentata* operating in the scene. In the hyper-iconic realm of *anime*, such decoded symbolism has no real place: that scene in

Wicked City: rendering the *female fatale* with unabashed pornographic fervour

Wicked City is a thrilling depiction of what it would be like to have sex with a woman who suddenly turns into such a sexy spidery monster. The erotic is always manifest and never latent in *anime* due to the art form's recourse to fantastic meta-physical depiction and its sexual tendrilation.

Wicked City is virtually a mockery of any accounting of its sexual symbolism – so much so that it is best read as film noir turned inside-out. That's not to say it is some fey tasteful 'erotic play with the noir genre', but that every flushed nuance and heated moment in the standard *femme fatale* manoeuvres of noir's entrapment of the male sex is here rendered with unabashed pornographic fervour. The 'inside-out' effect is ordained by *Wicked City*'s premise: the human world (sited in Tokyo) is on the eve of signing a treaty with the Black World's demon realm, but an extremist faction of demons are intent on subverting the treaty signing. Their malefic appearance transforms the earthy realm into an ulterior dimension of Otherness, destabilising detective Taki as he protects the diplomat Giuseppe Mayart. Taki's work is exacerbated by being partnered to the *femme fatale* of Makie, a sexy assassin who has defected from the Black World. His shifts from distrust to attraction to respect to love whirl his emotional tie to Mackie, and coincide with the incursions of Black World demons whose transgression is marked by their hideous necro-sexual violence.

Sex hangs heavy throughout *Wicked City*, regardless of which realm we are in. Giuseppe is a comically pathetic old lecher, desperate to get to the nearest massage parlour. Taki is hard-working but horny, a regular at pick-up bars according to his bartender friend at the start of the story. Mackie might be dressed in a black suit and tie, but her sexual aura is intense. The demons are grotesquely morphing monsters of penile and vaginal explosiveness, contorting external forms and internal organs into each other. Violence is a layer of action overlaid on this overtly sexualised world, clearly positing sex and violence as parallel entities. This open duality is something generally repressed in Western photo-fiction, where the cross-fertilisation of sex and violence is disallowed as desperately as the Black World extremists refuse the dimensional peace treaty. Emblematic of *anime*'s attachment to Japanese 'erotic grotesque' in literature and *manga*, *Wicked City* depicts a world where repression and subtext are the last of anyone's fears or concerns.

Feature
Genre: Mystical Horror
Dir/Anim/Chara: Yoshiaki Kawajiri; **Prod:** Kenji Kurata, Makoto Seya; **Scr:** Kisei Cho; **Score:** Osamu Shoji; **Sound:** Fukushima Onkyo; **Novel:** *Yojou toshi* (*Strange Beasts' City*); **Wr:** Hideyuki Kikuchi.

A Wind Named Amnesia (*Kaze no na wa Amnesia*)
Japan, 1990 – 80 mins
Kazuo Yamazaki

The history of every nation is based as much on what it forgets as what it remembers. Possibly the former is the defining mechanism that renders history mythical and not factual. Being futurist rather than historical, *A Wind Named Amnesia* is a haunting tale of loss that wells up in those who realise that what they have forgotten contains the seeds of what they have become.

Set in America at the close of the 20th century, *A Wind Named Amnesia* gives no explanation for why 'the wind' came. It simply did, creating a globe of mute primitives with no memory of anyone or anything about them. Wataru's name (meaning 'to go from place to place') has been given to him by Johnny, an experiment in advanced memory induction, who Wataru found when he stumbled into a military bio-weapons facility. Johnny teaches Wataru to speak, drive and shoot, but then dies, leaving Wataru to fend for himself.

Told through the experiences and new memories of Wataru, a journey of sorts unfolds as he travels across the States with a mysterious woman. Sophia is clearly not human, and appears to be studying Wataru to gauge how he can mobilise himself beyond the low level of existence which now defines life across the planet. This behavioural experiment becomes a philosophical quest for both Wataru and Sophia, as they effectively conduct social experiments to define life and humanity in a brutalised world on the brink of self-extinction.

In Los Angeles they befriend Little John, an ex-cop, and his daughter Sue, who has been assigned as a sacrificial bride to the 'god' Smasher Devourer. This 'god' in reality is a huge earth-moving mega-machine that someone stumbled across and accidentally discovered how to operate, from which a ruthless social ritual has developed in the now-feral LA wasteland. In the mid-West, they stumble across Eternal Town, the

Future Expo site for 2010. The only living people there are the elderly Mr Simpson who serves the young, beautiful Mayor, together enacting a series of mind-addled father/daughter scenarios. They inhabit a perfect world controlled by the Big Computer which requires no human maintenance. But like doomed marionettes upon a controlled stage, they live out their existence in a seemingly intelligent state while being mere shells of human existence and development.

Sophia has made a bet with Wataru that he will find no one to accompany him on their trek East to New York. She believes that once overcome by devastating conditions, humans are incapable of evolving past their debilitating predicament. But the humanist Wataru clutches to dim memories of how people once were, and that flicker of humanism keeps him seeking those with whom he can forge social growth. Like the return to ground zero which lines the subtext to so much *anime*, *A Wind Named Amnesia* is a study of how life must start from scratch, and how a nation needs to most remember what it is to live again when it has been reborn anew.

Feature

Genre: Eco Sci-Fi

Dir: Kazuo Yamazaki; **Prod:** Kosuke Kuri, Yashio Masumizu; **Scr:** Kazuo Yamazaki, Yoshiaki Kawajiri; **Anim/Chara:** Satoru Nakamura; **Mecha:** Morifumi Naka; **Score:** Hidenobu Takemoto, Kazz Toyama; **Sound:** Kazz Toyama; **Manga:** *Kaze no na wa Amnesia* (*A Wind Named Amnesia*); **Novel:** *Kaze no na wa Amnesia;* **Wr/Art:** Hideyuki Kikuchi.

Index

Page numbers in *italics* denote illustrations; those in **bold** indicate detailed analysis

List of Illustrations

Whilst considerable effort has been made to correctly identify the copyright holders, this has not been possible in all cases. We apologise for any apparent negligence and any omissions or corrections brought to our attention will be remedied in any future editions.

Adolescence of Utena, Be Papas/Saito Chico/Shogakukan Shokaku/TV Tokyo/Shojo Kakumei; *Akira*, Akira Committee; *Armitage III*, AIC/Pioneer LDC Inc.; *Barefoot Gen*, Gen Productions/Keiji Nakazawa; *Black Jack*, Tezuka Production Co. Ltd; *Blood – The Last Vampire*, Production I.G./SVW-SCEI-IG/Plus IGA/Manga Entertainment Inc.; *Blue Seed*, Ashi Productions Co. Inc./Production IG/Yuzo/Takada/Takeshobo/BS Project/TV Tokyo/NAS; *Bubblegum Crisis*, Artimic/Youmex; *Dangaio*, AIC/Emotion; *FLCL*, Gainax/KGI/Production IG/Synch-Point; *Ghost in the Shell*, Kodansha Publishing Company/Bandai Visual/Manga Entertainment; *Golgo 13*, Saito Productions; *Grave of the Fireflies*, Akiyuki Nosaka/Shinchosa Co./Studio Ghibli; *Gunsmith Cats*, Kenichi Sodona/Kodansha Ltd/VAP/TBS; *Kiki's Delivery Service*, Eiko Kadono/Nibariki/Tokuma Shoten/Nippon Television Network/Studio Ghibli; *Laputa – Castle in the Sky*, Nibaiki/Tokuma Shoten/Studio Ghibli; *Moldiver*, AIC/Pioneer LDC Inc.; *Neon Genesis Evangelion*, Gainax/Project Eva/TV Tokyo/NAS/Tatsunoko Productions Co. Ltd; *Ninja Scroll*, Yoshiaki Kawajiri/Madhouse/JVC/Toho Co. Ltd/ Movic Inc./Animaze; *Patlabor – Mobile Police*, Headgear/Emotion/TFC/Mad House Ltd; *Perfect Blue*, Mad House Ltd/Oniro/Rex Entertainment; *Please Save My Earth*, Saki Hiwatari/Hakusensha/Victor Entertainment; *Princess Mononoke*, Nibaraki/ Tokuma Shoten/Studio Ghibli/Nippon Television Network/DENTSU Music and Entertainment Inc.; *Sailor Moon*, Naoko Takeuchi/Kodansha/Toei Animation; *Samurai Champloo*, Manglobe Inc./Fuji TV/Shimoigusa Champloos; *Silent Mobius*, Kia Asamiya/Kadokawa Publishing Co. Ltd; *Spirited Away*, Studio Ghibli/NTV/ DENTSU Music and Entertainment Inc./Tokuma Shoten/Buena Vista International/ Tohokushinsha Film Corp./Mistubishi Commercial Affairs; *Vampire Princess Miyu*, Soeishinsa/Pony Canyon; *Wicked City*, Japan Home Video Co. Ltd.